HOME ON THE RANGE

A CENTURY ON THE HIGH PLAINS

JAMES R. DICKENSON

A LISA DREW BOOK
SCRIBNER
NEW YORK LONDON TORONTO SYDNEY TOKYO SINGAPORE

SCRIBNER
1230 Avenue of the Americas
New York, NY 10020

SCRIBNER and colophon are registered
trademarks of Simon & Schuster Inc.

Designed by Songhee Kim

Manufactured in the United States of America

10   9   8   7   6   5   4   3   2   1

Library of Congress Cataloging-in-Publication Data
Dickenson, James R.
Home on the range : a century on the high plains / James R. Dickenson
p.   cm.
Includes index.
1. McDonald (Kan.)—History.   2. Dickenson, James R.—
Homes and haunts—Kansas—McDonald.   I. Title.
F689.M344D53   1995
978.1'125—dc20   94-26800
                                                                CIP

ISBN 0-689-12194-6

CONTENTS

8 ⚞ CONTENTS

ACKNOWLEDGMENTS

A GREAT MANY PEOPLE HAVE GIVEN GENEROUSLY OF THEIR TIME AND effort in helping with this book, both providing information and insight and reading drafts of various chapters. First is my wife, Mollie Dickenson, a writer herself, who has given perceptive editorial advice and steadfast support and encouragement. I am also grateful to members of my family who read the drafts, including my sister, Elizabeth Raichart; my aunts Margaret Ritter, Fern Fields, and Opal Dickenson; my cousins Marcia and Danny Rueb, Jo Ann Wilford, Martha Stevenson, Wallace Ritter, and Terry Dickenson; and my mother-in-law, Norma McCauley. My cousins Bessie Madsen, Mildred Knapp, and Virginia and Bob Doll also gave great help and encouragement.

Many longtime friends in McDonald and people from other towns in northwest Kansas helped make the book possible. Primary among them is Ed Cahoj, a lifelong friend, who contributed crucial information, advice, a valuable reading of several chapters, and the generous hospitality of his farm home near McDonald. Claude Bell, before he died in January 1994, was an inexhaustible fount of knowledge as well as delightful company and provided a valuable reading of several chapters, as did his son, Ron Bell. I am also grateful to Owen Wingfield, president of the Peoples State Bank, for his friendship and his customary meticulous job of editing a draft. His colleagues at the bank, Elroy Osborne, Marlene Johnson, and John Powell, were also a great help in this regard. Les Loker, chairman of the Centennial committee, gave generously of his time and knowledge of that and many other matters pertaining both to the town and area.

11

Others in McDonald who provided a great amount of information and a critical reading are: Arlie Archer, A. B. Fisher, C. K. Fisher, Ray Johnson, Betty and Vance Lewis, the Reverend Gregory H. Moyer, the Reverend Clarence Swihart, Eleanor Swihart, Joan Tongish, and Leonard Vyzourek.

I am also grateful for the help and encouragement of Don Antholz, my high school classmate; Amelia and Bob Banister, longtime family friends; Henry Cahoj; Richard Cain, the high school principal and superintendent of the Cheylin school district; Bertie and Vernon Davis; Rick Frisbie; LaVerne Goltl; Marion Hallagin; Joan and Wayne Harper; Keith Headrick; Dan Hubbard; Dave Hubbard; Bob Johnson; Brenda Johnson; Lois Johnson; Vera Kacirek; Ruth and Laverne Klepper; and Dale and Ratha Lee Loker.

In Atwood, Bob Creighton, an energetic and civic-minded community leader, gave unstintingly of his time and encyclopedic knowledge of the area and its prospects, and provided a close reading of the draft. I am also indebted to other civic leaders, including the Reverend Delbert Stanton, president of the Rawlins County Economic Development Commission; Ruth Kelley Hayden, a historian of Rawlins County, organizer of the county historical association, and mother of former governor Mike Hayden; Marcille Currier, co-director of the Atwood Chamber of Commerce; Kathy Davis-Vrbas, editor of the Rawlins County *Square Deal*; Rosalie Ross, publisher of the *Square Deal*; Mary Holle, associate editor of the *Square Deal*; and Cynthia Dixson of the County Extension Service.

In Colby, Wayne Bossart, manager of Northwest Kansas Groundwater Management District Four, was an essential source of information and a discerning editor. So were Larry Barrett, chairman of the Colby Economic Development Commission, and Larry White, an architect and developer, both of whom provided valuable information and readings of chapter drafts. I also am grateful to city manager Carolyn Armstrong and Richard Wahl, extension agricultural economist with the Kansas Farm Management Association NW.

Friends and colleagues in the Washington, D.C., area who gave encouragement, critical reading of several chapters, and priceless suggestions include Nick Kotz, an author and friend who provided sage advice and early encouragement; Bob Day, a novelist and creative writing teacher at Washington College who brought his discerning novelist's eye to the manuscript; his wife, Kathy Day, an artist; Richard Harwood, a friend and former colleague at *The Washington Post*, who also teaches at Washington College; novelist Kate Lehrer and Jim Lehrer, newsman, playwright, and novelist; poet E. J. Mudd, who gave strong encouragement and discerning editorial advice early on when it was most needed; and Roscoe Born, a fellow Kansan and a friend, mentor, and editor at the *National Observer*.

I am deeply indebted to Professor Mark Lapping, formerly of Kansas State University and now director of the School of Planning and Public Policy at Rutgers University, who provided invaluable knowledge and insights into the history and problems of rural Kansas, encouragement at a critical point in the project, and a close and helpful reading of the draft. I am also grateful to Deborah and Frank Popper, also of Rutgers University, both for their help on the manuscript and for their valuable work in stimulating constructive thought and action on the future of the High Plains.

I am indebted to Ron Goldfarb, my agent, for his support, encouragement, and professional skill. Finally, I want to thank my editors at Scribner, Lee Goerner and Lisa Drew, for their faith in and support of this project.

INTRODUCTION

THIS BOOK BEGAN AS A FAMILY HISTORY BASED ON STORIES MY MATERNAL grandmother told me when I was young. I carried them around for nearly thirty years while the idea of someday writing about them germinated. As I set them down, however, it became apparent that the family's experience in settling the frontier made them part of an epic portion of the nation's history, so I begain broadening my scope.

This book is about life in a rural, wheat-farming community in western Kansas, a way of life that is gradually disappearing as the country has become industrialized and urbanized. In a sense, it recounts a historical cycle that seems almost to be coming full-circle. In the second half of the nineteenth century, my great-grandparents and grandparents were part of the stream of settlers who migrated to western Kansas after the Civil War to become wheat farmers. They broke the virgin sod, erected houses, barns, schools, churches, and towns, and made the area one of the most agriculturally productive in the world. A little more than a century later, the population has ebbed away from this area and many of the farms, schools, churches, and towns lie vacant, dilapidated, and boarded up like old boomtowns.

Home on the Range describes how the area was settled, how it changed and developed, where it stands now, and what the people are doing to try to save their small towns and way of life, as seen through the lens of my family and the history of my home town.

To a great extent, my writing this book is the result of one of those accidents of history that profoundly shape our lives: my father's death when I was two-and-a-half. At the time, we were living in Rolla, Kansas, in the southwest corner of the state, where my father and his brothers had settled and where my mother and he met while she was teaching high school there. My mother and I stayed on in Rolla for three years after his death while she continued teaching. My Grandmother Dickenson lived with us, a loving and generous presence who helped Mother and kept a fond eye on her grandson.

When it was time for me to start first grade, Mother and I moved north to McDonald, Mother's hometown, where she got a job teaching in the high school and we lived with my maternal grandmother, Mary Elizabeth Phipps, for several years before Mother remarried. So I grew up in McDonald, like Rolla, a town of about 400 population. Because of this and the fact that I stayed with Grandmother in her big house in town during the summers when I was a teenager working for my uncles and other farmers, we became very close. We had many shared experiences, including the stories she passed on. The tale that probably is the seed of this book is Grandmother's account of how she and Grandfather Phipps switched to the Democratic party almost a century ago.

I am grateful to her for many things. Among them is her bequest of her love for the Kansas prairie, the people who settled it, and those who still live on it and farm it.

CHAPTER ONE

GRANDMOTHER

THE WHEAT CROP IN THE SUMMER OF 1948 WAS A RAVISHING BEAUTY, coming off a winter of exceptionally good moisture. The stand was so heavy it seemed almost fluid, a great golden ocean stirred by the ubiquitous western Kansas wind into undulating waves as it reached to the horizon in every direction. To a farmer, it was a work of art, as lovely as a favored child. It was going to make fifty bushels an acre. It was a bumper crop by any measure.

Then, just a few days before the wheat was ready for the combines, the storm came.

Out on the High Plains, storm clouds are often as welcome as a lover's smile because they herald precious precipitation, which becomes scantier and less dependable in the westward progression from the Missouri River to the Rocky Mountains. Very often, however, there are malignant exceptions such as tornadoes, blizzards—and hail.

Hail. The specter of one of those lethal clouds boiling up ominously in the western sky, a baleful green apparition brushed with streaks of silver, is certain to induce despair in a farmer. At an early age, the children of the High Plains learn that those clouds are a threat to happiness and prosperity. Adults know that hail will dent their cars, rip the shingles off their roofs, reduce their bank balances—and break their hearts.

This storm barged through during the night, not as a nurturing, murmuring shower, but as a destructive agent that made any *sleeping* nightmare seem blissful by comparison. It was a reminder that the dawn is not always the harbinger of hope and renewal. And with the dawn, it was my glum duty to drive Grandmother Phipps out to inspect the damage.

In my life, I have contemplated root canal with greater relish. As always in the wake of such storms, the morning was all blue sky, golden sun, and ponds of sparkling rainwater, as fresh and clear a day as anyone has ever seen. Mother Nature, often so generous and benevolent, is also capable of capricious cruelty—and leaves in her wake a dazzling morning like that one as a sort of mocking smile, a reminder of who, after all, is boss.

Neither Grandmother nor I had much of an appetite, and we decided we could put off breakfast until after our inspection trip. She sighed and took her sunbonnet down from one of the coat hooks on the wall behind the kitchen door. We climbed into the dusty cab of the green International Harvester pickup, which we kept parked in her backyard, and rode with wordless dread to her farm three miles west of town.

Hail is spotty, so we had reason to hope that we might have escaped with only partial damage or even spared completely. Although the storm missed Grandmother's other two fields, one a mile north of her farm, the other just east of town, she had no such luck with the half section her farm was on; it was caught by the very north edge of the storm, which had swept through from southwest to northeast. The hail hadn't merely wreaked 100 percent destruction, it had virtually plowed the field and planted the next year's crop as well. It shattered the nearly ripe wheat berries out of their hulls, pulverized the straw, and then beat everything into the ground with such ferocity that the field looked as though it had been turned under with a moldboard plow.

With her first look, Grandmother's eyes welled up briefly. The financial loss involved was probably the least of her considerations; to my knowledge, the only interest in material goods she ever evinced was the wish to conserve her assets to pass on to her children. Uppermost was her farmer's disappointment and frustration over losing such a magnificent crop. But Grandmother had spent a lifetime in intimate contact with Mother Nature and the elements. She of all people had no doubt as to who had the final word, always.

"Well, Dickie-Doodle," she finally said, using her favorite nickname for me, able to smile after she'd assimilated the damage. "We might as well look on the bright side. It looks like the good Lord has plowed and drilled [planted] for us. We could have a good volunteer crop here next year."

I put the pickup in gear and, although still stricken by the sight myself, managed a rueful smile of admiration for her strength and resilience. "That's for sure, Grandma," I responded, knowing full well that it was a disaster.

⚮

For nearly ninety-one years, Mary Elizabeth Duling Phipps, who rests beneath the western Kansas prairie she loved so well, had something of a Ptolemaic view of the universe. Like everyone else, she was taught that the earth and the other planets circled the sun, but deep down she had the feeling that the sun and the rest of the cosmos really revolved around western Kansas. If anyone had suggested this in so many words, she'd have laughingly denied it, but it was implicit in her worldview. She took as the First Principle that bread, the staff of life, was one of the bases of existence itself, along with air and water. From this flowed the inescapable conclusion that wheat farmers were truly engaged in the Lord's work. She had a powerful sense of the land. She believed that if you didn't have land— good, rich topsoil you could pick up and run through your fingers, land that would grow crops to feed hungry people—you had nothing.

This tenet, with which she had been inculcated from childhood, had been reinforced by her life's experiences. Among them was the run of Populist party victories in Kansas in the early 1890s, which were a reaction to the drought and depression of those years and a revolt against the Big-City Business Interests Back East (the phrase was always spoken as though it were capitalized). One Populist movement leader, "Sockless" Jerry Simpson, a Kansas rancher, preached this credo at every campaign stop: "Man must have access to the land or he is a slave. The man who owns the earth owns the people, for they must buy the privilege of living on his earth. . . ."

Grandmother believed this without question and held on to her farm until she died in June of 1962. When it was sold shortly thereafter, her youngest son, Wayne, who ran it for her after Grandfather Phipps died, opined that selling it and putting the proceeds in a 5 percent passbook savings account would have produced a greater return than farming it had. My first reaction was, in effect, "What?" Was that why we'd all spent all those twelve- and fourteen-hour days broiling under the summer sun, eating the proverbial peck of dirt that every farmer supposedly consumes in his lifetime? But that was a fleeting thought, a mere twinkling. I knew that such a calculation would have been meaningless to Grandmother.

Hers was the devotion that keeps people farming despite all the heartbreak and obstacles posed by a capricious and frequently cruel climate, greedy and exploitative middlemen, and the vagaries of domestic politics and international markets, powerful forces over which the farmer, particularly the small or medium-sized, has little or no control. Only the most fortunate and successful begin to realize anything approaching the return on capital investment and sweat equity they'd realize in other enterprises.

It may have been easier to keep that Populist faith in Grandmother's day. At the time her seven children were born, around the turn of the century, about a third of the nation's population lived on farms, with agriculture as their occupation; forty years later, when America entered World War II, 20 percent of the nation's families—7.1 million—still lived and earned their sustenance on farms. By 1990, this number was down to about 2 percent as technology made the farmer ever more productive, all but eliminating the need for large numbers of hired hands and the large farm families that were a common source of manpower until two generations ago. This has also reduced the size of the small-farm-town society and has made many of its members feel like an endangered species.

I grew up amid strong, self-reliant women, including my mother and her sisters, Margaret and Fern; Grandmother Dickenson; my aunt Opal Mettlen Dickenson, who married my father's brother, Lawrence; and, of course, Grandmother Phipps. Strong women were the norm on the High Plains, not the least because it took strength to survive on the frontier. This phenomenon worked changes in local attitudes toward women. The custom of barring women from activities designated as exclusively masculine—business, politics, etc.—which was a matter of course back east, broke down on the frontier, where the women's help with the work was essential and valued. As a result, thirteen of the eighteen states (counting Missouri) west of the Missouri River granted women's suffrage as much as half a century before the Nineteenth Amendment was ratified in 1920. First was the Wyoming Territory in 1869, followed by Colorado in 1893; Kansas acted in 1912.

This was considered radical in the context of the times, but the West was given to radical and innovative political movements, such as Populism. There were reasons for this: the drastically different conditions the frontier settlers encountered and the concomitant requirement for new formulas for living and solutions to a whole new set of problems, the need to build a society from scratch out of the wilderness, the heritage of an initial period of lawlessness, and the sheer physical hardship. Historians such as Frederick Jackson Turner and Walter Prescott Webb speculated that a special spirit of democracy and equality grew up on the frontier, where women shared the work, isolation, and hardships. In addition to being partners in the work and hardship of the farms and ranches, the women also took the lead in taming the frontier by establishing community and cultural institutions such as churches, schools, and social, musical, literary, dramatic, and other cultural groups.

However, as Webb, the great historian of the plains, noted, "The evidence, such as it is, reveals that the Plains repelled the women as they attracted the men." There was an adage that the plains were great for men and dogs but hell on women and horses.

The accounts of the early homesteaders in my home county, Rawlins County, when it was still an empty, unpopulated frontier, tell of the homesteaders' wives left alone for months during the winter with the children in their sod huts while their husbands worked on farms and in towns as far as 250 miles away to help make the mortgage payments on their farms and finance their next year's planting and harvesting. The terror of their wintry isolation was exacerbated by severe blizzards. In O. E. Rolvaag's novel, *Giants in the Earth*, Per Hansa, the protagonist, achieves a state of near ecstasy over the fact of owning his own domain on the barren South Dakota plains; at the same time, his wife, Beret, steadily sinks into despair and madness as she looks out the window of her squalid sod home and contemplates the empty, desolate landscape of grass, wind, and sky, and, worse, the blank "whiteouts" of the fearsome Dakota winter storms.

Grandmother Phipps was the role model for her family. She was the dominant person in her children's lives, not through force of personality, but through her generosity with her love and time, her tolerance, her understanding, and her strength. She led by example. In many ways, she was the embodiment of the strong frontier woman. She wore long flowered dresses and old-fashioned sunbonnets. When a good dress became too worn for church and other social events, it became a work garment until it was worn out; "waste not, want not" was the credo of the frontier. She milked the cows, slopped the hogs, raised chickens, baked her own bread, cakes, and pies, canned the fruits and vegetables from her sizable garden, and made her own laundry soap (a brown, evil-looking concoction of cooking grease and lye that could take the paint off the walls), which she brewed up in an oblong copper washtub. She could hitch a team of horses, but she never mastered the automobile.

She was acutely attuned to the land and nature. She hated weeds because they deprived worthy plants of precious moisture, and she relentlessly pulled each one she spotted. "You've got to get it by the roots or it'll grow right back," she'd say, and I never knew her keen eye to miss a one. She pitched the water from her dish-washing basin onto the grass in the backyard despite her daughters' protests that the soapsuds might harm the grass and regretted that she couldn't drain the bathtub onto her garden. Her brother, my great-uncle Charlie Duling, liked to tease her by joking, "The reason Lizzie disapproves of people spitting on the sidewalk is that she can't stand the waste of moisture."

Fried chicken dinners unfailingly produced a family minidrama, which played out to the same conclusion time and again. When the platter came around to her, Grandmother would, without fail, reach for the back or the neck in order to leave the choicest pieces for others. Her daughters were long alert to this, however, and the inevitable wrangle over it was a family ritual.

In the summer of 1942, unusual and persistent rains caused seemingly interminable delays of the wheat harvest. The wind and rain bent the stalks nearly double in a soggy tangle, which along with the humidity kept the straw from drying out. The combines inched through this mess as slowly as the tractors pulling them could be throttled down, the tractors bucking slightly as their engines were on the verge of stalling. The rigs frequently had to stop to let slugs of damp straw thump their way through the combines' innards, causing the big machines to shudder as if in torment. When it came time to cut Grandmother's fields, she suggested, in her usual spirit, that the crews shouldn't cut a full swath if it was going to be hard on the combines. Uncle Wayne smiled—he knew his mother— and observed to others later that any wear and tear on the combines in that abnormally difficult harvest was nothing compared to the toll it was taking on his nerves.

❧

In 1905, Grandmother and Grandfather Phipps bought a 240-acre farm near McDonald, which was about 100 miles west of Long Island, Kansas, where they had lived for about twenty years, both before and after their marriage in 1888. The move to McDonald, where their two youngest children and most of their thirteen grandchildren were subsequently born, was a pilgrimage in horse-drawn wagons that took several days. Grandmother lived to fly—fifty-four years later at the age of eighty-nine, from Denver to San Diego on a Boeing 707—and enjoyed marveling at the fact that the flight took only half as long as the five-hour bus ride from McDonald to Denver.

Grandmother went to Sunday school and church every Sunday she was home, barring a blizzard or a rare bout of illness or some other out-of-the-ordinary event. She began her days, including Sundays, about five or five-thirty in the morning. In her robe and slippers, she would go out to the chicken yard in back of her house and snag a young fryer by the leg with a long wire that was bent into a hook on one end. She'd carry the hapless bird over to the buffalo grass in the backyard, grasp it by the head, and with a couple of quick twists of the wrist, swing it in a circle until the centrifugal force exerted by its weight decapitated it. The hen's body, its head still in her hand, would describe a gentle parabola to the grass. After it had stopped flopping, she'd pop it into a pot of boiling water and have it plucked, picked, cleaned, cut, floured, and ready to fry before leaving for church. The rest of us witnessed this sacrificial rite with horrified fascination and to the best of my knowledge no one else in the family was capable of it. When the chore fell to me, I copped out and used an ax and a chopping block. To Grandmother, however, it was just another routine of farm life—and she did make the best fried chicken on the face of the earth. Fortunately, my mother and the rest of the women in the family carried on the tradition—of frying chicken, not killing it.

Grandmother's other culinary efforts were less dramatic, although equally successful. Every Saturday, almost until the day she died, she baked several loaves of bread, depending on how many children, grandchildren, relatives, in-laws, friends, or other visitors were expected at the time. One of the greatest treats my cousins and I and our friends enjoyed as children was those first hot, fresh-out-of-the-oven loaves. We tailored our Saturday afternoon play schedule so that we'd be in the backyard near the kitchen door at 2:00 P.M., which was when the process usually came to fruition. Grandmother would cut into the first loaf out of the oven and spread the slices with butter, which melted immediately, and we'd sprinkle sugar on them. This was a treat that couldn't be matched by any candy we could buy downtown or at Roy Stark's "Gasoline Alley" filling station, which was less than 100 yards down the alley from her house. For us depression-era children, in fact, nickels for candy bars were relatively scarce, which heightened our appreciation of this homemade treat.

Grandmother also made doughnuts, which she'd shake up in a brown paper bag with sugar in it. I have no more pleasurable or sensuous memory than of coming into her warm, cheery kitchen on a snowy winter afternoon, all cold and wet from sledding and playing in the snow, and being given hot cocoa and melted marshmallows, along with doughnuts and the little round balls that had been the "holes," which were fresh out of the boiling grease. If anything, I liked them better without the sugar. Another of her favorite dishes was cornmeal mixed with milk and water and fried into an unleavened cornmeal mush. We'd spread our servings with butter, add pancake syrup, and enjoy one of the great breakfast dishes of the civilized world.

ᴈⱥ

I was very close to Grandmother Phipps because we spent so much time together when I was young. My father died when I was two and a half and my mother and I went to live with her for several years, until Mother remarried and we moved away. After that, however, I continued to return to Kansas in the summers of my high school and college years to work on my uncles' farms and stayed with Grandmother in her house in town; my cousin, Wayne D. Phipps, Jr., Uncle Wayne's son, who was three or four years younger than I, did the same when he was old enough. I also visited Grandmother on the frequent cross-country trips I made before I was married.

In June of 1943, nine years after my father died, Mother went to Cherry Point, North Carolina, where she married Cheston L. "Ert" Raichart, a man she had known when they were teenagers; as a young man, he occasionally had worked on the farm for Grandfather Phipps. A career Marine at the time of Pearl Harbor, Ert was stationed at the Marine Corps Air Station at Cherry Point, prior to going to the Pacific.*

I stayed behind in Kansas with Grandmother, and in late August, she and I took the train to North Carolina. It was a wartime train trip that turned into something of an epic for an eleven-year-old boy and his seventy-one-year-old grandmother. At 8:00 P.M. in Benkleman, Nebraska, thirty miles from McDonald, we boarded the Denver *Zephyr* to Chicago. We were on a Pullman car and I got the upper berth, which the porter pulled down and made up at bedtime. The dining car, where we had breakfast the next morning, was by far the fanciest restaurant I had ever been in. My memory is of blinding white napkins and tablecloths, sparkling crystal, and exotic dishes served by solicitous black waiters. Those traditional Pullman cars with the upper and lower berths were a particular wonder to a farm boy, and the spectacle of total strangers in their pajamas and robes sharing the bathrooms was an exotic novelty. You could even put your shoes out at night and wake up to find them freshly shined! Like many my age, I have had few travel experiences that match the wonder and excitement of the train rides of my youth.

Things started going downhill after we got to Chicago, however, because we had to take a cab to a different train station. We'd been to Denver a few times, but it wasn't a patch on Chicago for size and Grand-

---

*Ert's father was a farmer and schoolteacher versed in the classics; the nickname was a shortening of his middle name, Laertes.

mother was almost as overwhelmed as I was. She hadn't spent any of her life in big cities, or even small ones for that matter, except for infrequent shopping trips to Denver. Unfortunately, the cabdriver was confused as to where we had to go, which put us in danger of missing the connection to Cincinnati. Grandmother began to get panicky at the prospect of such a disaster and I wasn't far behind; for all we knew what to do, we might as well have been in the Congo or on the far side of Mars. The cabbie at various points was defensive, angry, placatory, and finally a little panicky himself as he came to the realization that he couldn't simply dump these two frightened, weeping rustics, just in from the godforsaken boondocks, out on the sidewalk. With resignation, he accepted the reality that the only way he was going to get rid of us was to deliver us to the right railroad.

We did make it, only to discover that if it wasn't one thing, it was another. The 300-mile leg to Cincinnati was in a non-air-conditioned parlor car, which wouldn't have mattered a great deal had the train left on schedule. It being wartime, however, we were sidetracked in favor of troop trains and other higher priority traffic, so we sat on a switching spur sweltering miserably in Chicago's blast-furnace midday August heat with the windows open in the futile hope of catching a breeze. It probably wasn't more than three or four hours, but it seemed like an eternity at the time, with the cars jammed with wartime traffic, lots of servicemen and civilians standing or sitting in the aisles.

At least we had seats, and a couple of things distracted me, if not Grandmother, from the ordeal. She knew there was one element of travel she could control and she had packed enough fried chicken and home-baked-bread-and-butter sandwiches—there is no better combination in the world—to feed a threshing crew. At age eleven, I had yet to see the disaster that home-fried chicken couldn't offset. That, and my boundless fascination with the servicemen's uniforms and insignia and my eavesdropping on their conversations, made that leg of the trip considerably more bearable for me than it was for Grandmother. She, of course, suffered from the conviction that an infinitude of unforeseen and inexplicable catastrophes lurked in waiting, a feeling inspired in part at least by her life's experiences. In due course, however, we arrived in Cincinnati and the next train was absolutely sybaritic. It was an air-conditioned Pullman and ran reasonably close to schedule on the twenty-four-hour ride to Goldsboro, North Carolina, where we were met by Mother and my new stepfather.

The trek ended with one final adventure. On the drive to Cherry Point, we stopped for supper at a roadside café, during which a drunken Marine started threatening the cook with a butcher knife. My stepfather, a Marine warrant officer, was in uniform; he stepped in, and ordered the Marine to put the knife down. Fortunately, the man wasn't totally out of control and retained some sense of military discipline. To me, of course, this was pretty exciting stuff, just like in the movies, and it confirmed my assumption that this phase of my life was going to differ substantially from what had gone before. However, for long-suffering Grandmother Phipps, who had assumed the responsibility for delivering her grandson halfway across the continent, it was just another reminder that calamity lurks around every corner and that be it ever so humble, there's no place like home. Like shipwreck survivors, Grandmother and I were bound even closer by this experience. We recounted it often in later years, in my case with ever-increasing embellishment, and I have no doubt that whatever pleasure she may have derived from the memory was in direct proportion to the passage of time, which gentles most memories.

☙

After I reached my teens, Grandmother followed my nascent social life with amused interest. She didn't miss much and I seldom failed to entertain her. There was good reason for her interest: She never knew quite what to expect. I was a piece of work as a teenager, no doubt about it, a hot dog and a half someone could have covered with mustard. I swaggered around town in my work costume of Marine Corps boondockers (field shoes), Marine dungaree (fatigue) trousers, and blue chambray work shirt with the tail out and unbuttoned to show off my tan and, hopefully, a few chest hairs. This getup was topped with a red felt hat with a "pancake" or flat crown and the front brim pinned up to the crown with a big gold safety pin the way John Wayne did in his cavalry movies. Grandmother regarded her peculiar grandson with her usual indulgent smile and the outfit seemed to entertain the other townspeople as well. John McCain, the mayor and owner of an auto-and-truck-repair garage, took his first look at that getup and laughed out loud: "Well, Dickie, we always know you're going to come up with something different."

One Saturday night, when I was seventeen or eighteen, Ed Cahoj and a couple of other friends and I set out for a dance in Bird City, the next town west of McDonald. We fueled up with a can of Coors apiece at the Highway Cafe, and I was feeling resplendent in a brand-new canary yellow sport shirt and light gray glen plaid slacks. The Highway Cafe was a restaurant and beer joint next to the Standard filling station on U.S. Highway 36, which runs along the south side of town. At that time, the station, like many others, had a "grease pit" next to the building instead of a hydraulic lift for oil changes and lube jobs. The grease pit was a rectangular, concrete-lined trench five or six feet deep and narrow enough that a vehicle's wheels could straddle it so that the station attendant could stand in it and work on the bottom of the car. It was a rainy night and we had parked on that side of the building. We ran out of the café to the car and somehow in the darkness and the storm, I managed to mistake the grease pit for a dark, rain-dampened stretch of sidewalk and sprawled into about an inch of greasy water that had collected in the bottom of it. Why I thought there was ten-foot stretch of sidewalk to nowhere in that particular location, which I'd known all my life, is still a mystery. In any event, the only thing hurt was my pride, so I decided to go home, clean up, and change clothes.

When my friends dropped me off, oily but unbowed, I obviously had a problem of explanation. I looked like something off "The Wreck of the *Hesperus*" and Grandmother was still up and listening to the radio in the living room. Naturally, stealing through the kitchen and up the stairs to my bedroom, getting a change of clothes, sneaking back down to the bathroom, and taking yet another Saturday night bath undetected was out of the question, but I tried. I called in from the kitchen that it was just me, that nothing was wrong, I'd just gotten a bit wet in the rain and had come home to change. She intercepted me before I could get to the stairs, of course. Once assured that her favorite greaseball was unharmed, she broke into laughter at the sight, remarking that I never got *that* filthy in a normal workday on the farm. So, I had to recount the whole miserable tale.

When I told her that my friends were waiting outside in the car, she invited them in while I cleaned up. From the bathtub, I could hear them laughing, at my expense, as they went through it for her one more time. When I emerged, once more presentable and considerably chastened, Grandmother Phipps started laughing again. "Now, be careful, Dickie-Doodle," she said. "Stay away from the Highway Cafe." By the time I arose the next morning, she had washed out the oil stains with detergent and the garments were presentable again. "Your mother will never know the difference," Grandmother assured me. And, "Stay away from the Highway Cafe" became our code for "Be careful and behave yourself."

I was good for a laugh lots of times. One day I was caught in the rain while running the tractor on her farm west of town. I didn't have the pickup that day and was riding the tractor from town to the field and back; it was an International Harvester W9 that had a road gear with a speed of about fifteen miles per hour and the trip took only ten or fifteen minutes. The rain caught me in the middle of the field and I got soaked, but that was the least of it. Mud had packed between the lugs on the big rear-wheel tires and when I shifted into high on the highway, the mud was flung free. On me, mostly. By the time I got to town, I looked like something that had just crawled up out of the primordial ooze. Unfortunately, I had to go down main street (Rawlins Avenue) to get home, the rain had stopped, and people were back out on the street. I was so plastered with black topsoil that probably no one would have recognized me except for the tractor and my red hat. When I got home, Grandmother laughed out loud, yet again, at the apparition that appeared at her kitchen door, before hustling me into a warm bath.

❧

There was one episode that was no laughing matter by any measure, however. The perils of farming, one of the nation's most dangerous occupations, were always in the forefront of Grandmother's mind. It was in August, when we were running the tractors long hours to get the summer fallow ready for drilling wheat in September. Often at that time of year, we worked around the clock with two or three of us operating in shifts. In this instance, however, I was working alone and wanted to finish up the field that had been hailed so badly. It took until after 9:00 P.M. and it was dark by then. When I started the pickup to drive to town, however, the headlights wouldn't go on. I assumed that the problem was a blown fuse, but a quick rummage through the glove compartment didn't turn up any spares.

Since I'd never had a fuse problem with that particular vehicle before, I had no idea whether there were any spares on hand. I tried to drive home in the dark, but had to go on U.S. Highway 36 and it was a cloudy, moonless night. I could barely see the other side of the road, and other vehicles certainly couldn't see me. It was going to be a long, slow trip, assuming I didn't kill myself or someone else in the process, so I pulled over onto the shoulder and made another search for fuses. Poking around in the quarter inch or so of dirt that was caked in the bottom of the glove compartment, I finally unearthed a little tin box of fuses. Fortunately, there also were matches for the benefit of smokers and I was able to locate the blown fuse in the fuse box on the fire wall and replace it.

Voilà! Lights!

I drove into town pleased that the problem hadn't caused me any more inconvenience, never thinking that I might have given anyone reason for concern—a typical teenager's attitude. So, I headed down the main street to Alfred Buck's drugstore to see if it was still open so I could pick up the *Omaha World-Herald,* as I did on workdays like that. A block or so from the drugstore, however, I was stopped by my uncle Vic Ritter, who was in his car coming from the other direction. With obvious concern, Vic asked where I'd been. This surprised me momentarily because I assumed that everyone in town, and certainly in the family, knew where I was spending my days—out on the tractor, like everyone else. But his manner explained itself. I quickly recounted what had happened, then said, "I'll get right home." Vic nodded his agreement.

Of course, with darkness having fallen and me an hour later than usual, Grandmother had the horrible fear that her grandson had fallen off the tractor, with the all-too-imaginable consequences of being run over by the implement, a chisel plow, in this case. She wasn't seeing ghosts, either. Such accidents are a part of farm life and we all were warned to be careful in operating our dangerous equipment. I had been instructed to shut down if I got sleepy in the afternoon—to lie down in the shade of the tractor or the pickup, take a nap, and take no chances of nodding off and falling off the tractor. So, fearing tragedy, Grandmother Phipps had called her daughter Margaret, who had dispatched her husband to investigate. When I arrived, Grandmother rushed to embrace me, weeping and speechless with relief. She confessed that she didn't know how she could ever have borne the ordeal of having to tell my mother, who had already undergone one major tragedy with the death of my father. That was one of the most poignant occasions of my life and certainly one of the most humbling. Although the incident was inadvertent, her tears of anguish and relief put me and my conceits in perspective. The last thing I ever wanted was to give Grandmother cause for grief or unhappiness.

The summer I was eighteen, Christian Endeavor, the Methodist youth Christian study program to which the McDonald Federated Church subscribed and in which I had participated, reentered my life, in a different context than when I was a child. C.E., as it was known, had been moved from Sunday to Wednesday evenings under the auspices of the Reverend Arthur Isbell, a new, young minister who had established a remarkable rapport with many of the teenagers of the town and surrounding farms. Attendance was good, despite my absence, for which the long days of farm work provided a rationalization. Then I learned that a certain girl was attending C.E.

I'd had a couple of dates with her, a handsome, statuesque girl from a family that farmed south of town. That made me the object of some envy by my friends, who privately referred to her as "Outlaw." This was in reference to a recently released, highly ballyhooed movie by that name, which starred the hitherto unknown Jane Russell, a handsome, statuesque actress. The girl of my intentions, however, was no outlaw by any definition. She was as bright and sensible as she was pretty—too intelligent by half to get very serious about the likes of me, as it turned out. I had finished my freshman year of college and she was a year or so away from college but already very interested in it. The opportunity to talk about college seemed to be the basis of whatever interest she had in our relationship, which was mildly romantic, quite pleasant, and completely platonic. It involved movies, dances, parking and a little necking—and a lot of conversation about college and matters of the mind.

In any event, Christian Endeavor was an excuse for us to get together in the middle of the week. We'd sit through the first session, then at the break, when everyone went outside for a stretch, we'd continue on out to the street and get into the pickup. We'd buy Cokes and potato chips at the Highway Cafe and head for the drive-in movie at Atwood, eighteen miles east, or go park on Grandmother's farm and talk.

Since I used the pickup for the farm work, I liked to joke that there usually was enough topsoil in the cab to plant a crop. That normally didn't matter, but as it was the only vehicle available to me, it had to be cleaned up for social use, the need for which normally was slight to nonexistent.

Naturally, Grandmother Phipps approved when I informed her that I was going to start shutting down a little early on Wednesdays in order to attend Christian Endeavor; I generally worked until about 8:00 or 8:30 P.M. when we were doing the field work. She also watched with interest as I carefully swept out the pickup's cab, went over it with a damp cloth, and hosed down the outside before driving off to the church. One reason for her interest was that the church was just a short block from her house. The only thing between them was Fran Miller's garage and John McCain's house, and an NFL quarterback could have broken one of the stained glass windows on the fly from Grandmother's back alley. It was at most a five-minute stroll if you weren't in a hurry, less if you were, and about the only thing likely to deter us from walking to church on Sundays would be a blizzard of a magnitude to threaten the livestock. In normal circumstances, that is.

Not necessarily being normal, I drove off into the dusk on those warm summer evenings, ostensibly on a spiritual quest. I really had no illusion that I was fooling Grandmother; I'd failed too often at that. Customarily, when I ventured out of an evening, I would walk, not drive, in the opposite direction from her house down to main street to check out the action and companionship. Finally, Grandmother could contain her curiosity no longer. "Who's the young lady?" she inquired one evening as I was heading out the door. Somewhat nonplussed, I stuttered and stammered and then gave up in the face of her amused smile. I told her and she nodded her approval, as I knew she would.

I have no idea why I thought I could run that one by her. A couple of years before, I attended my first dance at the Knights of Columbus Hall, which was located next to the Catholic church in the corner of a wheat field twelve miles northeast of town. Again, I tried to be secretive as to why I was getting all dressed up and where I was going. This was primarily because beer and other spirits were sold at KayCee Hall, the Catholics being considerably less inhibited about this than we Protestants, who, truth to tell, were somewhat scandalized by it (not enough to stay away, of course) but titillated, nevertheless. The next morning, I came down to breakfast to find that Grandmother had the *McDonald Standard* open to an ad publicizing the dance and an inquiring look on her face. Once again, I gave up. Actually, what she was curious about was who was there and what had taken place. She didn't mind a little gossip as long as it didn't hurt anyone.

Grandmother always expressed her hope and confidence that I would meet "Miss Right," and one of my great joys was that she lived to meet my wife. The last time I saw Grandmother, in fact, was about nine months before her death, when Mollie, my wife-to-be, and I were leaving after a visit at the end of the summer of 1961. Grandmother was nearly blind by then, but all her other faculties were sharp, and as we drove away that morning, she stood on the back porch wearing her sunbonnet and a long flower-print housedress, smiling and waving her handkerchief in our direction in farewell. I knew she couldn't make out much more than light and shadows, but she knew where we were.

🖎

However cavalier her grandson might have been about religion, Grandmother took it seriously. Her favorite hymns, "In the Garden," "Blessed Assurance," "Bringing in the Sheaves," "Love Lifted Me," "Whispering Hope," and the others, invariably trigger strong and poignant memories of her. Not surprisingly, these are my favorites and like her children and grandchildren I have adopted the ethic and culture of her religion, if not all the theology.

For all of this, a year or so before Grandmother died, she astounded me.

We were sitting at the dining room table when to my astonishment she confided, rather reluctantly and a bit sheepishly, that she wasn't sure she completely believed in Christianity's major tenet of life ever after for true believers. She had believed and she wanted to believe, she said, but . . . at some point she found that she no longer was sure that there was life ever after or a literal Heaven, where people would live in joy and ecstasy through all eternity.

I was not only stunned but saddened because I assumed that believing in John 3:16, which states that the belief—true belief—in the divinity of Christ guarantees eternal life, would be of great comfort to anyone regardless of age or circumstance. I had just read the chapters of Gibbon's *Decline and Fall of the Roman Empire* in which the great Enlightenment skeptic theorized that one reason for the triumph of Christianity was its promise of eternal life, of life ever after, to the people of the Dark Ages, whose temporal lives for the most part were nasty, brutish, and short.

Grandmother confessed that in her ninety-first year she still enjoyed this mortal life. She had worked hard since childhood and had endured more than her share of tribulation and sorrow, but she had always enjoyed good health and still did, except for the gradual loss of her eyesight. She took great pleasure from her large extended family and her circle of friends (the entire town and surrounding countryside), and she avidly watched, or rather listened to, the television news programs and her favorite soap operas. She felt fine physically and still had a good appetite. In fact, the two of us had just finished cleaning up after supper, which we had prepared together, something we had done countless times over the years and which we enjoyed enormously (even the cleanup—she washed, I wiped).

On reflection, her questioning wasn't surprising. She had spent a long life dealing with an often harsh reality and had a clear-eyed, rational view of the world. She was not inclined to be judgmental or moralistic. She was the most tolerant, understanding, and compassionate person her children and grandchildren ever knew. The only theology I ever heard her preach was the Golden Rule and I always thought of her as a Golden Rule Christian because she lived her life by it. Her instinct was to see the best in people and give them the benefit of the doubt. She disdained malicious gossip and believed that you got out of life what you put into it. Her life may have been hard, but she found it rich and fruitful.

✴

That conversation was just one of hundreds Grandmother Phipps and I had over the years. Many took place when the weather was nice as we sat in rocking chairs on the front porch and watched the sunset. I once joked that the only thing we lacked was chewing tobacco to spit over the edge of the porch the way Uncle Charlie did. This tickled her and thereafter her invitations to come visit were couched as proposals to "come on home and we'll sit on the porch and rock and spit." We spent a lot of time over the years "rocking and spitting."

Even after her eyesight began failing, she kept up with the news by listening to the radio and television, and she loved to talk about current events. When I was a graduate student in history at the University of Iowa, I became increasingly interested in the family history and she told me countless anecdotes, which turned out to be the inspiration for this book and many of which none of the other family members remembered having heard.

We did a lot together. We listened to the radio, sharing our amusement at Jack Benny's stinginess and Fibber McGee's hall closet. We played countless games of Chinese checkers, the board game with marbles, which was one of her favorites. But what we enjoyed most was just being together and our hours and hours of conversation. In addition to the normal love between grandparents and grandchildren, Grandmother and I were close friends.

✍

When she died, it was the family's melancholy task to break up her household, with each of us selecting the artifacts we wanted to remember her by. It was doubly anguishing for me because of the realization that I would never again be in the house in which I was born and raised and which represented warmth, security, and love.

As we finished up, I loaded the items to be thrown away into the truck and hauled them out to the town landfill, which was in a ravine a mile west and a half mile south of town. When I had finished unloading, I stood for a moment and looked around.

The inscrutable, brooding prairie stretched unbroken to the horizon, shadowed with blues and other dark hues in the late afternoon sun. As I took in the scene, I began to feel for the first time an almost mystic sense of it. For all the hours and days and weeks that I had spent working that ground under that sky, it was on that sad occasion that I first truly felt the spirit of the land that Grandmother had loved so deeply and to which she had just gone to her eternal rest.

CHAPTER TWO

"IS IT TIME TO PRAY NOW, MAMA?"

THE FIRST OF THE PHIPPS FAMILY FOREBEARS TO IMMIGRATE TO THE New World, Jesse Phipps, was born in Ireland in 1788 and came to Virginia in 1807, later moving to North Carolina. His wife was descended from a Robert Taliaferro, who came to Virginia in 1636 at the age of sixteen. The Taliaferro name was subsequently anglicized to Tolliver, which was my great-grandfather Phipps's first name.

Like many genealogists of families that originated in the United Kingdom, chroniclers of the Phipps family believe it traces back to William the Conqueror and his invasion of England in 1066. In this case, it was a French noble named Taliaferro, who was one of the Conqueror's lieutenants. The Dickenson genealogists have done the same, contending that the family is descended from another Conqueror subaltern, a duke, Walter de Caen, whose domain in Normandy included the Norman city of Caen, and whose oldest son, with inexorable Gallic logic, was know as de Caen's son. The genealogists theorize that many of the Dickensons, Dickinsons, Dickersons, Dicksons, Dixons, Dickasons of this country are descended from the de Caen's son line. It may be that most Americans whose forebears came from the United Kingdom are thirty-seventh cousins or so, God only knows how many times removed, related through their Norman ancestry.

The Dickensons emigrated from England to Virginia in the early eighteenth century. A century later, they crossed the Cumberland Gap on the Daniel Boone Wilderness Road to the West, paused for a generation near Nashville in Sumner County, Tennessee, then moved on to southwest

Missouri, where my father and his siblings, six boys and two girls, were born around the turn of the century. The boys then moved on to Morton County, in the far southwest corner of Kansas, at the time of World War I.

The Phippses also crossed the Cumberland Gap when they migrated north and west to Owen Country, Indiana, from North Carolina in 1834. They made the move with some Tolliver family relatives, their belongings loaded in oxcarts and wagons, with the men, women, and children walking alongside. To succeeding generations, they handed down the story of their leaving, of the grieving farewells to those remaining behind in North Carolina whom they'd never see again, the women weeping into their long white aprons. They also told of the hardships and pleasures of the slow 400-mile trek through the gap across the Cumberland Mountains and up through Kentucky to the Hoosier State. To succeeding generations, they handed down such items as a black walnut kitchen table and a blanket chest that they'd brought along in the wagons.

The Phippses set up farming near Freedom, Indiana, which is about twenty miles west of Bloomington, the site of the state university. Grandfather Phipps was born in Freedom in 1857. Grandmother Phipps's family, the Dulings, who came from Coshocton County, Ohio, also settled on a farm near Freedom twelve years after the Phippses, in 1846. The Dulings were of German descent and Grandmother referred to them as "Pennsylvania Dutch." She used some German words and phrases such as *Schmierkäse* for cottage cheese, the pronunciation of which she anglicized to "smearcase." The Duling forebears were Germans who had moved to Holland (thus the "Dutch"), landed in Pennsylvania in the early eighteenth century, and pushed west to Ohio and Indiana.

Both my maternal great-grandfathers served in the Union Army in the Civil War. On February 15, 1865, two months before the war's end, Tolliver Phipps, age thirty-five, enlisted in the 148th Indiana Infantry, which was recruited and formed up in Indianapolis in February 1865 and was mustered out the following September. Like many units from the western states, the regiment was part of the Army of the Tennessee and mostly pulled guard and garrison duty in middle Tennessee. Two men were killed in action and thirty-four died of disease in its brief history. Tolliver Phipps was a nonfatal disease victim. Two weeks after enlisting, he came down with pneumonic typhoid fever and was hospitalized in the Indianapolis city hospital in a scarlet fever ward. The illness left him with weakened kidneys, lungs, and eyesight—when he died of tuberculosis in 1914 at the age of eighty-five, he had been almost completely blind for years. He also got chronic diarrhea contracted by drinking bad water while his company was guarding a railroad bridge south of Nashville in August 1865. He received a federal disability pension for the last twenty-four years of his life, eight dollars per month at first, then raised to twenty dollars per month in 1907 as the result of a bill passed by Congress that year.

Tolliver Phipps's experience was typical of the Civil War, in which two soldiers died of disease for every one killed in combat, which was the case on both sides. This was partly due to society's total ignorance of germs and the importance of sanitation at the time and partly due to the packing together by the thousands of farm boys who had had no exposure to common diseases and therefore no immunity to them. In the Union Army, the farm boys were much more susceptible—about 45 percent more so, according to the records—to contagious diseases, including such childhood illnesses as mumps and measles, than their counterparts from the more densely populated northeastern and Middle Atlantic cities, who had had more exposure to the various bacteria and had built up greater resistance.

Grandmother Phipps's father, Collin C. Duling, enlisted in the 97th Indiana Infantry in 1862 at the age of twenty, was assigned to Company F, and went, as a family history put it, "to the front to defend his country." The 97th Indiana was recruited from the then Seventh Congressional District, which included Terre Haute and the west central part of the state. Like the 148th, it was part of the Army of the Tennessee, first under Ulysses S. Grant and then William T. Sherman. It participated in the siege of Vicksburg and the battles of Chattanooga and Kennesaw Mountain. In July and August of 1864, it was part of Sherman's force that besieged Atlanta, and was on the right flank of his "March to the Sea" in November and December of that year. It fought up through the Carolinas as Sherman pursued Confederate general Joseph T. Johnston in the final battles of the war. In January 1864, when the regiment and its parent unit, the 4th Division,* were at Scottsboro, Alabama, Collin Duling was transferred from Company F to the "Division Train" for logistics and communications, where he remained for the duration as a teamster.

According to the Indiana adjutant general's report of 1866, the 97th Indiana lost 46 men killed in action; 149 died of sickness and disease and 146 were wounded. Collin Duling emerged unscathed, was mustered out of service along with the rest of the regiment in June 1865, and married Sarah Matilda Kauffman two years later. Grandmother Phipps was born near Freedom in 1871, the second of six children.

---

*The 4th Infantry Division was among the first to land at Utah Beach on D-Day, June 6, 1944.

In 1876, when Grandmother was five, the Duling family moved from Indiana to Nebraska and in 1879 moved to Norton County, Kansas, where they took up a homestead just south of the Nebraska line, about sixty miles southwest of Red Cloud, Nebraska, Willa Cather's hometown. The mysterious, brooding prairie that Cather described so eloquently in *My Antonia* and *O Pioneers!* was the land the Dulings and Phippses settled. The Phipps family followed the Dulings to western Kansas three years later, in September of 1882, settling a few miles east of them, in Phillips County. This move was due in large part to my great-grandmother Margaret Ann Holbert Phipps, a deeply devout Baptist.

In 1880, the Kansas state legislature enacted an amendment to the state constitution "to absolutely and forever prohibit the manufacture, importation, and sale of intoxicating liquors as a beverage" in Kansas, which the voters ratified by referendum. Her Baptist minister convinced her that Kansas would always be a teetotal state and that sounded good to her. The preacher knew whereof he spoke. In 1881, U.S. senator Preston B. Plumb of Kansas was the first to propose a national constitutional amendment on prohibition. Kansas led the charge that succeeded in 1919, nearly forty years later, in getting the Eighteenth Amendment enacted, aided enormously by the World War I war effort.

Prohibition wasn't the work of religious and moral crusaders alone. Businessmen had become increasingly concerned about drunkenness and absenteeism in the industrial workforce, particularly among the poorly educated immigrants of the late nineteenth and early twentieth centuries. This worry, plus criticism that grain needed for the war effort and the people of war-ravaged Europe was being used by distillers, came to a head in the industrial war mobilization. Corporate money and leadership was a major factor in the passage of the Eighteenth Amendment. Nor was John Barleycorn the only agent of the devil with which Kansans struggled during that time. There were periodic attempts to ban cigarette smoking at the state universities, among public-school teachers, and in the military training centers in the state during World War I. There also were campaigns against dancing, particularly the decadent tango.

In their puritanism, the Phippses were in the mainstream of the state. The outside perception of Kansas at this time was colored by the emergence of the lurid cattle towns of Abilene, Newton, Ellsworth, Wichita, and Dodge City as the Union Pacific Railroad pushed west from Kansas City. These were the railheads through which Texas beef was shipped back east after the Civil War (Abilene was the first) and they actually were the settings not only of Wild Bill Hickock, but of Bat Masterson, Wyatt Earp,

Doc Holliday, Luke Short, and the Long Branch Saloon as well. The 1948 movie *Red River*, with John Wayne, Montgomery Clift, Joanne Dru, John Ireland, Walter Brennan, Ward Bond, and the rest of the John Wayne Western-movie repertory company, was based on a novel about the first cattle drive from Texas up what became the Chisholm Trail to Abilene.

The reality, however, was that the cultural and social fabric of Kansas was more the creation of New England puritans and abolitionists who came to the territory during the pre–Civil War period of "Bleeding Kansas," and of like-minded followers, such as the Phippses, than of fast-draw John Wayne types shooting it out on Main Street. The settlers by and large were puritanical and pious, and many, like the Mennonites, had migrated to escape religious persecution, repressive government, and military conscription. They were closer culturally to New England and Europe than to Texas. Jacob Eisenhower, who moved his family of six boys (one of whom grew up to be president of the United States) to the wild and woolly cow town of Abilene, Kansas, in 1878–79, was a member of the sober, pious Pennsylvania Dutch River Brethren sect. Until Dwight Eisenhower was named commander of the invasion of North Africa in 1942, Abilene's most famous son had been its marshal in 1871, Wild Bill Hickock. The railroad in many of these cow towns was the dividing line between the respectable folks and the cowboy saloons and brothels, giving rise to the concept of the right side and wrong side of the tracks.*

In addition to being a teetotaler in principle, Margaret Ann Phipps was concerned about her oldest son, James Matthew Phipps—my grandfather—who had married in 1876 at the age of nineteen but was widowed in 1880. Jim Phipps was described by one of his nephews as "perhaps the most agile, best-proportioned man" he ever knew. His mother, however, feared that without the gentling influence of his late wife, my grandfather was getting far too much enjoyment out of the saloons in Freedom, a rough-and-tumble—often violent—timber and sawmill town. One family member recalled that "Mother said that on a still evening they could hear the fighting and the roistering clear out to their farm, about a half mile from town. Those fellows went in for gouging out the loser's eye and Mother said there were a lot of one-eyed men around."

At first, it wasn't clear that the move to Kansas was the solution to that particular problem. For starters, the family had settled only twenty-five miles from three towns just across the line in Nebraska—one of which,

---

*In 1907, the *McDonald News* ran this bit of advice: "An anxious young lady asked what was the proper height for a lady to raise her skirts on a muddy day. For modest young ladies, possibly 3 inches . . . not more than that." This was a typical matter of concern of the time.

Orleans, was a railroad junction. Nebraska was a state that didn't share Kansas's passion for abstinence. According to family recollections, it didn't take long for Grandpa and his brother-in-law, Marion Hicks, a free-spirited young homesteader who also operated a blacksmith shop in his backyard, to discover this.* The Hicks family's pilgrimage had paralleled that of the Phippses. They came from southwest Virginia, not far from the Phippses, who had been just across the state line in northwest North Carolina, and the two families had known each other before moving west. The Hicks family also migrated to Freedom, Indiana, and then to western Kansas.

Shortly after the Phippses arrived in Kansas, Tolliver Phipps bought the timber off part of a stand of trees near his new farm and dispatched Grandpa and Marion to cut it. One of the trees they cut fell between two stumps and was going to have to be lifted out, which appeared to be impossible without a team of horses or some other aid. The man who owned the timber stand derived considerable humor from their predicament, but while Grandpa was talking to him, Marion straddled the fallen tree and hefted it to see how heavy it was. When Grandpa, who was facing Marion, saw that he was able to lift the tree over the stumps, he bet the landowner a gallon of whiskey that one man could hoist it free. The man gleefully took the bet and Grandpa and Marion shortly thereafter were a jug of whiskey richer, if not wiser. The landowner's sense of humor took a definite downward turn.

Tolliver Phipps accepted his son's escapades somewhat more philosophically than his wife did. Before they moved to Kansas, Grandpa, Marion, and some of the boys had done a bit of carousing in Freedom one Saturday night, which had sparked talk around town the next day. Grandpa was complaining to his father that the accounts were greatly exaggerated, in some cases completely fabricated, and wondered why people didn't just mind their own business and shut up. When Grandpa finished, Tolliver Phipps observed, "Well, if a man makes a jackass out of himself, he can't blame people for trying to get on and ride."

Grandpa's marriage to my grandmother in 1888, six years after he moved to Kansas, changed all that, however. He became a highly respected and successful farmer and a deeply religious man (as ultimately did Marion Hicks). He was the Baptist church Sunday school superintendent, mayor of McDonald, a member of the co-op board, and a longtime

*Marion's weight lifter's physique and strength were legendary. One family account cites several witnesses who claimed to have seen him hold his 225-pound anvil by the horn out at arm's length with one hand. The term *grain of salt*, however, comes to mind.

member of the school board. In his obituary, he was described as "a pioneer of the west," a man with a "rugged, self-reliant type of friendly and kindly disposition," one who had a "deep understanding of the frailty of human nature and had that charity of heart that made it his disposition to help rather than censor the wrongdoer."

His youngest son, my uncle Wayne, thought Grandfather Phipps was "undoubtedly the smartest man in the world. He didn't try to impress anyone, he'd just comment in a quiet way about events and people." My mother has a considerably sterner memory of her father. She remembers a strict disciplinarian looking for a switch with which to punish his youngest child, Fern. Aunt Margaret, Grandpa's second-youngest daughter, remembers "a stern parent who didn't like or tolerate foolishness. He was strict and we behaved around him." Fern herself recalls a stern paterfamilias who set a time for her to be home on dates when she was a teenager and could be counted on to be sitting up in the living room to ensure the curfew was met.

I have just a handful of memories of a big, formidable man with a walrus mustache who towered above the corn in the field just west of his farm, which to me at the age of three or four seemed like a forest of trees. I can recall trying manfully to stretch my legs enough to walk in his tracks as I followed him from the farmhouse to the barn, which prompted one of the hired men, Audrey Klepper, to laugh, "That boy's really trying to follow in your footsteps, isn't he, Mr. Phipps?"

When Grandmother and Grandfather Phipps were married on September 13, 1888, he was five days shy of his thirty-first birthday and Grandmother was a month away from her seventeenth. They had seven children, four boys and three girls, the youngest of whom was born when Grandpa was almost fifty-eight and Grandmother was nearly forty-five, twenty-seven years after they were married.*

The Phippses and Dulings had known each other in Indiana and got together again after the Phippses arrived in Kansas. Tolliver Phipps bought two quarter sections from the federal government, one for $1,325 ($8.28 per acre), the other for $4,000 ($25 per acre). Grandfather Phipps farmed and traded in land, buying and selling quarter sections, some in partnership with his brother-in-law, Charles A. Duling, Grandmother Phipps's older brother.

Like everyone else who migrated to western Kansas in the late 1870s and early 1880s, the Phippses and Dulings enjoyed the abnormally abun-

---

*This youngest child, Fern, was younger than two of her nieces and one of her nephews, her oldest brother's three children.

dant rainfall of the 1880s and then were rudely jolted into reality by the decade of drought that began in the summer of 1887. This followed the disastrous blizzards of 1886–87, which killed about 80 percent of the range cattle. This, in effect, ended the free-range cattle industry, although its days were numbered anyway because of the advent of the homesteaders and other small farmers who could cheaply fence off their land with the invention of barbed wire. The hard times of drought and depression lasted through the 1890s until the first years of the twentieth century, when nearly two decades of good crops and high prices, lasting through World War I, marked the so-called "Golden Age" of American agriculture.

Unlike many of their neighbors, who in the 1890s had to give up and return in defeat and discouragement to their homes back east, the Phippses and Dulings managed to survive the hard times and avoid bankruptcy and foreclosure; Tolliver Phipps left an estate of land and other holdings to his surviving children, my grandfather and his sister, Addie. In addition to farming wheat, Tolliver Phipps was a highly respected cattle breeder and set out a large orchard of plum, apple, peach, apricot, and cherry trees. He had a reputation as a naturalist—one of his grandsons was told years later by one of his elders that only the lead character in the novel The Yearling knew more about nature than Tolliver Phipps. This closeness with nature made him more farsighted than his peers; he worried about soil erosion in northwest Kansas long before enough native sod had been turned under to make it a problem, which happened a half century after he moved there, and with a vengeance. This caused many to consider him eccentric because they didn't foresee wind erosion and couldn't imagine that there would ever be rain enough to wash the topsoil away. After farming near the town of Long Island, Tolliver and Margaret subsequently moved into town, where they were active in the community and church.

In 1905, Grandfather and Grandmother Phipps bought a 240-acre farm about 100 miles west of Long Island and three miles west of the town of McDonald in Rawlins County, where I was born. My mother, their fourth child, was only four at the time, but vividly remembered that 100-mile trek west despite her tender years. By that time, there were graded roads between the towns, including what is now U.S. Highway 36, which runs east and west parallel to the fomer Chicago, Burlington and Quincy Railroad line (now Burlington Northern) through McDonald. There also were wagon trails on the section lines (a section is a square mile) that subsequently became graded and graveled roads.

The family swung a bit out of their way, to the south of the railroad and highway route, in order to stay with relatives and friends who were located along the way, as was the custom in those days.* Grandpa and the three oldest children—my uncles, Chester, than sixteen, Blaine, twelve, and Asa, eight—were in the hayrack, a big wagon for hauling hay, which was loaded with the family's possessions. Grandmother, Mother, and Aunt Margaret, not yet a year old, rode behind in a buggy hitched to the hayrack.

The most memorable moment of the pilgrimage was when the buggy came unhitched in the middle of a creek they were fording. The hayrack continued across the creek and was the only sign of life at that point on the vast prairie. "Oh, Lord, Lord!" Mother recalled Grandmother exclaiming. "Lord, please help us now!" Then, recalling the precept that the Lord helps those who help themselves, a principle she lived by, Grandmother splashed into the creek and ran to catch up with the hayrack. Every time they came to another creek on the trip, Mother would ask anxiously, "Is it time to pray now, Mama?" That evolved into a family joke and whenever Grandmother would exclaim, "Oh, Lord!" as she did occasionally when something untoward happened, the girls would laugh and respond, "Is it time to pray now, Mama?"

The new farm was virgin sod, the tough, wiry buffalo grass and other short grasses of the region. Grandpa and the oldest boys broke the sod into strips and then cut it into blocks with which they constructed a sod house. Reflecting the economic priorities of the time, the farm had a frame barn and outbuildings for the animals well before there was a frame house for the humans.

The easiest way to build a "soddie" was to burrow into the side of a hill or rise, preferably on the east or south side, which got the sun and was alee of the wind, and build just the front section out of the sod blocks. On the High Plains, however, there wasn't always a hill or rise where it was most convenient and most soddies were built from the ground up with sod blocks. The settlers broke the sod with a steel breaking plow that cut it into strips about eighteen inches wide and three or four inches deep, leaving the grass and root system intact. They cut these strips into slabs about three feet long and stacked them on top of each other grass side down,

*It was a custom my mother came to loathe as an adult because friends and relatives, still operating under the old habits but far more mobile thanks to Henry Ford, would drop in unannounced, blithely assuming that they would be put up for the night—or two or three. Grandmother shared this assumption, or at least acquiesced in it, but Mother had a more up-to-date view. Being a woman of diamond-tipped will as well, Mother managed to put a chill on a number of warm Kansas evenings, which no doubt induced heartburn in her gentle, easy-going mother.

with the tough, thick roots and grass holding the slab together. The walls were secured by staggering each tier the way masons do bricks, laying every third slab crosswise, and pinning the slabs together with stakes driven through them at the corners and at intervals in between. Loose dirt was tamped in as mortar to level the slabs and seal the cracks between them.

As wood became available, the settlers put in wooden floors and roofs. Otherwise, they made do with thatched or sod roofs supported by a ridge pole and rafters made of whatever scraps of wood were available, including poles cut from the cottonwood, ash, hackberry, and elm trees that grew along the creeks. Thatching was made of willow brush and prairie hay from the creek bottoms with sod blocks on top to keep it from blowing away in the strong, persistent Kansas winds and, hopefully, to help make it waterproof. The walls and ceiling were lined with burlap or heavy white muslin and every couple of weeks or so, all the furniture would have to be moved outside and the muslin linings and room partitions would be taken down and boiled and scrubbed.

The soddies had the virtue of being well insulated against the cold and heat, but that probably was their only one. They were dark. They were leaky and sections of the roof would occasionally collapse. There also were snakes, lizards, centipedes, ground squirrels, prairie dogs, and other burrowing critters that didn't realize they were intruding and would pop unexpectedly through the ceiling and walls into the muslin lining, often at night when it was most disconcerting. The hope that a soddie would be waterproof was only a hope, and the cloth linings had the virtue not only of catching the occasional visitor, but of funneling the water into buckets and washtubs when it rained. Mother particularly feared that a snake would fall through the muslin at some point, and occasionally this would prompt her to climb into bed with her grandfather, Tolliver Phipps, who had come out to live with them shortly after they moved. She later confided that for years afterward, she had dreams about snakes, which probably was common to many soddie dwellers.

The family lived in the sod house from 1905 to 1910. Wayne, the youngest son, was born in it in 1908. In 1910, Grandpa put Grandmother and the youngest children on the train to go stay with his sister and her husband on their farm back in Phillips County over the winter while he and Chester, Blaine, and Asa built a three-room frame house. The older children continued to use the soddie as a sleeping annex until he built a two-story addition a couple of years later which had a living room, dining room, and main bedroom downstairs and two bedrooms upstairs. The girls shared one of the upstairs rooms, the boys the other. Chet, the oldest son, married in 1910 and lived in the soddie with his bride for a time after the addition was put on the frame house.

Grandpa and the boys broke the sod on that farm at first with horses, mules, and hand plows. It took brutal, unrelenting, muscle-popping exertion to keep the plow cutting a straight, eight-inch furrow, and the farmers' lives were enormously eased when the walking plows were superseded by six-horse teams and riding or "sulky" plows. In 1915, when Grandpa bought another half section of buffalo grass a mile south, which also had to be broken, the job was made far easier by his new gasoline-powered tractor.

Gradually, the family improved the farm, enlarging the house, adding outbuildings, and digging an ice cellar. This was about fifteen feet long, twelve feet wide, and eight feet deep, with a roof. It was filled with huge blocks of ice cut from a man-made pond on the Archer farm two miles south or nearby creeks and rivers, or shipped in by boxcar from further east. Insulated with straw between the layers of blocks and on top, the ice would last the summer and some was used to chill the iceboxes that preceded electricity and refrigerators. Later, machine-made ice, generally sold in 100-pound blocks, could be bought year-round in town. Butter and milk and other perishables also could be kept cool in summer by lowering them into the well. Ice cellars or icehouses were used until the Rural Electrification Administration wired rural areas, a project begun before World War II and completed in the years just after. In 1925 the *McDonald Standard* carried a farm advice column from the Department of Agriculture with instructions for building and insulating icehouses and cutting ice off a pond; for keeping cream it recommended a half ton of ice per cow, for milk a ton and a half per cow (a ton is forty-five cubic feet).

From 1905 to 1913, the younger children attended a one-room country school, which was located a mile north of the farm and whose eight grades were taught by a neighbor's daughter. Asa, the third son, didn't make it all the way through, however. When he was in the eighth grade, in the school year of 1910–11, he became angry at the teacher over something, stood up, made a speech announcing that he was through with school, and walked out.

Although many teachers generally had fond memories of their experiences, the job had its drawbacks, one of which was boys like Uncle Asa. Older boys often were a hazard to the young women, many of whom were just in their late teens and whose training consisted of taking a normal course of one to three months and then passing the teacher's examination. Eighth-grade boys who tried to sneak a chew of tobacco in class were not uncommon and many teachers recalled how older boys often tried to trick them to reveal the shallowness of their preparation. In those early years of the century, the teachers were paid as little as fifteen dollars a month and were often put up by farm families in return for helping with the housework, sometimes even sharing a bed with a younger child.*

Asa wasn't a troublemaker, he just didn't have any use for school; he had a reputation, in fact, for merriment and being something of a class clown, and old family photos almost invariably catch him laughing and cutting up. He did go to school in town for a couple of years with the younger children after Grandpa and Grandmother decided they could get a better education there than in the one-roomer out by the farm, but he didn't finish high school. As did the children of other farm families, Asa, Mother, Margaret, and Wayne drove the three miles to town in the buggy or a spring wagon behind a team of horses, which they put up at a livery barn. They arrived back at the farm in the late afternoon in time to help with the milking, feeding the livestock, chopping wood, and other chores.

McDonald opened its high school in 1915. Until then, high school students had to go to the county-seat towns of Atwood, eighteen miles east, or St. Francis, in Cheyenne County, twenty-three miles west. McDonald High's first graduating class, in 1917, consisted of one: William Roy "Link" Lyman, a son of the town's leading land agent, who was also a large rancher. Link may have felt somewhat lonely at times, but he filled a lot of space just by himself. He was a big, handsome football star who got his nickname when he was enrolled at the University of Nebraska in Lincoln, where he was an all-American tackle. He went on to play professionally for thirteen seasons for the Canton Bulldogs and then the Chicago Bears, where he was a teammate of Red Grange and Bronko Nagurski and, like them, is in the National Professional Football Hall of Fame. He was two years ahead of my mother in school and was her first boyfriend.

The Phipps family had a mixed record on education. Not surprisingly, the family put increasing emphasis on education as it tamed its frontier farm and life became easier. Blaine, my mother, Wayne, and Fern went to college and only Blaine, whose attendance was interrupted by military ser-

*The McDonald News of October 4, 1907, has an account of the outcome of the trial in Goodland, fifty miles away, of a "demure little school marm" who was sued for whipping a boy for disobedience and won. "Hands were clapped and a purse and bouquet presented. If more teachers had the pluck and nerve of the little Sherman County teacher, there would be less need of reform schools and state prisons," the story concluded.

vice and his untimely death, failed to graduate. Mother and Fern became teachers, of English and music respectively. Uncle Chet, the oldest, never went to high school, although he briefly attended business college in Grand Island, Nebraska, where he confessed to Wayne that the only thing he learned was the elegant penmanship of the time. Asa's ambitions were to farm and get to the war in 1917.

Blaine went to high school in St. Francis, roomed in a private home, and was visited by his parents or came home on weekends, a two- or three-hour trip one way by horse and buggy. He was in a class of ten whose class yell was "Bachelors three, Old Maids seven—we're the Class of 1911." A brilliant student, he worked briefly for a newspaper in Houston, then attended the University of Illinois, where he worked his way as a telegrapher and hotel night clerk. A big man (about six feet four), he was on the Fighting Illini varsity football team and a member of the ROTC, which was compulsory at land grant universities.

Mother went off to college after graduating from high school in 1919, first to Frances Shimer in Illinois, where she spent two dreadfully home-sick years, then to Ottawa University, a Baptist school in Ottawa, Kansas. Uncle Wayne also graduated from Ottawa, class of '29, where he distinguished himself primarily by playing end on the varsity football team and breaking his leg jumping off a porch one evening with the intention of making an ice-cream run.

Margaret dropped out of high school at the end of her junior year at the age of eighteen in May 1923 to marry a handsome young man named Hugh Victor Ritter. Vic was a man of many accomplishments. Besides being musically (violin and vocal) and artistically inclined, he was a dedicated entrepreneur who, with his brother, built and opened a grocery store and movie theater on Main Street after they moved to McDonald from Arkansas. It was a classic small-town courtship and marriage.

"I got so I liked to go down and get the groceries," Margaret recalled, laughing, more than sixty years later. "I'd sit on the counter and visit with Vic. I was only about sixteen or so. He was six years older. He'd also deliver groceries to the house and I kind of liked that. I remember he wore dark blue denim overalls. You remember how men used to wear overalls in those days? I thought he looked pretty good in those overalls."

It was love at first sight. Their first date was a high school basketball game. They'd go to community and school plays. Driving around the countryside on Sundays was a favorite form of entertainment. They courted for more than a year. "Sometimes we'd sit around the room and the folks would go to bed and Vic stayed a little too late one night, I guess, and Dad walked from the bedroom right through the front room past us and Vic decided it was time to go home. He could take a hint."

They were married by the Federated Church minister in the living room of Grandpa and Grandmother's house in the middle of a weekday. "After the ceremony, Vic had to play a violin solo at some program at the school," Margaret recalled. "I waited out in the back there. As soon as he got through playing, we got in the car and drove to Goodland and spent the night. Then we went on to Colorado Springs and spent a couple of weeks there. Vic's folks had a cabin up at Manitou [Springs] and we stayed there. His aunt was living there, but she moved out when we came and let us take over." It was a long, happy marriage that produced a close-knit family of three boys and three girls.

🕮

Those were good years for the Phipps family and for farmers in general. Money and credit were easy, crops were good, and prices were high enough that the first two decades of the twentieth century were one of the few times that the farmer's buying power matched that of the rest of society. The ratio of agricultural commodity prices to the farmer's expenses of this period is the basis of farm "parity" and price support payments today. This "Golden Age" of agriculture was a brief window of tranquillity and prosperity between the hard times that had preceded it and those that were to come. But at this point, their move to Kansas was looking good.

CHAPTER THREE

CENTENNIAL

THE PARADE BEGAN AT 10:00 A.M. SATURDAY, RIGHT ON SCHEDULE. The high school band passed Pete Holub's big auto-and-tractor-repair shop at the intersection of Lincoln Avenue and main street on the north end of town and, followed by the 125 other floats, it wheeled south down the west side of main street (which for some reason is named Ralwins Avenue, although it's never called that) then back up the other. The number of entries—bands, floats, classic autos, horsemen on thoroughbred steeds—was astonishing, and all the town's business establishments, clubs, and organizations, as well as many of its families, were represented. So were the chambers of commerce, civic and service clubs, and business establishments from nearly every neighboring town in northwest Kansas, eastern Colorado, and southwest Nebraska within 50 to 100 miles. The centennial celebration of McDonald, Kansas, was under way.

Ronald McDonald of the fast-food chain, resplendent in his clown costume, huge shoes, bulbous red nose, and fright wig, drove crazily through the otherwise orderly affair in an eccentric-wheeled (and eccentrically painted) clown car, a Model A Ford whose engine periodically bucked and wheezed and emitted steam and acted as though it were about to expire or explode. McDonald's, which participates with towns and people of the same name who are celebrating anniversaries and memorials of this sort, also donated $2,000 cash, which helped finance a high-tech sound system capable of coping with the whistling prairie winds that otherwise would have drowned out the performers in the outdoor patriotic cantata on Saturday night. The centennial's organizers also got word to NBC's Willard Scott, who mentioned it on the *Today* show.

Keith Headrick, an old schoolmate of mine who has lived in Denver for years, noted admiringly: "If somone had tried to tell me that anyone could organize a parade this big and this good out here and that this many people would come to see it, I'd have told them they were crazier than hell. I was at a parade in Denver a couple of weeks ago that wasn't half as good as this." No one was inclined to disagree and as the parade progressed, civic pride swelled accordingly.

🌾

It was the weekend of June 10, 11, and 12, 1988, that my hometown of McDonald commemorated its 100th year on the High Plains of western Kansas. The skies were blue and the golden sun baked the prairie, ripening the endless fields of wheat as the summer solstice drew near. For forty-eight hours, God was in his Heaven and all was right with the world for the centennial celebrants—residents, former residents, friends, and neighbors of this little farm town of about 200 souls that perches precariously on the vast, windswept plains thirty-five miles east of the Colorado line and fifteen miles south of Nebraska.

In its heyday, McDonald's population only got up to 435, but the head count for the outdoor hamburgers and the barbecue lunch and dinner the Lions Club served on Saturday came to about 3,000, most of whom hadn't lived in the town in some time. We packed the streets, having journeyed from as far as California, Florida, and Washington, D.C., to commemorate our hometown's 100th birthday. When one of the organizers, welcoming us back home, noted in a flight of rhetoric that many had come "from the four corners of the earth," one member of the audience murmured to his neighbor that as a matter of fact they had come *to* one of the four corners of the earth, and a far corner at that. A joke that made the rounds was: "The good news is that McDonald isn't the end of the earth. The bad news is that you can see it from here."

Be that as it may, everyone seemed to be quite happy to be back where they could, figuratively, peer over the edge of the earth if they wished. The festivities were abetted by the fact that a bumper wheat crop was less than a month away from harvest, the area having escaped the drought that was parching vast areas of the Dakotas, Minnesota, and the corn triangle of Iowa, Illinois, and Indiana. No matter how long ago people had moved away, among the first questions they invariably asked were: "How's the weather?" and "How's the wheat?" those concerns being innate to people from the High Plains.

Wallace Stegner, the great environmentalist and writer, spoke for me, and I think for most of the rest at our centennial as well, about the small towns of the West:

> The loneliness and vulnerability of those towns always moves me, for I have lived in them. I know how the world of a child in one of them is bounded by weedy prairie or the spine of the nearest dry range. . . . I know how precious is the safety of a few known streets and vacant lots and familiar houses. I know how the road in each direction both threatens and beckons. I know that most of the children in such a town will sooner or later take that road, and that only a few will find it back.

For many of us, our formative years in McDonald gave us the strongest sense of security and community we would ever experience. At any given moment my mind's eye can picture McDonald's every street and house, its stores and people, for they are as familiar to me as my innermost thoughts. And for one weekend, at least, quite a lot of us found that road back to the safety of those few known streets and familiar houses, and were reminded of what we'd left behind.

The celebration actually got under way early Friday evening with family picnics on the school grounds. The music was provided by a local bluegrass band led by a young man named Eldon Pickett, a member of one of the town's oldest families. Many of the out-of-towners approached the festivities somewhat uncertainly. They stared into the faces of old friends and former classmates, pulled identifications out of their memories, and, tentatively at first but with growing confidence, renewed old friendships and shared memories.

As it turned out, the centennial was a rip-roaring success from start to finish. The fact that some had been apprehensive about how it would go, however, was a reminder that growing up in that part of the country, where Mother Nature and remote economic forces are often harsh and capricious, can foster a turn of mind that tends to view the glass as half empty rather than half full. The event—and its success—stirred mixed feelings of affection and nostalgia for the town and dismay about its overall decline; the years have not been kind to small farm towns like McDonald, which have steadily grown smaller since World War II.

Historically, High Plains settlers have suffered from feelings of physical and psychic isolation and the conviction that they are often the victims of global political and market forces and weather phenomena over which they have little control and which more often than not seem to do bad things to them. Thus, they battle a sense of defensiveness, a feeling that people from the cities, and possibly even some of the native-born who have moved away, either don't acknowledge that they exist or secretly scorn them. In fact, some former residents did approach the centennial with some trepidation, partly because they didn't know how the town would look, and, frankly, wondered if the good folks there could pull it off.

O Ye of Little Faith! The centennial's spectacular success was a tribute to the community's civic dedication and two years of hard work by a committee of townspeople and farmers led by, among others, Chairman Les Loker, a hard-driving regional insurance executive; Mayor Raymond Johnson; Gene Sramek, a farmer and chairman of the Centennial Historical Committee; and about twenty-five others. Their accomplishment intensified the celebrants' affection and memories of a time when they still were young enough to believe almost literally that McDonald was at the center of the universe.

McDonald is an ordered and well-laid-out town, and when I was growing up there every house was occupied and well tended. As a youth, I nurtured a secret, chauvinistic belief that our street, Decatur Avenue, which runs north and south, had the best houses in town. Grandfather and Grandmother Phipps's big two-story house, in which I was born, was next door to a bungalow that she and Grandpa built in the early 1920s, while across the street was the even larger Voorhies house. South of us were the big houses of the Lymans, the Morelands, the Harpers, and to the north were the Madsens, Kacireks, Caswells, Benklemans, Harrisons, Dobbses, Wingfields, Bucks, and other leading families; I took piano lessons from Hertha Benkleman in her living room and before I was old enough to work on the harvest crews mowed lawns and weeded gardens for the Benklemans, Harrisons, and Dobbses. In fact, most of the blocks are a mixture of large, medium, and small houses; the Voorhies house, which has fallen into a sad state of disrepair although it's still occupied, was next to two tiny "shotgun" cottages. Although considerably diminished over the past three decades, the town still is neat and orderly, even though Main Street is deserted at night and on Sundays after church. This makes it seem somewhat barren, which is apropos to the High Plains. However, it doesn't have the unkempt look of Herndon and Ludell, the two other dwindling small towns in Rawlins County, whose business districts by comparison seem overgrown by trees and have a sort of weedy, gone-to-seed look to them.

To begin with, McDonald had been spruced up for the centennial as it hadn't been in years. Part of the sadness of a declining town is the concomitant physical decay, with abandoned buildings, weeds, and junk piling up in some of the vacant yards and empty lots. The weeds were cut and all the old, rusting farm vehicles and implements that had accumulated over the years were hauled away—rod weeders, one-way plows, wheat drills, harrows, and disks; McCormick-Deering, John Deere, Case, and Oliver tractors; Dodge, GMC, Ford, and Diamond T farm trucks and pickups; and old Chevy, Ford, and Plymouth automobiles, some still mostly intact, some stripped down to their frames and chassis. The people gave their houses and yards the spring cleanup of their lives, and the town was turned out for the event like a senior prom queen ready for the ball.

The cleanup actually began in 1985 when the sewer system was installed. When the ditches for the system were dug, the alleys were cleared of trash barrels and outhouses, some of which had survived even to that late date. Every house in town was repainted for the centennial, with the exception of one hard-headed holdout who owned one of the biggest houses in town, one my uncle Vic and aunt Margaret Ritter and their six children had lived in for several years during World War II. A two-story former boardinghouse on Main Street across from the old McDonald Hotel building, it was not a house anyone was likely to miss, either. I wasn't in the least surprised to learn that the holdout was Lester Powell, a hulking, barrel-shaped farmer with aquiline features who could be a formidable presence. And he often was. Les, who was a year or so behind me in school, frequently displayed what you might call a confrontational personality and spent a good bit of his time swimming upstream against the rest of the world. The committee leaders also decreed that the tufts of grass that had sprouted in the cracks in the sidewalks on Main Street be pulled out because the NBC television affiliate newspeople from Oberlin, fifty miles to the east, told them they would stand out on television. Grass growing in the streets and sidewalks, as William Jennings Bryan noted in his famous "Cross of Gold" speech nearly a century before, is a sign of decline.

True, there were a distressing number of empty buildings on Main Street, including the old L-B movie theater (for the owners, Lee Latta, a farmer, and Alfred Buck, the drugstore owner and a longtime civic leader), which had given us all so much pleasure; sitting up in the balcony, where smoking was allowed, was part of my rite of passage as a teenager even though I didn't smoke. Where once there had been a grocery store, the pool hall and barbershop, and a couple of restaurants, there now were empty lots. Many of the residences were as well kept, and in some cases as imposing, as ever, but others were run-down, a few abandoned, and there were several vacant lots where substantial dwellings once stood; they always make me think of missing teeth. All the vacant buildings and lots had been spruced up, however, and none was unsightly—just a melancholy reminder of the decline of small-town America.

_____

The parade on Saturday morning was a source of apprehension for some, who feared that it would consist of little more than the high school band, the fire engine, and a few farmers showing off new tractors and combines—not, God knows, that the ability to afford them is not good and sufficient cause for celebration at any time in that country. The centennial committee, however, had specifically banned proud farmers and their new machinery from the parade. There wouldn't have been room for them, anyway.

At about eight o'clock Saturday morning, the celebrants began emerging from their homes or drifting into town (many stayed on the farms of friends and relatives or in motels in neighboring towns like Colby and Goodland, both fifty miles away) to begin the festivities with coffee and doughnuts at the senior citizens center in the old hotel building. They found their small hometown transformed into a carnival wonderland. The floats, bands, and other entries literally overran the town as the parade formed up on the school playgrounds on the east end of town next to the school buildings—the red-brick grade school and the blond-brick high school, both of which I attended, and the field house between them, which was built after I moved away—and on two of the three streets that run the town's full east-west length of nine blocks. Wandering among the floats, I thought back to the hundreds of recess and noon hours I'd spent in that school yard playing softball, football (tackle, without pads and helmets), and Pom-pom Pull Away ("Come away or I'll pull you away!"), which for some reason we rendered, "Pump Pump Pole Away."

The parade wended the four blocks west from the school yard to main street. It trooped down main street, past the hardware and farm machinery store, the liquor store, the bank, the post office, the grocery, an antique shop, Les Loker's insurance office, the McDonald Hotel, a former auto-and-tractor-repair shop that is now the city office and maintenance equipment storage building, the two-story Masonic temple (which at one time had a blacksmith shop on the ground floor), and other buildings that once had housed implement and auto dealerships, dry goods and grocery stores, cafés, and auto-and-tractor-repair shops. At the railroad tracks on the south end of town, the entries wheeled around in front of the co-op grain elevator office, and doubled back up the east side of the street past the American Legion Hall, an auto-repair garage, the fire department and town jail, the building that for decades housed Hattie West's grocery and notions store and at the time of the centennial was the site of the "Frosty Mug" café and tavern, and the old telephone exchange building. The applauding spectators lined both sides of the street, seated in temporary bleachers and lawn chairs or standing on the curb.

In sum, the parade was glorious. In the hour and a half it took for all the entries to parade down one side of main street and up the other, some of the floats stirred emotions stronger than the normal pleasure of a parade. For my family, the Phippses, who turned out more than two dozen strong, nearly all of us from out of town,* the emotional high point was when the American Legion post members marched past behind their color guard, resplendent in their navy blue overseas caps and shirts that had the Legion emblem and the words "Chester Phipps Post Number 229, McDonald, Kansas" emblazoned in gold on the backs. Chester "Little Chet" Phipps, Jr. (his father, my mother's oldest brother, was "Big Chet"), won the Silver Star and was subsequently killed in action on a submarine in the Pacific in World War II; prior to that, the post had been named after an uncle, Asa Phipps, who died in World War I.

For the most part, the family floats celebrated their longevity in the community. One featured a young farmer wearing a cowboy hat, boots, and chaps and pulling a child's red coaster wagon on which he'd fashioned a canvas Conestoga wagon top. His young daughter, who appeared to be four or five and was dressed in a long pioneer woman's dress and sunbonnet, rode in the wagon. Her older brother walked alongside his father, also wearing a cowboy outfit and carrying a Daisy air rifle modeled after the famous Winchester carbine. The signs on the sides of the wagon read: "Pulling the Fifth Generation. 85 Years on the Same Farm." The young farmer was Mike Sramek, a member of a large family, one of many in the country, that had immigrated to Kansas in the late nineteenth century from Bohemia and Moravia, where they had also been wheat farmers. He is a cousin of Berdean Sramek Wilkinson, a girl on whom I'd had a crush when we were in grade school. Berdean lives north of town with her farmer/rancher husband in an area known as North Divide and is the

---

*Four decades earlier, at the end of World War II, there were more than two dozen Phipps family members and in-laws, spanning four generations, living in McDonald or on farms nearby. By 1988, only one, my aunt Margaret Ritter, a widow who was eighty-three at the time, still lived in town.

North Divide reporter for the county weekly newspaper, the *Square Deal,* which is published in Atwood, the county seat.

Another popular float, which particularly touched me, was that of Laverne and Ruth Klepper and their family. It was built on Laverne and Ruth's pickup and had a sign on each side that read: "Thanks, McDonald, for Being Our Home Since 1926. McDonald Is Our Kind of Place." A blown-up color photo of Laverne and Ruth and their children and grandchildren, twenty-five in all, adorned the vehicle's hood.

When the last float had cleared Main Street, the spectators flooded into the street in search of old friends and acquaintances. I first looked for Laverne Klepper and Claude Pickett, with whom I'd worked when I was a teenager and who had a strong influence on me in those formative years. Not surprisingly, I found the two old cronies together in the middle of the street. They were dressed alike, in gray cotton herringbone bib overalls and caps with the centennial logo on the front.* Although they had long been best friends—both were about eighty at the time—Claude and Laverne were physical opposites, real-life versions of Mutt and Jeff. Claude was a tall, raw-boned, taciturn man with a weather-beaten face and square jaw, while Laverne is short, stocky, and powerfully built, with a cheerful, gregarious disposition he inherited from his father.

My memories of them and the town and the rest of its people are of an active, hard-working community working its way out of the Great Depression and the Dust Bowl to participate in the triumph and prosperity of World War II and the postwar economic boom. At the time of the centennial, I was a national politics reporter for the *Washington Post* and had lived in Washington, D.C., for more than a quarter of a century. I hadn't lived in McDonald, the town of my birth, for nearly forty years, but the pull of that road back had gotten stronger, if anything, in the preceding decade, a process, I'm told, that often comes with maturation. Over the ten or fifteen years preceding the centennial, I'd had dreams at night about the town, that it was a growing, prospering community; in one version of the dream, its downtown business district had expanded to include two or three streets parallel to the main street. Alas, this was only a dream.

I felt a deep attachment to the community even as a child. I had been familiar with every face and every square inch of the town; it was the center of my universe. In the course of those conversations that young people

*An escutcheon bearing the name of the town and the centennial dates, 1888–1988, a rooster pheasant, sunflowers, ears of corn, a rolled diploma lying across an open book that had the state motto, "Ad Astra Per Aspera"—"To the Stars Through Difficulties"—along the top of the pages, a horse-drawn reaper, and a farm with house, barn, windmill, and silo and billowy clouds in the background.

of high school age have about what they want to do with their lives, I expressed the wish to live there as an adult, although I knew even then that in career terms it would never be feasible. Many of my peers held the opposite view and emphatically voiced their determination to bolt at the first opportunity, generally on graduation from high school; ironically, some, like Bob Johnson, who had voiced this sentiment strongly in those days, are still there, four decades later, many operating their fathers' farms, in Bob's case in partnership with his sons.

I, on the other hand, had taken that road Wallace Stegner evoked and while I visited frequently when I was in my twenties, the demands of career and family made trips back to western Kansas infrequent for two decades. In the quarter century between 1962, when Grandmother Phipps died, and the centennial, I had gotten back to McDonald only twice, once to do a story on the wheat harvest in 1966, once for a family reunion in 1985. Given the intensifying call of my roots, however, there was no doubt that I'd attend the centennial. In addition to simply wanting to be there for the party, I also wanted to get reacquainted with the people, starting with two of my mentors, Claude Pickett and Laverne Klepper.

Claude's family moved to the area about the time the town was founded. He was born on a farm near McDonald in 1907 and lived in the town until his death in 1993. He saw the town grow to its peak of population and prosperity during World War II and then begin its decline in the 1950s. He served on the city council for thirty years and on the township board for forty. He had farmed, owned a dairy, been the town plumber and electrician, and at the time of the centennial still farmed a quarter section of wheat ground (160 acres) owned by the town. There weren't many things that needed doing in that town and its environs that Claude Pickett couldn't do.

For about fifteen years, one of Claude's enterprises was serving as overseer of my family's farm operations after Grandmother Phipps's two surviving sons moved away. The youngest, Wayne, managed it by long-distance telephone to Claude and Grandmother and frequent commutes from Boulder, Colorado. The Phipps operation benefited greatly in countless ways from Claude's calm common sense and hands-on expertise; his approach was to prevent trouble as much as possible by anticipation and foresight, an approach that hadn't always guided the operation before him.

The Phipps family boys who worked on the farm during their teens also benefited from Claude's knowledge and guidance. This took several forms. Having been born to farming, he knew the land, the climate, and the crops instinctively. He was a good mechanic who taught us to understand, operate, and appreciate the expensive, complex machinery with which we were entrusted. He taught us to maintain our tools and implements and clean them up after using them: His admonition that "you can tell a lot about a man by the way he takes care of his tools" was one I never forgot. He also demonstrated the value of taking a break from a difficult repair job that somehow wouldn't come together, to smoke a cigarette or drink a Coke and think about something else for a few minutes, and then after you went back to work—*presto!*—it somehow would fall into place. But possibly most valuable of all, he comprehended human nature and passed on to us lessons about life in general.

Working together with livestock and machinery, fixing fences, repairing buildings, or any of the thousand and one things a farmer must do to avoid being eaten alive by his acres, gives males many opportunities to talk. Claude was raised under a code that decreed treating others with courtesy and understanding and according them the benefit of the doubt. For him, these rules held doubly true for the aged, the young, and the weak and powerless. He believed that women and the elderly were to be treated with courtesy and respect, the young and infirm with sensitivity and compassion.

Claude was taciturn in the sense that he didn't talk for the pleasure of hearing the sound of his own voice. This backed up his message, which was that people are truly judged on their actions, not their words. He was also given to understatement. If Claude's evaluation was, "Yes, sir, that's just a pretty fair job you've done there," that was pretty fair reason to feel that it was pretty darn good, in fact. In the motion picture *The Last Picture Show*, there is a character played by Ben Johnson who was an ethical guide and counselor to the teenage boys of the small Texas town in the movie. I recognized Claude and Laverne in that role.

Laverne is a retired rural-route mail carrier. In his hours off the mail route, he hired his many skills out to farmers and townspeople, including the Phippses, and I had the opportunity to work with him on many occasins. Like Claude, Laverne had been a role model for me. When I brought my wife-to-be to McDonald for the first time, no one was more eager to make her feel welcome than Laverne—and to make sure she realized what a sterling chap she was getting tied up with.

Laverne inherited his affable temperament from his father, who had been a grandfather figure to several generations of the town's schoolchildren. Mr. Klepper—his first name was Orval, but to my knowledge none of the children ever called him anything but Mr. Klepper—was the grade school custodian for years. He was known for his sunny disposition, which eased the sometimes difficult passage through school for many of the kids. For years, a running joke between Mr. Klepper and me whenever we met on the street was to accuse each other, with elaborately feigned sarcasm, of planning to sneak off to go fishing instead of working: "Well, hello, fisherman! On your way down to the crick, I suppose?" was our standard greeting and for years we addressed each other as "fisherman."

Laverne's younger brother, Audrey, was equally amiable. "Aud" had worked on the farm for my grandfather before World War II, during which he was a turret gunner on a B-17 in the Eighth Air Force over Europe. He was one of my first childhood heroes even before he went off to war, and in the summer of 1945, when he was freshly discharged from the Army Air Corps, Audrey and Mr. Klepper were hired to shingle the Fritz's house on the south edge of town. To my delight, they took me on as a helper. Aud helped make the time pass by relating some of his war experiences to an eager audience and, as a thirteen-year-old, I got some expert instruction in carpentry as well. Part of the indoctrination had to do with workmen's humor. Occasionally, as I was sitting there on the roof engrossed in nailing on the new shingles, one of them would surreptitiously tack the bottom of the nail apron I had tied around my waist to the roof and wait for my reaction when I tried to move. Anything to break the monotony.

I also learned something else. Mr. Klepper was a music lover and one of the Fritz's daughters was a professional singer who paid a visit home while we were working there. Mr. Klepper insisted on stopping work and going down to listen a couple of times when she was practicing, which may have been my first realization that even out on that frontier setting "real" men could have aesthetic interests.

This, incidentally, is one of the great benefits of growing up in a rural milieu—the opportunity as a youngster to do adult work with adults. It does wonders for a teenage perspective; young people begin doing adults' work at an early age and are ready to become adults sooner. As a result there is far less juvenile alienation from the grownups and the rest of society. The loss of this is one casualty of our urban lives.

There were a number of others I wanted to see as well. One was Claude Bell, whose family had been close to mine. It pleased the family that Claude bought Grandmother Phipps's farm when she died in 1962. His brother, Clarence, taught high school agriculture at both Bird City and McDonald and was my "ag" teacher my freshman year; Clarence died shortly before the centennial, but I had seen him at the 1985 high school alumni reunion weekend and, fortunately, had the wit to write him afterward and tell him what a good teacher he had been and how much I had learned from him. Claude, a graduate of Kansas State, as was Clarence, also taught high school—math and physics—both at McDonald and St. Francis, twenty-three miles west. In addition to being one of the area's most successful farmers, Claude had a highly sucessful political career as a state senator and as a Republican candidate for lieutenant governor.*

Another I wanted to see was the banker, Ross Wingfield. Movies and popular literature often portrayed small-town bankers as villains, but that stereotype never applied to Ross. Although universally addressed by his first name, Ross was highly respected as well as well liked. He is a distinguished, well-groomed man who moved to McDonald in 1933, when the Peoples State Bank, which had to close in December 1930, was reopened. Ross soon established a reputation for being careful and conservative but caring and creative as well. He was a banker who helped solve the farmers' and businessmen's problems, rather than adding to them.

When he turned the operation of the bank over to his son, Owen, in 1979 at the age of eighty-two, several hundred farmers and townspeople attended a ceremony in his honor. Ross's stewardship was best described by a leading farmer with the simple tribute, "He's taken care of our community." Some recalled his granting extensions of their notes in bad years. Bob Banister, whose grandsons are the fourth generation on the family farm, remembered asking for a loan to expand his irrigation system and recalled, with a laugh, that "Ross told me one irrigation system is enough. 'You don't need more with your heart problems.'"

Ross was a classic instance of doing well by doing good. In a town whose population and businesses had declined in numbers in the quarter century prior to the centennial, the Peoples State Bank is today a modern operation with a large addition that was built in 1976 with matching yellow bricks from the former post office building, which had been torn down the year before. Its deposits, $32,000 when Ross arrived in 1933, totaled about $6.5 million when he stepped down nearly a half century later.

I had my own gratifying experience with Ross. In 1946, Owen returned from his World War II Army service in Europe and was scheduled to arrive on the train in Colby, fifty miles southeast. Some business matter arose and Ross couldn't drive over to meet him, so he asked me to go in his stead. I was fourteen, the minimum age for a Kansas driver's license, and flattered beyond description at being so entrusted; needless to say, I never forgot it. In addi-

---

*Both Claude Pickett and Claude Bell died five years after the centennial. Claude Pickett was eighty-five, Claude Bell eighty-three.

tion, I liked Owen a lot. He worked in several wheat harvests for us in high school and while he was finishing up at Kansas State on the GI bill. He was and is thoughtful and good-natured and, six or seven years my senior, was like a kind and helpful older brother to me. He had also been one of my mother's favorite students when she taught high school at McDonald.

One of Ross's clients was the area's wealthiest and most successful farmer, Clarence K. "C.K." Fisher. By the time of the centennial, C.K. and his son, A.B., owned and operated 24,000 acres of wheat, corn, feed grains, and pasture and as a major cattle operation ran several thousand head of cattle and three large feedlots. Because of his wealth, C.K. has been a source of speculation and envy by some, but I've always liked him and admired his acumen and capacity for hard work.

C.K. came to McDonald in 1928 as the high school agriculture teacher, fresh out of Kansas State University in Manhattan. He and A.B. are models of what it takes to survive and prosper as a farmer and rancher on the High Plains: steady growth of the operation, a shrewd sense of when to expand and when to avoid becoming overextended, the managerial ability to absorb and efficiently administer this growth—and a limitless capacity for hard work. C.K. was eighty-one at the time of the centennial and could still be found out in the feedlots or on the tractor every day. His farm is just half a mile north of town and he owns several quarters west of town. His big, well-maintained buildings and feedlots are plainly visible looking up Main Street, and the cemetery is on a corner of one of his sections. The Memorial Day ceremonies every year take place in the midst of one of the Fishers' wheat, corn, or milo crops.

For me, seeing Claude, Laverne, Ross, Claude Bell, and C.K. was not only pleasant but appropriate because they personified so much of the town's history. They could have been made honorary centennial marshals, but that could have been said of so many others as well.

Actually, the first person I wanted to see was Ed Cahoj, who is my oldest friend. We began in grade school together back before World War II. A star athlete in high school, Ed has a taste for locker-room humor and as I was standing around at the picnic Friday evening talking to people and wondering where he was, I heard a familiar voice over my right shoulder: "By damn, you ain't any better lookin', you damn sure ain't any younger, and I doubt like hell you're any smarter. But you couldn't have gotten any dumber, either."

That's his standard greeting, no matter how much time has elapsed since our previous meeting, hiding in ambush and then slipping up behind me, regardless of whom I might be talking to. My response is not to turn around but just say, "Hello, Cahoj. I'm surprised to see you. Are you still in the federal witness protection program?"

As teenagers we played sports, chased girls, and drank beer together. Over the years, when I came back on visits, we spent a lot of hours wandering around the back roads in an auto, enjoying the western Kansas countryside and shooting the breeze. Cahoj is a big, raw-boned man of impressive strength and agility and was one of the most formidable high school football ends (all–Northwest Kansas) and basketball centers (twenty-five points per game) the area has produced. ("He's a real horse," Claude Pickett once noted admiringly when Ed was still in high school.)*

Another of my high school classmates, Wilbur "Chick" Enfield, also betrayed no indication that any significant amount of time had passed since we last saw each other. He greeted me with "Well, hello there, Dick-Richard, my boy," the name and mock-patronizing older-brother tone of voice he had affected with me back when we were teenagers. It amused me then and still did all those years later. Chick looked—and talked and acted—much as he did back when we were eighteen. He still combed his black hair straight back with the part in the middle and, in his mid-fifties, had the upturned nose, freckles, and guileless manner of a mischievous boy.

He remained one of the great raconteurs and commentators on the passing scene. He employed the same phraseology—an Enfield account of any sort of collective commotion almost invariably included the declaration, "Why, they was just a-hootin' and a-hollerin' and a-bellerin' like a buncha lost calves." The topics of his always entertaining, nonstop commentary seemed to have picked up where we had left off thirty-five years before. It ranged from fishing up at Ogallala (Nebraska), one of his passions, to U.S.-Soviet relations, with stopovers about the "mess in Washington" and the joys of making and selling furniture at home, another passion after he turned his farm operation over to his two sons.

❧

There is a remarkable variation in the way physical appearances change between youth and middle age. Some people are instantly recognizable. Others change so much that it's almost impossible to tell who they are until they start talking, when the voice is the giveaway. Even when physical

---

*When I wrote a story in the *Washington Post* about the high school alumni reunion in 1985 and mentioned Cahoj by name, I got a call from Vice Admiral Daniel Wolkensdorfer at the Pentagon, who at the time was chief of the Navy's antisubmarine warfare division and is now retired. He is from Herndon, a little town about forty miles east of McDonald, and was astonished to see McDonald and Cahoj mentioned in the *Post.* His memory of playing football against Cahoj was, "Trying to figure out a way to block that big SOB without getting myself killed in the process."

appearance changes a great deal, voices, gestures, and mannerisms don't, and a reunion is a remarkable demonstration of how mannerisms and characteristics are set in the early years.

I ran into Chick at our high school class reunion party hosted by Don Antholz, another of our classmates. It was attended by nine of the fourteen of us who had entered high school together, and our spouses, plus Berdean Wilkinson and her husband.* Berdean had gone through grade school with us, then attended a Catholic girls' high school in Denver; since I hadn't graduated with the class, either, she and I were sort of honorary guests. I was struck by how relatively little most of my classmates, particularly the men, had changed over the years.

The party wound up in Don's huge new machine shed. Although the day was bright and sparkling and there wasn't a cloud in the sky, we finally had to move the picnic tables into the machine shed and grill the steaks there because of an unrelenting twenty-five-mile-an-hour wind blowing out of the northwest. It was a wind you could work in without thinking much about it, but it proved to be too much in a social situation; the concrete slab of a nearby prefab building that had been blown down in a recent storm was mute testimony, if any was needed, to the weather on the High Plains.

Cahoj had remained close friends with Chick. At one point, he asked Chick if he was having trouble letting go of his farming operation and turning it over to his sons. Ed had a similar situation—he had taken over his dad's farm thirty-five years before and in turn had passed it on to his oldest son, Phil. "Hell, no," Chick snorted. "They can sink or swim just like I did." The inheritance of farms was a common experience for several of my high school classmates. Don Antholz had taken over his father's farm and is operating it with one of his sons. Another, Russell Marshall, whose father had given me my first full-time harvest job when I was thirteen, had also inherited his dad's place. A fifth, Deroy Hubbard, had taken over his father-in-law's sizable operation; Deroy's sons, Dan and Dave, in turn, operated it after his passing and, in addition to being successful farmers, are tireless workers in the community and church, including serving as volunteer firemen. Inheriting the family holdings is about

---

*The first of the fourteen in the class to die was Clifford Carpenter, who was killed in a construction accident when in his twenties. Deroy Hubbard, whose twin brother, Harlan, was in the class and at the reunion, died of a heart attack a few years before the centennial. Another, Tommy Johnson, was in a hospital in Topeka in the terminal stages of Pick's disease, which is closely related to Alzheimer's. The other absentee was Marilyn Larson, who couldn't make it at the last minute because of the death of her father. Finally, it seemed a particularly cruel irony that shortly after our reunion Chick died of cancer, which came on and took him away suddenly.

the only way most young people can get into farming today. Chick was the exception. He inherited nothing from his father, a mechanic, and put his holdings together entirely on his own.

On Friday and Saturday nights of the centennial weekend, as Chick would put it, there was "a-hootin' and a-hollerin'" aplenty in the normally sedate little town. On both nights, there was a country-and-western band and dancing on main street, which turned into a big communal tailgate party until well after midnight. On Saturday night, there was also a rock band and dance for the younger set in Dale Loker's machine shed on the east end of town. That band could be heard loud and clear all the way across town between the country band's sets. For that matter, it probably could be heard all the way to Nebraska and Colorado; young people from neighboring towns, in fact, did come over to join the festivities both nights.

After I returned to Washington, a friend from the *New York Times* remarked that she assumed I had been regarded as a celebrity at the centennial. Quite the contrary, I responded. Despite what I supposed were their lifelong suspicions that I was going to wind up doing something weird—like living in Washington, D.C.—they treated me as they always had, as I knew they would and which was all I wanted.

☙❧

In the days of our youth, McDonald had an encompassing sense of community, which added intensity to such events as high school football games with rival towns such as Bird City. The centennial sparked other memories of our close-knit community—the importance of the schools and their social and cultural events, of birth announcements and funerals, bumper wheat crops, disastrous droughts and wind- and hailstorms, kindnesses and cruelties, everything in the context of a remarkable feeling of community and security. On summer Saturday nights after World War II, the town was packed with moviegoers, women shopping for groceries and dry goods, and men crowding the pool hall waiting for a turn at the snooker tables. Outside, the sidewalks on main street were so jammed when the movie theater let out at 10:00 P.M. that people had to walk in the street if they wanted to get anywhere in a hurry.

Along toward the witching hour on Saturday night, I was standing in front of the Frosty Mug with Cahoj and another old friend from our school days, Keith Headrick, whom we all had known as "Hayrack." I looked down main street, which, for two evenings, once again had displayed its former vitality, and I was reminded of the past. Once again, possibly for the last time, it was jammed with humans and autos. Apparently, we were thinking about the same thing.

"Remember how on Saturday nights main street used to be completely parked up like this on both curbs with a row of cars down the middle?" Keith suddenly asked. "Sure do," I responded. "It made it hard just to drive up and down main street," Cahoj recalled. It's not hard to drive up and down main street on Saturday nights anymore; since the 1950s, it's been a rare Saturday night that a cannon could be fired down the middle of main street with any danger of hitting anyone. It was a bittersweet reminder that now it takes the magnitude of a centennial celebration to match what used to be a normal Saturday night.

In those days, the 1930s and 1940s, most of the celebrants, like me, had large extended families living in town or on nearby farms, including grandparents, aunts and uncles and their children, and in-laws. By the time of the centennial, however, many of these families had no surviving members remaining in the area and others had just one or two, many of whom were elderly and just living out their days. We took our rural culture for granted and assumed that it would go on forever. Over the past few decades, however, it seemed that events and developments had conspired to destroy or at least greatly reduce that culture. These included steadily developing technology, global oil shocks that drove the prices of everything up, every twitch of world markets, every attempt by the federal government to use U.S. agricultural exports as a diplomatic tool. Every drought or hailstorm seemed to be the final blow that drove another farmer or merchant out of business.

Everyone recognizes the problem, but there's been little progress in solving it. Some academics and other students of the situation have proposed buying out marginal farmers on the High Plains, a geographical area bounded roughly on the east by the 98th meridian, which cuts Kansas in half east and west, and on the west by the Rocky Mountains. There is much marginal land in the region, but a great deal of it is one of the most agriculturally productive areas in the world. The High Plains is home to only one-fortieth of the population of the United States, but it comprises about one-fifth of the area of the contiguous forty-eight states and is the world's fourth-largest wheat producer, the seventh-largest beef producer, and the sixth-largest oil producer.

One idea is to turn much of the High Plains back to its original grasslands and reintroduce the bison and other indigenous animals and plants, a plan that goes under the rubric of "Buffalo Commons." Along this line, one Denver think tank envisions a future High Plains "archipelago society" of urban "islands"—a few surviving medium- and large-sized towns—on the interstate highways, surrounded by a sea of wheat, corn, and grass. The small towns like McDonald would disappear and return to the earth; dust to dust, in the words of the Book of Common Prayer.

This, needless to say, has aggravated the people out here and exacerbates the feeling of isolation and alienation that white settlers on the plains have experienced since they first began crossing the Missouri River early in the nineteenth century. Even after the recovery from the farm crisis of the early 1980s, morale remained low for a time in much of the Midwest farm belt. The counselors and comforters—the clergy, community leaders, older family members—had to battle feelings of alienation, hopelessness, and burnout in themselves. Fortunately, with the cyclical upturn of the farm economy in the early 1990s, signs of hope appeared anew and communities like McDonald stepped up their efforts to invigorate and restore themselves.

⚞

All of that was on our minds as we stood on the sidewalk in front of the Frosty Mug. "Think there'll be another party like this a hundred years from now, a bicentennial?" I asked. "Who knows?" Cahoj responded. "A hundred years from now there could be wheat growing and pheasants nesting right here where we are, and no one will know there'd ever been a town here at all."

That thought had been expressed by several celebrants during the weekend. But for forty-eight hours at least, we were able to remember things as they were when we were young. Albeit briefly, we had found the road back home and were deeply thankful of it. It was the best party I've ever been to.

CHAPTER FOUR

FOR MUCH OF ITS HISTORY, KANSAS HAS HAD AN IMAGE PROBLEM—the image of being dull, square, old-fashioned, ordinary, mediocre even. It was the leader of the prohibition movement. With a few exceptions, such as U.S. Senate Republican leader Bob Dole, its twentieth-century politicians, Republican and Democrat alike, have generally been moderately conservative, and polite and colorless as well. They always seem to call Calvin Coolidge to mind.

Many who have never been to Kansas think of it as a monochrome of conventional conformists who inhabit a dreary, boring stretch of unrelieved flat prairie that has no apparent redeeming social value. For that matter, many who do visit there share that view because they fail to appreciate its variety and natural beauty. They think the only excitement the state offers is tornadoes and watching the haircuts down at the barbershop. Certainly, Hollywood shares this prejudice. The movie *The Wizard of Oz* is in vivid Technicolor except for the Kansas scenes at the beginning and end, which are in black and white.

Yet Kansas has a powerful hold on its natives. In 1902, Carl L. Becker, one of the great American historians of the twentieth century, accepted a post at the University of Kansas after a brief, unsuccessful term on the faculty at Dartmouth. Although a native of Iowa, to Becker, KU seemed akin to exile to Siberia, so on the train from Kansas City to Lawrence, where KU is located, he was astonished when a coed in the seat in front of him broke off her talk with her companion to gaze out the window, then turned and said with deep emotion, "Dear Old Kansas!" Becker subsequently wrote an interpretive essay in which he concluded that Kansas was not a geographical entity, but "a state of mind, a religion and a philosophy in one." Becker, a scholar of the eighteenth-century Enlightenment, was subsequently hired by Cornell, where he went on to make his reputation, in part because of this essay, according to Kenneth S. Davis, a Kansas historian.

Davis recounts the experience of another historian, Dudley T. Cornish, then chairman of the history department at Kansas State College in Pittsburg, now Pittsburg State University. In 1957, Cornish, a native New Yorker, was on a bus with about thirty Kansas schoolteachers, with whom he had toured New England and Canada. When the bus crossed the state line, Cornish reported that the teachers burst into "Home on the Range," the official state song, with "unashamed tears of joy on the singing faces." Kansas also occasionally got an emotional hold on some most unlikely partisans. In 1913, one Boris J. Patchjieff, a Turk who had graduated from KU, was promoted to commander of one of the Ottoman Empire's battalions in Bulgaria. For his unit's battle cry, he adopted the KU pep yell, "Rock Chalk, Jayhawk, Kaaay Yeeeeew!" ("Rock Chalk" refers to the limestone deposits in eastern Kansas.)

This emotional attachment was not evinced by Kansas's early visitors, however. In 1541, Francisco Vázquez de Coronado, governor of Nueva Galicia in New Spain (Mexico), set out for Quivira, as Kansas and the territory of the Wichita Indians was then known, to discover the gold of the legendary "Seven Golden Cities of Cíbola." The gold turned out to be as legendary as the cities, and while Coronado praised the area as "the best I have seen for producing all the products of Spain . . . the land itself being very fat and black, and being well watered by the rivulets and springs and rivers," the Spanish lost interest in it when they found nothing that could be minted into doubloons.

After the United States acquired the area under the Louisiana Purchase, Daniel Webster opposed development of it, asking in a Senate debate:

> What do we want with this vast and worthless area, of this region of savages and wild beasts, of deserts, of shifting sands and whirlwinds, of dust, of cactus and prairie dogs; to what use could we ever hope to put these great deserts, or those endless mountain ranges . . . ?

Zebulon Pike, who had been sent in 1806 to explore the territory between the Missouri River and Santa Fe, New Mexico, filed a report in 1810 on his exploratory expedition. He saw no possibilities for white settlements in the arid portions of the Louisiana district: "These vast plains of the western hemisphere may become in time as celebrated as the sandy deserts of Africa. . . ." Indeed, the Great Plains did become known as the "Great American Desert," in part because of Pike.

At the end of the nineteenth century, in 1895, William Allen White, the famous newspaper editor from Emporia, described a family, defeated by the drought and depression, that was straggling back east through Emporia:

> The stock in the caravan would invoice four horses, very poor and very tired, one mule, more disheartened than the horses, and one sad-eyed dog, that had probably been compelled to rustle his own precarious living for many a long and weary day. . . . These movers were from western Kansas—from one of those counties near the Colorado line which holds a charter from the state to officiate as the very worst, most desolate, God-forsaken, man-deserted spot on the sad old earth.

One of those counties, in short, where the Phippses and Dickensons settled.

Nevertheless, much of Kansas's history is as colorful as that of any state. The first white family in Kansas was that of Daniel Morgan Boone, son of the famous frontiersman, who was sent by the U.S. government in 1827 to teach agriculture to the Kansas Indians in what is now Jefferson County, just west of Leavenworth. The first white child born in the territory was Boone's son, Napoleon, who was born on August 22, 1828.

The westward push of the frontier in the first half of the nineteenth century was a major factor in precipitating the Civil War because it exacerbated North-South sectional tensions by raising the question of whether the new territories would be free or slave. The Kansas-Nebraska Act of 1854, which created the territories of Kansas and Nebraska, made Kansas a major focal point in the "irrepressible conflict" over slavery. The act succeeded the Missouri Compromise of 1820–21, which admitted Maine as a free state and Missouri as a slave state. The Missouri Compromise also prohibited slavery in the rest of the Louisiana Purchase north of 36 degrees 30 minutes latitude, which is approximately the Missouri-Arkansas line. The Kansas-Nebraska Act opened this area to slavery, leaving it to the voters of the two territories to decide whether they would be slave or free.

Because of the general assumption that Kansas would be slave and Nebraska free, the Kansas Territory became a pre–Civil War battleground for bloody clashes of abolitionists and proslavery Southerners, the Free-

Soil "Jayhawkers" and southern "Bushwhackers," which caused Kansas to become known as "Bleeding Kansas."* John Brown's killing of five proslave men at Pottawatomie Creek, in 1856, in what became known as the "Pottawatomie Massacre," is the most famous of the many shootouts between the two sides between 1854 and the end of the Civil War.

The proslavers, many of whom were from just across the border in Missouri, predominated at first. The first territorial legislature, elected with the help of Missouri proslave guerrillas, enacted what became known as the "Black Laws," which decreed the death penalty for anyone who helped free a slave and a prison sentence for anyone who openly criticized slavery. The Free-Soilers included New England abolitionists whose expertise in frontier agriculture was marginal but who came to Kansas appropriately armed with Sharps rifles, which became famous as "Beecher's Bibles."† The antislavery forces ultimately prevailed, however. The 1860 census reported a population in the territory of 107,206, of whom about 70 percent were antislave. After the Free State party–dominated legislature adopted a constitution that declared, "All men are possessed of equal and inalienable natural rights, among which are life, liberty, and the pursuit of happiness," Kansas was admitted as the thirty-fourth state on January 29, 1861. For all this, some historians contend that disputed land titles, a staple of life on the frontier, may have cost as many lives in Kansas as slavery.

The state fought on the Union side in the Civil War and although sparsely populated it contributed the most fighting men to the Union and suffered the highest number of fatal casualties per capita of any of the northern states. Walter Prescott Webb, one of the leading historians of the plains, suggested that there is a historical irony in the pivotal role the Kansas-Nebraska Act played in the great North-South sectional conflict. Webb argued that while the South won politically with the Kansas-Nebraska Act, and the Compromise of 1850 before it, it lost economically. Because of the area's subhumid and semiarid climate, which wouldn't support the cotton economy, the Kansas-Nebraska territory actually was a barrier to slavery, not an opportunity. If it had been better adapted to slav-

---

*The term *jayhawker* comes from the pre–Civil War raids of militant abolitionist guerrillas, such as John Brown, on slaveholders and their property. This came to be known as "jayhawking" and its perpetrators as "jayhawks." Some contend that the name is a combination of the jay, a gaudily plumed and aggressive bird, and the fierce hawk, which, they argue, perhaps tongue in cheek, aptly symbolizes the average Kansan.

†They were named for the Reverend Henry Ward Beecher, the brother of Harriet Beecher Stowe, author of *Uncle Tom's Cabin*. When a highly publicized party of seventy abolitionists set out for Kansas from New Haven, Connecticut, in 1856, Beecher's Congregational church in Brooklyn gave each a Bible, a hymnal, and a Sharps rifle.

ery, the South would have fought harder for it, and its history might have been different, he concluded.

Another major factor was that the construction of the railroads, primarily on an east-west axis, ruptured the commercial ties between the South and the West, which had been formed by shipping agricultural surpluses south to New Orleans on the river networks. The Northwest territories' new bond with the Northeast helped swing them into the antislave camp; shipments of corn, pork, wheat, flour, and other farm commodities to the East increased by as much as sixfold between 1850 and 1860, while shipments to the South remained relatively stable.

⚡

After the Civil War, many Kansas towns were the railheads for the big cattle drives up from Texas. Abilene, in 1867, was the first, and between 1867 and 1871 alone, about 1.5 million Texas cattle were driven there. A total of about 4 million cattle were shipped east from Kansas railheads during the twenty years of the "Long Drive," 1867 to 1887, when the age of the open range ended.

Much of the legend of the winning of the West that so caught the nation's—and Hollywood's—imagination is based on Kansas history: Dodge City, Abilene, Wyatt Earp, Bat Masterson, the Long Branch Saloon, Miss Kitty and her girls, and fast-draw shoot-outs on Main Street. The cow towns did have their day. They even shocked some Texans. Robert Day, a Kansas-born writer, tells of one Washington, D.C., editorialist of the time. This worthy noted the towns' plethora of tarnished angels, who were known as "doves" and their places of business as "roosts." He was shocked to have to report that "the Texas cattle drovers . . . loiter and dissipate sometimes for months and share the boughten dalliances of fallen women."

The Wild West aspect of Kansas history has probably been considerably blown out of proportion, however. The towns and their leading citizens were business-oriented; Joseph G. McCoy, an Illinois meat dealer, was the entrepreneur who chose Abilene as the first railhead on the Kansas Pacific west of Kansas City and imported the lumber to build its stockyards, loading chutes, livery stable, and hotel for the cowhands. As the cattle business became increasingly profitable, its hardheaded entrepreneurs cracked down on the towns' early lawlessness and maintained a balance between law and order and offering enough trail's-end entertainment to keep the drovers' goodwill. Firearm ordinances were enforced, gunshot deaths were kept to a minimum (just forty-five between 1870 and 1885, sixteen of which were by law officers), and the Main Street shoot-out was primarily a fiction of pulp literature and the movies; most gunshot deaths and injuries were inflicted by gunners shooting from behind cover. In their heyday, Abilene had eleven saloons (and three brothels, with twenty-one girls) and Dodge City had eight. Most were crude holes-in-the wall that served cheap whiskey; the famed Long Branch in Dodge and the Alamo in Abilene were among the few well-appointed places with long bars and gaming tables.

Some spectacular elements of the state's history, alas, are all too true. Kansas was the scene of much of the swift, ruthless extermination of the great bison herds that blackened the High Plains until the 1870s—estimates of the national total run as high as 60 million, with a major concentration on the great mid-grass and short-grass commons bordered by the Arkansas River in Kansas on the south, the Platte River in Nebraska on the north, the Rocky Mountains on the west, and the Missouri River on the east. Santa Fe Railway freight reports indicated that the haul of buffalo bones, used in making fertilizer, from Kansas alone in the 1870s and 1880s was 300,000 tons, which would account for about 31 million buffalo. In 1872 and 1873, an estimated 1.25 million buffalo hides were shipped east by the three major railroads.

It was, as one historian noted, a melancholy tale for those who would have mankind live in harmony with nature. It should also be noted that many contemporary Kansans were sickened by the spectacle, including the state's most famous hunt. This was by the Grand Duke Alexis of Russia, son of the czar, whose large hunting party toured western Kansas, southwest Nebraska, and eastern Colorado on a luxurious special train. Kenneth Davis noted that one hunter reportedly killed 120 buffalo in forty minutes.* There was sufficient outrage that the legislature passed a buffalo protection law in 1872, but it was vetoed by Governor James M. Harvey, who accorded the grand duke one of the few state dinners in Kansas's history.

This slaughter met the short-term goals of providing meat for the white settlers and railroad construction crews and supplying the enormous sudden demand for buffalo robes and hats. It also coincided with a shortage of cattle hides and an expanding market in the eastern United States and Europe for tough, durable leather from which to manufacture many products, including drive belts for the rapidly growing number of steam-

---

*Buffalo were susceptible to wholesale slaughter because they were curious and weren't spooked when one of their number went down. Instead, they tended to gather around to see what was going on.

powered factories; many settlers also helped pay their homestead mortgages by shooting buffalo and selling the hides and bones. In the long
term, the extermination of the buffalo enabled the white settlers to raise
wheat and cattle on the enormous buffalo common between the Missouri
River and the Rockies, which obviously wouldn't have been possible with
millions of bison as regular commuters back and forth through it. Finally,
it eliminated the major source of food and shelter of the Plains Indians
and greatly aided the tragic process of their subjugation and abasement.
This was accomplished, in the words of Ray Allen Billington, a leading
historian of the frontier, "at a cost in blood, wealth, and human decency
which will forever stain the annals of the American frontier."

Several millennia earlier, the Indians themselves had been immigrant
intruders who crossed over to North America on the temporary land
bridge from Siberia that was a result of the last ice age. They brought
with them the hunting skills and metal-tipped weapons and tools they
had developed on the Euro-Asian continent. As the historian John
Steele Gordon has noted, this "emerging biological superpower" was a
major factor in the extinguishment of many North American species, including horses, mastodons, mammoths, elephants and camels, various
species of deer, bison, and antelope, ground sloths, glyptodonts, and giant
beavers, as well as their predators, saber-toothed cats, giant lions, and
cheetahs. The ecology was able to adapt to these superhunters and return to its evolutionary equilibrium, however, because there were far
fewer of them compared to the hordes of Europeans who streamed to the
New World in the nineteenth century. And, they didn't have mechanical
technology such as repeating rifles and steam power to aid their assault
on the environment.

Indians ceased to play any dramatic part in Kansas history after 1878,
when a band of northern Cheyenne, one of the most advanced of the
Plains tribes, left the reservation to which they had been assigned and
trekked north to their historical home in the Dakotas. Harassed by cavalry and local militias along the way, they killed a number of white settlers
in Kansas and finally several of them were killed by the cavalry, which
caught up with them in western Nebraska. Their two chiefs, Dull Knife
and Little Wolf, were jailed and threatened with hanging, but the sentence was not carried out.

Kansas, still mostly virgin prairie with just a narrow margin of settlement along the Missouri border at the end of the Civil War, was settled all
the way to the Colorado line by the end of the century owing to the white
immigrants' insatiable hunger for land and economic opportunity. That

drive, of course, was a major reason for the near-extermination of the buffalo and the tragic treatment of the Plains Indians, who were herded onto smaller and smaller reservations that were inevitably established on arid, unproductive land the whites didn't covet. Often treaties were negotiated in good faith by white officials only to be abrogated—welshed may be a more appropriate term—a few years later because of the political pressure of the never-ending waves of white settlers and their irresistible demand for whatever valuable land there was on the reservations.

🖾

It is doubtful that even a few Americans today have any idea of the intensity of the hunger for land that propelled the white settlers out beyond the forest belt onto the vast, trackless—and treeless—High Plains. O. E. Rolvaag probably expressed it most lyrically in his epic novel, *Giants in the Earth.* This is the ecstasy experienced by Per Hansa, the Norwegian fisherman who is the novel's protagonist, during his first summer of breaking the sod and building a two-room sod house (in one of which he kept the livestock) on his South Dakota homestead:

> That summer Per Hansa was transported, was carried farther and ever farther away on the wings of a wondrous fairy tale—a romance in which he was both prince and king, the sole possessor of countless treasures. . . . He found his tasks too interesting to be a burden; nothing tired him, out here. Ever more beautiful grew the tale; ever more dazzlingly shone the sunlight over the fairy castle. How could he steal the time to rest these days? Was he not owner of a hundred and sixty acres of the best land in the world? Wasn't his title to it becoming more firmly established with every day that passed and every new-broken furrow that turned? . . . Such soil! Only to sink the plow into it, to turn over the sod—and there was a field ready for seeding. . . . And this was not just ordinary soil, fit for barley, and oats, and potatoes, and hay . . . indeed it had been meant for much finer and daintier uses; it was the soil for *wheat,* the king of all grains! Such soil had been especially created by the good Lord to bear this noble seed and here was Per Hansa, walking around on a hundred and sixty acres of it, all his very own!

In the meantime, Per Hansa's wife, Beret, saw only a savage, barren wilderness as she steadily succumbed to madness and despair. Per Hansa and Beret, along with their fellow immigrants, came from a culture that viewed the wilderness as hostile and distinctly separate from "civilization." Subduing it was a matter of survival and became Holy Writ for the world's religions. The Book of Genesis spelled out the charter: "God said unto them [Adam and Eve], Be fruitful, and multiply, and replenish the earth, and subdue it; and have dominion over the fish of the sea, and over the fowl of the air, and over every living thing that moveth upon the earth." Their forebears having done just that in Europe over the millennia, the nineteenth-century immigrants bent their efforts to the same goal in the New World. The numbers tell the story: From 1607 to 1870, about 407 million acres were settled in the United States and 189 million acres put under cultivation; between 1870 and 1890, 430 million acres were settled, with 225 million under cultivation. In the late nineteenth century, this westward expansion and settlement of the continent was a secular, geopolitical credo: Manifest Destiny.

Technology, of course, played a major role in this drive to carry out the Good Word on the High Plains. The railroad was crucial, as was the steel sod-breaking plow. The plains probably couldn't have been settled without three other inventions—the Colt six-shooter, the windmill, and barbed wire. The six-shooter (and the Winchester carbine, a short, lightweight weapon designed for horseback) enabled the white man to fight the Plains Indian on horseback and win. The windmill enabled him to harness the wind to draw water from underground. Barbed wire was a cheap and efficient way to fence farms and pastures and keep the cattlemen's herds from overrunning the homesteaders' crops; it ended the brief, twenty-year open-range cattle era on the Kansas plains and made settlement of the area by humans possible.

☙

For a number of reasons—the capriciousness of the weather, which makes farming on the High Plains far riskier than back east, where the rainfall is more abundant and more dependable, and the economic power of the railroads, bankers, millers, and others—Kansas has been the scene of periodic farm revolts, first the Granger and Greenback movements of the 1870s and then the Populist uprising of the 1890s.

Walter Prescott Webb told of the disorientation experienced by many immigrants from the watered and forested East when they crossed the Missouri and entered the strange, dry, treeless plains. Their lips and nostrils dried and cracked, water supplies were few and far between, green was not the dominant color, and their estimates of distances were wildly in error because they were unaccustomed to the enormous space. In his book, *Blue Highways*, William Least Heat Moon observed that:

the true West differs from the East in one great, pervasive, influential, and awesome way: space. The vast openness changes the roads, towns, houses, farms, crops, machinery, politics, economics, and naturally, ways of thinking. . . . The terrible distances eat up speed. Even dawn takes nearly an hour just to cross Texas.

The 1880s were to the early settlers of western Kansas what a lucky streak at the beginning of a Las Vegas holiday is to gamblers: possibly the worst thing in the world that could happen to them in the long run because it fosters the fatal idea that they're in a game they can win. From 1878 to 1887, the state experienced a decade of above-average rainfall, which led to the conclusion that the Kansas climate must be much like that of Iowa and Illinois. This misapprehension was due primarily to the simple fact that no one knew what the normal rainfall west of the 98th meridian was because, obviously, no one had been there to keep records and the climate is so volatile and fluctuating that it takes years to establish accurate patterns. Reflecting this erroneous assumption about the climate, the counties in the High Plains states, for the most part, were laid out the same size as those in the states of the Northwest Territory, generally thirty-six by thirty miles, under the assumption that they would have the same relatively dense population. Because of that wet cycle, Kansas enjoyed a spectacular real estate boom in the 1880s.

This fostered the ridiculous and, in the end, destructive notion that "the rain follows the plow," that breaking the sod and planting trees somehow would stimulate increased rainfall. The crackbrained, pseudoscientific rationalizations for settling the High Plains and transforming Pike's "Great American Desert" into a "Great American Garden" were almost as numerous as the buffalo. One was that the steel rails of the railroads and the telegraph lines would alter nature's electrical cycles and induce rainfall. Many Civil War veterans, recalling the rain that followed the Battle of Gettysburg, convinced themselves that there was a cause and effect relationship between it and the intense cannon fire of the battle. They argued that if General William T. Sherman would only use more artillery on the Indians, it would have the secondary benefit of causing more rain.

Various charlatans and boosters, including the railroads' land departments, state immigration agencies, and steamship lines, which had agents and advertisements in the ports of Europe, depicted the area as an ever-blooming Garden of Eden with verdant soil that would be amply watered by countless artesian wells, in addition to being rich in valuable minerals, including gold and silver. The Dakotas were transformed into a paradise where "mocking birds and gorgeous paroquets and cockatoos warble musical challenges to each other amid the rich foliage of the sweet-bay and mango trees." The illusion that a great underground river, rushing down from the Rocky Mountains or possibly the Arctic glacier, was available to water the High Plains persisted in some minds up into the twentieth century; what actually was there was the Ogallala Aquifer, whose water moves slowly southeast from the Rockies through strata of gravel and rock and other geological formations at the rate of a foot or two a day. The aquifer couldn't be seriously tapped until the advent of centrifugal pumping technology powered by internal combustion engines.

Rainfall on the High Plains is as unpredictable as it is scanty, and in 1887, there began a decade of drought in which the rainfall was as much below the average as it had been above it in the preceding ten years. The settlers learned the hard way why Pike called it a desert. The 98th meridian is the approximate isohyetal line between the humid Midwest and the arid West, where the average annual rainfall is twenty inches or less, twenty inches being the minimum for dependable unirrigated dryland farming; it is also less than half the forty inches or more that falls in the Missouri River valley and on east. Although western Kansas farmland is as good as any in the world, it is a lonely, windswept, treeless land with a cruel climate, both winter and summer. The High Plains area is a steppe, not a desert, much of which is suitable only for grazing and generally not arable for crops such as corn without irrigation.

Geographers define the High Plains, which includes the western half of Kansas, as having three characteristics: It is relatively flat, it is treeless, and it has a subhumid or semiarid climate, i.e., twenty inches of rain per year or less. From the Texas panhandle north to the Dakotas, it is a gradual, relatively flat, 600-mile stretch that rises 4,500 feet in elevation between the Missouri River and Denver, at the base of the Rocky Mountains. It was—and still is—formed by the slow disintegration of the Rockies. One of the many hard lessons for the pioneers was that at the twenty-inch minimum there wasn't much margin for error or bad luck; a shortage of just an inch or two at a critical time in plant development could be the difference between success and failure. And, to add insult to injury, the rain sometimes came at times when it was harmful to developing plants; at the wrong time it can inhibit the formation of protein in wheat.

In the 1870s, however, no one knew, or could know, what the climate of the High Plains was. Blissful ignorance, the sales pitch that the area was an Eden on Earth, and the hunger for cheap land together proved to be a powerful magnet for the millions of entrepreneurial Europeans who between Appomattox and Sarajevo made the great pilgrimage to the High Plains from the eastern states and Europe. In the 1870s, 347,000 settlers moved into Kansas, the most of any of the western states and territories, and its neighbors' populations increased proportionally. Most came from the nearby states to the east such as Illinois, Indiana, and Missouri, and the populations of the states along the Mississippi River declined or remained static during the decade.

☙

The settling of the continent was greatly abetted by the communications revolution of the second half of the nineteenth century. The development of the steam engine revolutionized rail and ocean transport and speeded the transit of mass amounts of goods, aided by the new telephone and telegraph systems. This technology reshaped the world—and world agriculture. Investment in these technologies led to the opening of virgin land in the American West, Canada, Australia, and Argentina and a search for new markets. The result was the creation of an unprecedented world agricultural market, world agricultural overproduction that resulted in a global agricultural depression from 1873 to 1896, and resulting international agrarian discontent. The construction of 110,000 miles of railroad in the United States between 1870 and 1890 was probably the single greatest factor in this revolution. The explosive growth of U.S. agricultural production—and surpluses—had an enormous and disastrous impact on world economic markets and was a major factor in the agricultural depression. This plus bad harvest years in Europe and the migration of rural populations to the cities plus radical changes in the systems of land tenure there contributed to the steady growth of emigration to America. Unwittingly, the settlers of the High Plains contributed to their own problems, beginning with the farm surpluses, and the vagaries of the world markets bedevil their descendants to this day.

These matters were causes of intense concern and debate in the United States at the time and were part of the context of Frederick Jackson Turner's famous frontier essay of 1893. The American frontier, defined as the delineation of the area beyond which the population was two people per square mile or less, was pronounced closed after the 1890 census. Turner's thesis was that America's democratic institutions and character had been profoundly shaped by the frontier experience with its dream of opportunity, betterment, and a second chance, and he speculated on what the new era portended. The public domain, the free or cheap land of the frontier, was also considered by many to be a great safety valve and its exhaustion was a major issue of the day.

Much of the discussion, as it had been before in American history, was centered on the waves of immigrants in the late nineteenth century, which were increasingly from eastern and southern Europe. Proponents of immigration restriction couched their arguments in rhetoric that was astounding by today's standards; the current term *politically incorrect* doesn't come close to describing it. "The refuse of the murder breeds of southern Europe" will result in "the spoliation of the native pedigree stock"—i.e., Anglo-Saxon—one orator fulminated. The question for many was whether with the disappearance of the frontier the nation could continue to digest and purify "the depraved dregs of European civilization" if they were concentrated in the cities rather than on the free lands of the frontier. History has answered that and there is no question of the value of the contribution of these immigrants both to the nation's cities and to the High Plains.

Famine and repressive government in Sweden and poverty in Norway prompted many Scandinavians to migrate to the New World, many of whom landed in Kansas. In 1871, Czar Alexander II revoked the military exemption of the so-called "Volga Germans," whom Catherine the Great had lured to Russia a century before with the promise of free land and exemption from taxation and conscription. Many of these German Catholic and Mennonite emigrants to the American Midwest had a profound impact on American agriculture. The Mennonites brought a strain of hard red winter wheat from southern Russia known as Turkey Red because of its color and because it had originated in Turkey. With its adaptation to the climate of the Ukraine, which is similar to that of the High Plains, Turkey Red was well suited to western Kansas. It was more resistant than its predecessors to cold weather, or "winterkill," insects, and disease. Because of its protein and glucose content, it milled into excellent flour and was the parent of the varieties of hard winter wheat subsequently developed and grown on the High Plains.*

Wheat farmers also migrated from Germany, Austria, Moravia, and Bohemia, and their descendants are still prospering in western Kansas. Members of all these groups settled in northwest Kansas and one colony of Czechs who homesteaded in Rawlins County near what is now the town of Ludell named their original settlement "Prag," or Prague, while another

---

*Ironically, some are named after the great Plains Indian tribes, which didn't grow wheat and were displaced to make room for the wheat-farming culture–the Cheyenne, Comanche, Pawnee, Wichita, with other strains bearing such names as Red Chief and Chieftain.

near what is now the town of Herndon briefly named their settlement "Pest," for Budapest. Another group of settlers was the 30,000 blacks who fled their poverty and persecution in the Reconstruction South in 1880; the movement was known as the "Exodus" and its members as "Exodusters." Among their descendants were composer Lorenzo Fuller; football stars Gale Sayers, of the University of Kansas and the Chicago Bears, and Veryl Switzer, the first black to play for Kansas State; and E. P. McCabe, a Kansas state auditor believed to be the first black politician elected to statewide office in the North.

Also into western Kansas came my forebears, the Dickensons from Virginia and the Phippses from Ashe County, North Carolina.

🖎

The drought and depression of the late 1880s and the 1890s, however, forced many of these settlers to return east in the wagons that had borne them west, carrying signs with such messages as "In God We Trusted, in Kansas We Busted." Kansas's population declined as the state's early history proved the state motto, *"Ad Astra Per Aspera,"* to be appropriate. Some counties in the western two-thirds of the state never again matched their 1890 census levels. Kansas has experienced three major boom and bust cycles, which culminated in the depressions of the 1890s, 1930s, and 1980s, and several smaller recessions, in the early 1920s and the 1960s. The average population of the counties in western Kansas today is only about 8,000 and it's that high only because of a few counties that have large towns, such as Finney (33,000) with Garden City, Ford (27,500) with Dodge City, and Ellis (26,000) with Hays; the 1990 census for Rawlins County was 3,371.

Those who stuck it out in the 1890s were swayed by Populist politicians such as "Sockless" Jerry Simpson, a rancher from Medicine Lodge, and Mary Elizabeth ("What you farmers should do is raise less corn and more Hell") Lease of Wichita. The Populists began winning elections in normally Republican Kansas in that decade. William Jennings Bryan, the 1896 Democratic presidential candidate who co-opted the Populists' message, including the free coinage of silver, easily carried the state that year.*

Not everyone, of course, was persuaded by the Populists. In August of

---

*The Populists and other prairie radical movements were presaged by the Patrons of Husbandry, an organization that was divided into local units called "Granges." Membership in the Granger movement exploded during the depression of 1873. This panic was caused in part by the collapse of Jay Cooke's banking house due to mismanagement and corruption in its financing of the construction of the Northern Pacific Railroad.

1896, William Allen White, then a plump, conservative, and strongly opinionated young man of twenty-eight, wrote an impassioned anti-Populist editorial in his *Emporia Gazette* that began a half-century career on the national political stage. Smarting from losing an argument, both on fact and logic, with more than a dozen shabbily dressed Populist farmers in his *Gazette* office, White angrily responded with a diatribe entitled "What's the Matter with Kansas?" in which he fumed that the Populists had made the state the laughingstock of the nation:

> We have another shabby, wild-eyed, rattlebrained fanatic who has said openly in a dozen speeches that "the rights of the user are paramount to the rights of the owner." . . . Then for fear some hint that the state had become respectable might percolate through to the civilized portions of the nation, we have decided to send three or four harpies out lecturing, telling the people that Kansas is raising hell and letting the corn go to weeds [a reference to Mary Elizabeth Lease]. . . . Whoop it up for the ragged trousers; put the lazy, greasy fizzle who can't pay his debts on the altar, and bow down and worship him.

This is one of the most famous editorials in U.S. history, but many were not persuaded by it; small-town merchants of the Midwest and South shared the farmers' resentment of the railroad freight rates, the bankers, and the elevator owners, who arbitrarily set the farmers' commodity prices, plus their demand for government regulation. There is no record of the reaction of Grandfather and Grandmother Phipps to it, if any, but they were obviously taken by the ragged-trousered rattlebrains and switched their party loyalty from Republican to Democrat.* The transition wasn't always a pleasant matter, however. Grandmother regularly spent her Thursday afternoons in the church basement with the other members of the ladies' quilting society. This was also where the children's Sunday school classes, teenagers' Christian Endeavor meetings, and the various church dinners, bake sales, and other events were held. The quilting bee ladies, most of whom were Grandmother Phipps's best friends, were also mostly Republicans. They would spend two or three hours gossiping over coffee and cookies while making quilts to be sold at the church and Sunday school fund-raising bazaars. This was a high point of her week—except for a certain period in the summer. That was when the area got its seasonal infesta-

---

*Their youngest son, Wayne, who subsequently owned and edited the *McDonald Standard,* became an admirer of his fellow Kansas editor, however. On the wall of his office, he had a copy of White's equally famous and eloquent editorial on the occasion of his teenage daughter's tragic death when her skull was fractured by an overhanging tree limb while riding horseback.

tion of flying ants. These were minor but aggravating nuisances that swarmed around a farmer's head when he was on the tractor or the combine or, in the ladies' cases, while they were walking down the street or working in the yard. Among themselves, the men referred to the insects as "piss ants." Not so the quilting society ladies, of course. Instead, being Republicans, they called the ants "Democrats," as in, "I'll be glad when those Democrats get out of here and go back where they came from." This would cause Grandmother Phipps, one of the few Democrats in town, a measure of irritation, and she would come home and privately fume at this inadvertent insensitivity, but, typically, she never remonstrated.

In 1961, the year before she died, when I was a graduate student in American history at the University of Iowa, I would drive down to Mc-Donald to visit her during the Christmas, spring, and summer breaks. One pleasant evening that summer, we were sitting and talking in her rocking chairs on the front porch and got to talking politics. I asked her how it was that she had become a Democrat; my mother was Grandmother's only child who grew up to be a Democrat. Grandmother responded that the year she was twenty-five, she and Grandpa, at that time a registered Republican whose father was a Union army veteran (as was hers) drawing a partial disability pension from his military service, were impressed by the Democratic presidential candidate. The candidate was from Nebraska, had adopted much of the Populist platform, and was sympathetic to the plight of the drought- and depression-ridden farmers of the Midwest and South. So, when they read in the newspapers that he was making a campaign stop in Topeka, more than 300 miles and a long-day's train ride from their farm then in Phillips County, Grandmother and Grandpa got on the train, attended the candidate's rally and speech the next day, then rode the train back home to western Kansas. As soon as they got back, Grandfather Phipps changed his party registration to Democrat.

Nor was that the only fallout from that trip. They were not only taken by the candidate's politics, but also by his devout religious faith (he was Presbyterian, although his mother was Methodist and his father Baptist). So, arriving at a decision they had been considering, they sought out Brother Hughes, the Baptist preacher in McDonald. They "witnessed" or "testified" to their acceptance of Christ as their savior, as evangelic Protestants put it, were baptized by Brother Hughes (full immersion, of course), and became born-again Christians. I knew that Grandmother was born in 1871 and was about to make an exclamation, but she beat me to it. "Yes, William Jennings Bryan," she concluded musingly. "A fine, upstanding Christian gentleman."

I sat there momentarily dumbfounded. From the movie *Inherit the Wind* I had gotten an image of Bryan as a pious, self-righteous, gluttonous buffoon, although as a graduate student in history, I was in the process of having that impression corrected. The movie portrayed Bryan as the chief prosecution witness in the famous 1925 Scopes "Monkey Trial" in Tennessee, testifying against the teaching of evolution in the public schools and arguing for the literal Biblical version of Creation. Bryan, in fact, backed many progressive programs during his career, including women's suffrage and the graduated income tax. In 1896, what my grandparents saw was a tall, slender, handsome man of thirty-five who wore a black alpaca suit and low-cut vest. He was blessed with a surpassing charisma and oratorical talent and his powerful, mellifluous voice and grandiloquent gestures had been polished on the Chautauqua circuit.

Although not a leading candidate when the Democratic convention met that year, Bryan won the party's presidential nomination with one of the most famous orations in American history, the "Cross of Gold" speech, which first mesmerized the delegates and then set them into a nominating frenzy:

> Burn down your cities and leave our farms, and your cities will spring up again as if by magic. But destroy our farms and the grass will grow in the streets of every city in this country. . . . You shall not press down upon the brow of labor this crown of thorns, you shall not crucify mankind upon a cross of gold!

With his advocacy of free coinage of silver, Bryan spoke for the hard-pressed debtors on the nation's farms, including the Phippses. I had read a lot about the dramatic 1896 presidential campaign but until that moment on the front porch I had no idea of the impact it had on my family. I was also surprised that my grandparents would go to that much trouble to see a political candidate, but subsequently learned that the Populists were remarkably sophisticated students of the economic system.

The Populists came to the realization that the farmers' troubles were primarily caused by the nation's financial system. Their analyses and criticisms of the money and banking systems, in fact, were a major factor that led to the formation of the Federal Reserve System in 1913, although the Fed is considerably more conservative than the system the Populists proposed. Incredible as it seems today, until 1913 the major eastern commercial banks and bankers, led by J. P. Morgan, functioned as the nation's de facto central bank, which controlled the money supply and set interest rates. The Populists believed, with reason, that Morgan et al. made monetary decisions that favored eastern business interests at the expense of farmers. The Populists wanted to eliminate the private bankers from the money and credit distribution system entirely, but failed; the commercial banking system is still very much a major factor in the process.

That turn-of-the-century battle between the gold and silver forces was replete with irony. Free coinage of silver and the issuance of paper money unsecured by precious metals, which the Populists advocated, seemed impossibly radical to the Republicans, conservatives, creditors, businessmen, city folks, and others in the coalition that elected William McKinley over Bryan. It was much less radical, however, than the Populists' "subtreasury" proposal, which would have taken the control of credit and the money supply away from the big private commercial bankers and turned it over to the people and the federal government.

Under this plan, farmers would be able to get loans at 1 or 2 percent interest, paid out either in federal paper "greenbacks" or in negotiable certificates of deposit. These loans were not to be secured by either gold or silver bullion. They were to be secured by either the farmer's land or his crops, which would be stored in the federal warehouses or grain elevators (known as "subtreasuries"). These concepts of government purchase and storage of crops and subsidized credit for farmers were incorporated into the New Deal agricultural programs that saved Grandfather and Grandmother Phipps's farm forty years later. In fact, the Populists' proposed loan program, secured by crops, is basically the farm price support system in place today.

The farmers' struggles in the late nineteenth century were partly the result of post–Civil War deflation and contraction of the money supply due to the return to the gold standard, which Lincoln and the Congress had abandoned in 1861 in their financing of the war effort. During the Civil War, prices rose by about 75 percent and farmers in the North prospered. The gold standard was reimposed after Appomattox, however, and by 1884 prices were back down at their 1860 level. The scarcity of money drove farm prices down, interest rates up, and the farmers to desperation. The rich (business) got richer and the poor (farmers) got poorer. Ironically, the Panic of 1893 was to a great extent caused by fear resulting from the drawdown of the gold bullion reserve kept in the Treasury building in Washington to back the greenbacks in circulation. Because of dwindling federal revenues after 1890, this reserve fell below $100 million, the arbitrary safety line, which set off a national panic that caused banks to close, the stock market to crash, and employers to lay off workers.

The farmers finally got relief in the late 1890s, when the rains returned and crop failures in Russia boosted world demand for American wheat. This bit of good fortune for American farmers was substantially abetted by a historical fluke—the discovery of the enormous gold fields in Alaska, Colorado, and South Africa, which doubled the world's stock of gold between 1890 and 1914. This increased the money supply, as the Populists had unsuccessfully sought to do through the political system with free coinage.

As a result, the first two decades of the twentieth century were a time of unparalleled stability and prosperity for American farmers after the drought and depression of the 1890s, particularly from 1910 to 1914. Future government programs based farm subsidy prices and crop loans on "parity," the relationship of the farmer's expenses to prices for his crops. Farm parity is still based on the farmer's purchasing power of this period. This prosperity accelerated with the onset of World War I because of increased demand for agricultural imports due to wartime needs and disrupted production in Europe. The resulting high prices combined with good weather and crops in the United States furthered the prosperity of the prewar years.

By 1917, the price of wheat was $2.74 a bushel, more than triple the price in 1914, and farmers in western Kansas, including my family, were breaking virgin sod almost round the clock with tractors. The *Topeka Daily Capital* reported that "gas tractors were tearing the whole country upside down" in southwestern Kansas and that the native short-grass pasturage of that section would soon be gone. This was an exercise in greed that came back to haunt Kansas and the rest of the High Plains fifteen years later during the Dust Bowl.

⚒

Grandfather and Grandmother Phipps's political conversion by the "Boy Orator of the Platte" was rewarded forty years later during the Great Depression and the Dust Bowl. After Grandpa died in 1936, Grandmother was able to keep their debt-ridden farm, thanks to a low-interest federal loan, compliments of Franklin Roosevelt's New Deal. With the end of the Dust Bowl and the economic recovery from the depression that began with the World War II buildup a few years later, Grandmother was able to repay the loan quickly, and she kept the farm until she died.

There were staunch Republicans in that part of the country, including some of her relatives, who refused to accept any New Deal aid from "that man," as those who hated FDR referred to him, and some may have lost their farms as a result. Grandmother Phipps was never much for gloating over others' misfortunes, but I always wondered if she didn't harbor the thought that some of them who had prospered during the 1920s and hadn't been particularly reticent about it just might have gotten about what they deserved.

CHAPTER FIVE

A "JERKWATER TOWN"?

In the summer of 1916, forty years after the first white settlers in Rawlins County—five immigrant men from Germany—staked out their homesteads on the virgin prairie, life was good for the Phipps family. In the eleven years since their move to Rawlins County, the family had grown, with the addition of a boy and a girl, for a total of four boys and three girls, and the farm operation had expanded as well. In addition to their original 240 acres, Grandfather Phipps had bought another half section—320 acres, or half a square mile—weather and crops were good, and prices were high owing to demand created by the Great War in Europe. Life in the first two decades of the twentieth century was better for American farmers in general, not just the Phippses, than it had been since the Civil War or would be again until World War II.

The mighty engine that powered the settling of the continent was the European immigrants' hunger for land and economic opportunity. Some acquired land through the Homestead Act of 1862, which provided a quarter section of free land to any settler who "proved up" on it, that is, lived and farmed on it for at least five years. The Timber Culture Act of 1873 enabled an individual to acquire another quarter of the treeless prairie if he would plant forty acres of trees on it; because of the difficulty of this, the requirement was reduced to ten acres. In addition, individuals could buy more land from the federal government for $1.25 to $2.50 an acre.

The Homestead Act was intended to encourage the settlement of the West by making land easily available to anyone who wanted to farm it; the amount of land in the country devoted to farming more than doubled between the end of the Civil War and the turn of the century. The act never accomplished what its creators hoped for, however, because 160 acres wasn't nearly enough to be economically feasible west of the Missouri River. Ironically, the Land Survey Ordinance of 1785 had set the sales of federal lands to settlers at a minimum of 640 acres—a square mile—at the price of $1 per acre. In subsequent land acts, however, Congress lowered the acreage minimum, primarily because most families in the eastern United States with its ample rainfall couldn't farm a full section with nineteenth-century technology. In the well-watered east, even 160 acres could be more than a single family could manage.

A quarter section, however, is but a fraction of the land—2,000 acres or more today—that is the minimum for wheat and cattle ranching on the subhumid High Plains. As a result, the required five years of homestead residency became known as the "period of starvation." Walter Prescott Webb wrote that what the Homestead Act came down to was that "the government is willing to bet the homesteader one hundred and sixty acres of land that he'll starve to death on it in less than five years." John Wesley Powell, the nineteenth-century explorer of the West who wrote a definitive—and regrettably ignored—report on the region's climate and resources, thought the minimum should be two to four square miles, 1,280 to 2,560 acres.

Many early settlers in Rawlins County homesteaded, but most Kansas farmers and ranchers bought their land in larger parcels from the federal government, the railroads, or private brokers; some did use homestead acquisitions to augment their larger holdings. As an incentive to build westward, the government gave the railroads 181 million acres of federal lands, more than 10 million acres in Kansas. The railroads got an alternating block of ten to forty square miles, or sections, along their rights-of-way for each mile of track; these created swaths twenty to eighty miles wide, ten to forty miles on each side of the tracks, under railroad control. The railroads sold it cheaply, for $1.25 to $2.50 per acre, realizing their profit from passenger and freight revenues after the lands were settled.*

These sales were through their land departments and land agents, of

---

*In addition, corporations and individual speculators received another 340 million acres of federal (and Indian) lands, much of which was choice land near rivers and the railroads. This is compared to only 80 million acres patented to homesteaders, most of which was in poorer locations. Historians and economists calculate, however, that while this land subsidy gave the railroads a 1.1 percent greater return on investment, the social return to the nation in increased economic growth was at least 24 percent.

which each town had at least one in the early years. They plastered the newspapers in Chicago, Omaha, St. Louis, Des Moines, Kansas City, Topeka, and other cities back east with advertisements and arranged to show prospective buyers around. The agents from the towns, including McDonald, that were on the spur of the Chicago, Burlington and Quincy Railroad that runs from the main line at Orleans, Nebraska, to St. Francis, Kansas, 150 miles west, often met their prospective clients at the Orleans junction.

Competition among these agents was fierce. They kept jealous track of each other, and the enterprise sometimes included attempts to intercept each other's prospects at Orleans or some point along the line and present them with a better deal. The employment of whiskey and other entertainments to entice prospects to look at land near, say, McDonald rather than their original destinations in some other town was not unknown. Out and out chicanery also was not unknown.

My uncle Wayne, who owned and edited the town newspaper, the *McDonald Standard*, for several years, recounted such an event, which occurred shortly after the turn of the century. It was told to him by a lifelong friend, Edwin Lyman, who for years was McDonald's leading land agent and a major landowner himself. Lyman concocted an elaborate plot to steal away four big investors from the agent in Bird City, the first town west of McDonald. The Bird City agent had them lined up to buy up separate sections of the huge Dewey ranch south of McDonald, which was owned by a Chicago millionaire named C. P. Dewey, a kinsman of Admiral George Dewey, the hero of the Spanish-American War battle of Manila Bay. Lyman had learned about the deal in the course of his normal gossiping over whiskey and cigars with ranch foremen and cowboys when they came to town.

Lyman's scheme was in retaliation for the Bird City agent's earlier hijacking of some of his prospects. The plot involved Lyman's posing as an investment banker and boarding the east-bound train in Atwood, the first town east of McDonald. He introduced himself to the Bird City agent's assistant, who had been assigned to meet the prospective buyers in Orleans and escort them to Bird City. Alas, the assistant didn't know Lyman, whose first step was to engage him in talk about high finance and then propose a congenial drink of high-quality whiskey—and then another and another—to help while away the 150-mile train ride. It worked exactly as intended. More drinks at the hotel bar in Orleans led to a long-night's sleep for the Bird City assistant and allowed Lyman to greet the investors early the next morning and pass himself off as the Bird City man.

He sent a telegram to the Bird City agent, in the name of the assistant, informing him that the party had been delayed for twenty-four hours. He then bundled the prospects onto the first train to western Kansas before the real Bird City man was up and about. The party got off at McDonald, which is the town closest to the Dewey ranch, went to the ranch, and met with its owners. By the time the unsuspecting Bird City agent and his hungover assistant tumbled to the fact that their clients had been shanghaied, the buyers were at the ranch, the deal had been struck—in great part through Lyman's intimate knowledge of the ranch and what each buyer wanted—and neither the satisfied sellers nor the investors were inclined to undo it.

Lyman had moved to McDonald from Nebraska at the turn of the century and became one of northwest Kansas's leading citizens. He eventually bought 10,000 acres of the Dewey ranch himself, adding it to his holdings, which ultimately totaled about 30,000 acres. He established the town's first bank, a grain elevator, and a lumber and coal yard, and was a leading real estate and insurance broker. He built a large house and barn in town, which still is known as "the Lyman place," served on the school board, and contributed heavily to the building of the Federated Church.

His oldest son, William Roy "Link" Lyman, was the first graduate of McDonald High School, in 1917, and Ed's brother, Ashley Lyman, dean of the University of Nebraska School of Pharmacy, came out to deliver the commencement address for the graduating class of one.

🖎

The town of McDonald came into being in 1888. Like much else in the West, it was the fruit of a union of water and the railroad plus the desire of a large rancher, Rice McDonald, for a touch of immortality. The town site was in the area of three huge ranches, the Dewey ranch, one owned by the John D. Rockefeller family, and one belonging to the McDonald clothing manufacturing family in St. Joseph, Missouri, and managed by Rice McDonald. Together, the three spreads occupied a good share of the northwest corner of the state, and the town's early history was intimately entwined with them.

The town of McDonald actually was a re-creation of the town of Celia, which had been established in 1885 on what its founders thought would be the railroad right-of-way. To their astonishment, however, the railroad ignored their town, laid its tracks a half mile north, and dug a 200-foot-deep well three miles west for a watering station for its locomotives. The reason was simplicity itself: The underground water at the well site had a stronger flow than that at Celia, and in the West water is king. The well was dug by hand and lined with stone in a little more than three months, from July 6, 1888, to October 25, 1888. Maintenance platforms were built in the walls every 10 feet with ladders down to them and when the well was completed, the citizens celebrated by having a square dance on them, the caller and musicians on one platform, the dancers on the others.

With the advent of diesel locomotives and the refusal of the state to approve it as a drinking water source for the town because it was lined with rock and not cement, however, the well was filled in after World War II, an act of historical shortsightedness the citizens came to regret; Greensburg, Kansas, which had more foresight, now boasts the largest hand-dug well in the world, an honor McDonald might have claimed.

Given this history, McDonald literally came into being as a "jerkwater town," the term the railroad men used for their watering stops; it refers to the fireman's pulling down the water tank's long spout that delivered the water to the locomotive boiler.

If the mountain wouldn't come to Muhammad, then Muhammad would go to the mountain, as the railroad knew it would. The well site was on the McDonald family's 9,000-acre ranch and Rice McDonald offered to donate the land, 160 acres, for the town on the railroad right-of-way. His condition was that the town be named after him.* Several buildings in Celia, including the hotel, restaurant, post office, newspaper office, and grocery store, were moved to the railroad well site in 1888. The isolation and hard life on the High Plains seemed to be conducive to conspiracy theories, and to this day the citizens of McDonald suspect that Celia had to move because of collusion between McDonald and the railroad—McDonald for reasons of ego, the railroad because Celia balked at donating as much land for the town as the Lincoln Land Company, which had the construction contract for the line, wanted.

Nearly every town on the line, including Bird City and St. Francis to the west, started out this way—being founded on one site and then moving to where the railroad was. Atwood, the Rawlins County seat, was something of an exception. The railroad tried to bypass Atwood by building the line a mile north of it because the Lincoln Land Company owned lots in the hamlet of Blakeman and wanted the county seat moved there.

*Edwin Lyman bought the McDonald ranch, in 1916.

The citizens of Atwood fought back, however. They extended the town's limits out to the tracks and the state railroad commission forced the railroad to build a depot there. The state supreme court also ruled that the county seat would remain in Atwood.*

Such relocations and power struggles were common in the settling of the continent, and the one in Rawlins County was relatively peaceful as those things went. The pro-Atwood faction got a delay at one point, when it appeared the railroad would prevail, by swearing out a warrant for a pro-Blakeman county commissioner, which charged him with carrying a concealed firearm. They had no idea whether he was armed or not; as luck would have it, he was packing a loaded six-shooter at the time. In some Kansas counties, however, the county seat fights went beyond questionable legal tactics and were resolved by actual gunplay.

The citizens' confusion as to the railroads' intentions is understandable. In the 1880s, Rawlins County was surveyed by the Union Pacific, the Chicago, Rock Island and Pacific, the Oxford, Kansas and Nebraska, and the Burlington and Missouri, and there were rumors of surveys by the Kansas Pacific, St. Joseph and Western, and Kansas Western lines. The sight of survey crews pitching their tents outside of town as they moved through the county was not uncommon during the decade.

These strains between the railroads and their builders and the citizenry, however, didn't extend to the train crews. This spur of the Chicago, Burlington and Quincy was known locally at the time as the "Beaver Valley Line" because it ran alongside the Beaver Creek from western Kansas to where it emptied into the Republican River near Orleans. Early settlers fondly recalled that when a Beaver Valley Line conductor had a hungry baby on board, he would stop the train at the first nearby cow, get out and milk it, and then heat the bottle on one of the potbellied stoves that were in each car. The crews were also known to shoot rabbits for the passengers' lunch.

🖎

In 1898, the owner of the Dewey ranch, C. P. Dewey, sent his son, Chauncey, then twenty-one, to manage his huge holdings in northwest Kansas. C. P. Dewey, whose father had been a law partner of Edwin M. Stanton, Lincoln's secretary of war, made his fortune in Chicago real estate follow-

*During this fight, several buildings were moved to Blakeman in anticipation that it would become the county seat, but they were moved back to Atwood after the issue was resolved. One store building was cut in two to facilitate its move to Blakeman but was moved back and reassembled after the decision in Atwood's favor.

ing the great fire of 1871 and also owned an 11,000-acre cattle ranch near Manhattan, Kansas. Contemporary accounts indicated that while C. P. Dewey commanded respect because his check was good for any amount, he was heartily disliked in Riley County where he was known as "the man from Chicago."

Chauncey, a sophisticated—and, in the view of many, arrogant—young graduate in the classics from the University of the South, was similarly regarded in Rawlins County and reinforced his status as a rich eastern outsider by stocking his ranch house with volumes in the classics and fine art. According to Dewey family accounts, he was hurt by his lack of acceptance and didn't comport himself as an effete eastern dude. In fact, he was an active, hands-on cattleman who loved ranching and the West and would ride to town with his guard of cowhands, all of them decked out in boots, spurs, and chaps and armed with Winchester carbines slung to their saddles and Colt six-shooters strapped to their waists. Shortly after taking over the ranch, Dewey and a dozen of his cowboys drove 4,000 head of cattle 300 miles from Dalhart, Texas, up to the Dewey ranch, the last cattle drive from the Lone Star State up to Kansas.

The Dewey ranch was the largest in Kansas. They controlled about 700,000 acres, 300,000 of which they owned and the rest of which they leased from the federal government and private owners. The spread was centered near the four corners conjunction of Rawlins, Cheyenne, Sherman, and Thomas counties and covered part of all four counties. At some points, it extended as much as twenty-four miles north to south and thirty-six miles east to west. The Deweys ran 10,000 cattle and 40,000 sheep and employed eighty cowboys, many of whom were former soldiers, veterans of the Indian and Spanish-American wars.

The cattle industry, however, was dealt a major blow in the 1880s by the big blizzard of January 1887, which was one of the worst in the nation's history. It destroyed an estimated 80 percent of all the cattle on the High Plains range from the Dakotas to Texas, many of which had been weakened by the severe preceding winter and the drought of the summer of 1886. The winter of 1886–87 resulted in the bankruptcy of thousands of cattlemen, including some of the biggest cattle companies, and brought an end to the open-range cattle industry. A major factor, however, was greed—the open range had been drastically overstocked and overgrazed in the two decades following the Civil War because of the demand for beef and other foodstuffs in the rapidly growing industrial cities of the East, whose populations were growing at twice the rate of the nation's farm population.

Another was that the cattle business was also plagued by the fact that the Texas longhorn cattle were carriers of a disease known as "Texas fever," which was borne by ticks that burrowed into the animals' hides. The longhorns had developed immunity to the disease, which was fatal, but the cattle in Kansas hadn't, and in 1861 the state legislature enacted a quarantine prohibiting Texas cattle in the summer and fall, when the ticks were most active. The postwar demand for beef, however, forced a loosening of the quarantine to allow the great post–Civil War trail drives up to the new Kansas railheads. The new quarantine law allowed Texas cattle west of the 6th principal meridian, which is a reference point of the U.S. surveyor general for surveying public lands and runs north and south just east of Abilene. The drives later went up the Western Trail, a branch of the Chisholm that ran through Rawlins County up to Ogallala, Nebraska. As Kansas cattlemen moved west with the settlement of the state, the quarantine line on longhorns had to be shifted westward and was extended to the Colorado line in 1884.

Nevertheless, the Deweys harbored the modest ambition of owning or controlling the entire northwest corner of Kansas, an area measuring about 60 miles east to west and 40 miles north to south, more than 2,000 square miles. It would have reached from Atwood west to the Colorado line, and from the Burlington Railroad 30 miles south of McDonald up to the Rock Island line from Denver to Chicago, which was 20 miles north of McDonald, just over the Nebraska line.

According to their enemies, the Deweys had ruthlessly driven many homesteaders off their land, buying some out, purchasing mortgages on others and then foreclosing on them during the drought and depression of the 1890s, and acquiring some at tax sales. The Deweys frequently found their fences cut, water tanks punctured, wells poisoned, buildings and pastures set afire, and horses and livestock killed. On one occasion, Dewey found twenty purebred Hereford bulls shot, eleven of which died. It was a common homesteaders' charge that the large cattle herds trampled and ate their crops and that the cattlemen fenced off government land and then harassed the farmers with charges of trespassing and rustling. Twice, armed parties of settlers, one seventy strong, rode to the Dewey ranch to warn Dewey to go easy in his acquisitions or expect more trouble.

The conflict between wealthy cattlemen and poor homesteaders is a familiar theme in our popular culture; it is the plot of the movie *Shane*, with Alan Ladd and Brandon de Wilde, and is a subplot in the Broadway musical *Oklahoma* ("The Farmer and the Cowman Can Be Friends!").

The Deweys didn't just tangle with poor sodbusters, however. They were as cavalier with the Rockefeller family. Frank Rockefeller, a son of John D. senior, acquired a 13,500-acre ranch that adjoined Dewey's on the north. With it, he also acquired a substantial portion of grief. On one occasion, Dewey cowboys drove seventy head of Dewey cattle to graze on Rockefeller range and kept them there at gunpoint. Another time, Dewey cowboys cut the four-strand barbed wire fence between the two ranches, contending that it was on the wrong side of the survey line. Once again at gunpoint, they cut the wire at every fence post on a four-mile stretch. When Rockefeller appealed to Governor Willis J. Bailey, the governor advised him to seek judicial rather than executive relief.

A poor homesteader named Daniel Barry gave the Deweys far more trouble than the Rockefellers did. Berry's farm, and that of one of his sons, Alpheus, was five miles west of the Dewey ranch house, just across the Cheyenne County line and surrounded by Dewey holdings. In 1903, the feud between Dewey and the Berrys came to a head. It was the last of the western range wars and a classic confrontation of big wealthy ranchers who resented the encroachment of poor, hardscrabble, dirt-farming homesteaders on their water holes and free range.

Daniel Berry, however, had proved unusually stubborn and tenacious, both personally and legally. The Dewey-Berry feud erupted in a shoot-out over a wooden water trough for horses that one of Dewey's cowboys bought for $5 at a sheriff's auction sale of some of Alpheus Berry's property. When Dewey and nine of his cowboys, armed as usual with six-shooters and Winchester and Sharps rifles, went by Alpheus Berry's place to get the trough the day after the sale, they were greeted by Berry, three of his sons, and a nephew. Dewey testified at his trial that the Berrys shot first at him and his men and that they only fired back in self-defense. The Berrys contended that the Dewey party shot first, ambushing them in Alpheus's yard from behind the remnant of an old sod wall. Dan Berry and two of his sons, Alpheus and Burchard, were killed; the other son, Beach, was wounded; and the nephew, Roy Berry, escaped unharmed. None of the Dewey party was hit, although Dewey's horse was killed by a wild shot by Roy Berry.

Despite Dewey's contention that the Berrys shot first, he and two of his cowboys were indicted for murder. The Berrys' funeral in Bird City drew a huge crowd, with lines of mourners on horseback and in wagons a quarter of a mile long approaching the town from different directions. An armed Populist mob of about 150 that later formed up at Berry's place prompted Governor Bailey to dispatch Company K of the Kansas National Guard to help a sheriff's posse protect the Deweys when they were transported to the Cheyenne County courthouse in St. Francis; Dewey provided wagons from his ranch to carry the militia infantrymen.

Because of inflamed public opinion, the trial venue was moved to Norton, seventy-five miles east of McDonald. After a long series of complicated legal maneuverings, Dewey and his cowboys came to trial the following year, in 1904. They were acquitted of one murder charge and the others were dropped, a major factor in the verdict being testimony that the Berrys had a history of firing warning shots at creditors who came around to collect. An outraged mob burned the jurors in effigy when the verdict came down.*

The Dewey-Berry feud had an ironic resolution. Beach Berry, the surviving son, and Roy Berry, the nephew, testified at the trial that they all were unarmed but thirty years later, in 1934, admitted that they had fired warning shots over the Dewey party's heads and didn't expect them to be returned. In his efforts to clear his name, Dewey persuaded the Berry boys to execute affidavits that they had started the shooting, and Beach Berry agreed on one condition, according to Dewey.

"You know, Chauncey, I ought to get something out of this," Beach responded. "For thirty years I've wanted to fish on Dewey Lake [a man-made lake on the ranch]." Dewey agreed, recalling that "I told him, when you get ready to fish, you let me know and I'll take the day off and go with you. And he called me just a few weeks later and we went. People came and stood on the hill and watched a Dewey and a Berry fishing together. They couldn't believe it."

The feud was the high-water mark for the Deweys. Their ranch was subsequently broken up and sold off in parcels, as were the McDonald and Rockefeller holdings. After his acquittal, Chauncey Dewey moved back to Illinois, where he became a power in the Republican party as a leader of the Cook County GOP and a backer of Theodore Roosevelt. He and his family held on to several thousand acres, however, and after serving in the Army in World War I—he enlisted as a private and came out a major, serving on the staff of General Leonard Wood—Dewey moved back to northwest Kansas and lived there until his death in 1959.

For several years, he operated the ranch as a dude ranch. He built a

*The last lynching in that area was of a man in April 1932, who confessed to the rape and murder of an eight-year-old girl from about fifty miles away. He was taken from the jail in St. Francis by a mob of about forty men who overpowered the sheriff and was hanged from a large tree on the part of the Dewey ranch south and east of McDonald that Edwin Lyman had acquired. Lyman had his own problems as a rancher; a disgruntled ranch hand set fire to his barn, destroying the building and killing several horses.

twelve-room stucco Spanish-style mansion, modeled on the Alamo; the house burned to the ground two years before he died, the result of faulty electrical wiring rather than outraged Populists or resentful ranch hands. Dewey unsuccessfully ran for U.S. senator from Kansas in 1944 and in 1952 was the Kansas state chairman of Senator Robert A. Taft's campaign for the Republican presidential nomination.* The last large portion of the ranch, 6,000 acres, is owned by one of Dewey's sons, Otis.

⚔

Diseases such as Texas fever and blizzards that destroyed herds weren't the only hazards the settlers faced on the High Plains. The drought and depression of the 1890s almost did in the fledgling town of McDonald. As family after family gave up their homesteads and businesses, by 1900 the population had dwindled to twenty-eight people—seven families—and a handful of businesses. Rainfall and prices began picking up at the turn of the century, however, and in 1905, the year Grandfather and Grandmother Phipps moved there, McDonald was booming. In 1905 and 1906, it added eighteen new homes and barns, fifteen new business buildings, a new school building, which cost $5,000, and a second grain elevator. These were raw-looking frame buildings with false fronts that rose starkly and precarious-looking on that vast, endless prairie, unbroken as it was by trees or any traces of landscaping. With the ramshackle, one-story buildings, dirt streets, and hitching posts, old photographs of the town look like a set for a Western movie.

It is a measure of the number of farmers who could sustain themselves on relatively small holdings in those labor-intensive, premechanical days that in 1907 that "city of 160 [population] on the CB&Q Railroad, between the North and South Beaver Creeks," as the *McDonald News* described the town, boasted two general stores, two hardware and implement dealers, a lumberyard, a furniture store, a music, millinery and novelty store, a bank, a meat market, a restaurant, a hotel with another under construction, a drugstore, two telephone systems, a printing office, two real estate offices, two churches, a barbershop, a livery barn, two blacksmith and wagon shops, a harness- and shoe-repair shop, and the post office.

---

*Shortly before his death, Dewey was asked why a man of his background chose to live in such an obscure corner of the High Plains. "I never knew anyone who lived in the West who didn't want to go back," he responded. "I like the life, the country, and the people. The air is clean. Out here, it is hard to imagine that there is any big city, its hustle, noise, and dirt."

The precariousness of their environment inspired a relentless booster-ism in the townspeople in the early years of the century. Their cheerlead-ing took many forms, including diatribes against the mail-order firms such as Sears, Roebuck and Company whose lavishly illustrated mail-order cat-alogs, or "wish books," gave even the most isolated homestead family a glimpse of a wondrous fairyland of material goods beyond imagining. These companies were viewed as a competitive threat to local merchants, however, and Sears was referred to in the local newspapers as "Scars, Raw-back and Co."*

One measure of the improving times was an ad in the November 22, 1907, issue of the *McDonald News* for a lawyer to come settle in town and help expedite the increasing volume of business. However, it did reflect a certain ambiguity about the legal profession that probably rings a bell with many today: "Wanted—An Attorney! Good opening for the right man, no opposition, plenty of legal work to do. No grafter need apply! Boozer not wanted!"

The town did experience its share of grafters and boozers over the years, but it continued to grow and in the early years of the twentieth cen-tury the area enjoyed its greatest growth and largest population. The growth of the town continued slowly but steadily until after World War II, with a pause after the crash of 1929 and the onset of the Great Depression and the Dust Bowl.

By the outbreak of World War I in Europe, most of the settlers had moved out of their "soddies" into frame houses. Amenities such as the gramophone, or "graphophone," as the phonograph was originally known, and lace curtains were commonplace. People had coal delivered to their houses by the ton rather than scavenging the creek beds for fire-wood and the pastures for dried buffalo- and cow chips, the early sources of prairie fuel. Most still read by the light of kerosene lanterns, but some had battery-powered generators that powered lightbulbs, which didn't re-quire daily cleaning as the lamp chimneys did. There also were gasoline-powered water pumps and washing machines to ease the drudgery of housework.

Despite the growing number of amenities, the people in the area never forgot for long how far out on the edge they were, however, as revealed by this social item in the *McDonald News* shortly after the turn of the century: "Mr. and Mrs. A. B. Stewart took Sunday dinner with their son John and

---

*The fact that the mail-order catalogs were a major source of toilet paper in the outhouses of the time was considered appropriate by many of these boosters.

wife. On their way up there they saw a large wolf with a big hen in its mouth."

In 1919, McDonald constructed a fair grounds, which was the site of the annual county fair during the 1920s and remained in operation until 1940. Also in the 1920s, a number of enterprising citizens constructed a golf course in Joe Cahoj's pasture (the farm is now owned by his son, Ed) a mile south and a mile east of town. The greens were of sand, quarried from local pits and made fast with applications of used motor oil. The fairways and roughs were of the native buffalo grass. In the late 1930s, the course was moved to another pasture two miles west of Cahoj's.

Buying groceries and other goods was known as "trading," which was a literal construction. Going to town on Saturday afternoons to "do the trading" was a weekly ritual for farm families, and main street was packed with their wagons and carriages, and, increasingly, automobiles. Like my grandparents, they'd bring milk and cream and eggs and other truck to the store, which would credit it to their accounts. The storekeeper put the milk and cream into ten-gallon cream cans and shipped it east to the creameries in ice-cooled railroad cars; as late as the outset of World War II, McDonald still had three creameries.

"Mother would give Ed Dobbs [the general store owner] her grocery list and he'd pack it in big egg crates," my uncle Wayne recalled. "We'd pay the bill at the end of the month and he always gave us a great big sack of candy at the time."

There were signs of a new order of merchandising that was emerging, however. In February 1916, a Leavenworth newspaper reported that "Grocerterias" were the latest thing in the grocery trade. In this revolutionary concept, "the customer helped himself and paid for the purchase on exit" rather than handing a list to the grocer who would get the items down from the shelf himself. This was just one of the harbingers of change that would relentlessly alter small-town society in the rural Midwest as the century progressed.

Concern for the well-being of the towns in the westward movement was an integral part of the history of the frontier. From the beginning, town fathers kept an anxious eye both on the hopeful new settlers who were moving in and on the discouraged ones who were packing up to return in defeat to their homes in the east. Civic cheerleading was the order of the day, as in this worried editorial in the October 4, 1907, edition of the McDonald News, which preached the urgent need for the town's businessmen to get out and sell the surrounding farmers on trading in McDonald rather than in the neighboring towns:

Blaine Phipps in University of Illinois ROTC uniform, c. 1915.

Left: Uncle Asa, seated center, with Harry Archer (*l.*) and George Calnon (*r.*). They went into the Army together in 1918. Asa and George died of the flu on the same day in October, 1918. Harry lived into his 90s. *Right:* Roy "Link" Lyman, All-America tackle at Nebraska, c. 1920, fifteen years with the Chicago Bears, member of the Pro Football Hall of Fame, first graduate of McDonald Rural High School, 1917.

Above: The Phipps farmhouse, 1917. Grandfather and Grandmother are standing. Asa is sitting on porch at left, with Margaret, Mother, Fern, and Old Shep (really).

Right: Mother and Dad near Plains, Kansas, in October of 1929. She was teaching high school. They were married on December 28, 1930.

Dad and the author, 1932.

Little Chet home on leave, October, 1942, the last time we saw him. *Left to right:* my mother, his sister Bessie, Aunt Margaret, his wife Irma, his sister Mildred, Aunt Fern. At grandmother Phipps' house.

Dad and the author, 1933.

Right: Mary E. Phipps and the author in her front yard in McDonald, c. 1941. *Below:* April 14, 1935, "Black Sunday," the worst day of the Dust Bowl. Looking northeast from the water tower in Rolla, Kansas. The high school where my mother taught is at the lower right. We lived across the street, south of it.

*Above:*Main Street, McDonald, Kansas, summer 1925, looking north. Model Ts and horses and wagons are the vehicles. The dots northwest of town on the left are straw stacks from threshing wheat, which is in progress. *Below:*McDonald today: Main Street (Courtesy Rawlins County *Square Deal*)

The Cheylin Cougars sign shows McDonald's civic spirit, as evidenced by its enthusiastic support of its student athletes. (Courtesy Rawlins County *Square Deal*)

Junior and Dee Dewey, proprietors of the Frosty Mug, outside the old McDonald Hotel in which the bar and restaurant are located. (Courtesy Rawlins County *Square Deal*)

Home of Mrs. Mary E. Phipps, birthplace of the author, in September 1994. (Courtesy Rawlins County *Square Deal*)

The trade territory [of McDonald] depends upon the enterprise of the merchants and residents. The town will gain a reputation for being awake and it will forge to the front. It is the men in the towns, not the men living within a certain number of miles from it, that make the town.

That cognizance, if not the hope, proved prophetic. A century after the town's founding, the productivity of the land and its people had steadily increased, but the technology that made this progress possible had wreaked a drastic change in the support community and social fabric of the area. The county seat towns enjoyed relative prosperity but not the smaller ones; the 1990 census showed that McDonald's population was 184, having fallen back almost to its 1910 level after reaching a peak of more than 400 during and just after World War II.

At the turn of the century, however, the area was embarked on a period of sustained growth and prosperity that most assumed would continue forever. Not until the second half of the century did it become apparent that this parabola had a downward arc, one that unfortunately shows no sign of being reversed.

CHAPTER SIX

"JESUS WEPT"

Whenever I go back to western Kansas, I am struck by how many of the people there, including my contemporaries and members of my family, profess and practice a devout religious faith and seem to assume that most others do too. Many say grace before each meal at home. One farm family with whom I had lunch one day while they were harvesting corn clasped hands during grace; there were three generations at the table, all partners in the family farm operation.

At the death of Claude Bell, a man greatly admired and liked in the community, his family and friends drew comfort from the thought that he and Marie, his beloved wife of fifty-three years who preceded him in death by three and a half years, were together again, this time in Heaven; it is often observed of elderly widows there that they are waiting to be reunited with their husbands. Many carry their Bibles to church so they can follow the sermon's text, a typical one by the Reverend Gregory H. Moyer, pastor of the Federated Church in McDonald, being on a familiar theme, "Trials and Temptations: James 1:2–18." Bob and Amelia Banister, whose family and mine have been friends for three generations, punctuate their accounts of their children's triumphs and tribulations by thanking the Lord that, however things have gone for them, good and bad, "they grew up as God-fearing, church-going citizens."

My family is Protestant, but there is a large number of Catholics in the area, mostly descendants of immigrants from Germany and the Czechoslovakian provinces of Bohemia and Moravia, plus a few from Ireland. The Protestants are primarily Methodists, Baptists, and Lutherans, with a scattering of more fundamentalist denominations. Grandmother Phipps's brother, my great-uncle Charlie, used to refer to my grandparents' faith as "that old-time religion with the bark still on it." Uncle Charlie was describing the fundamentalist Protestantism of Puritanism and Victorianism, moral absolutes, literal interpretation of the King James Version of the Bible, and no compromise on doctrine. It invoked both the stern and angry Old Testament God of swift retribution, and the New Testament God of love, salvation, and redemption through Christ.

It has always seemed to me that the intensity of devotion in those times—and these as well, for that matter—was in proportion to the difficulty of people's lives. Given the harsh life of the nineteenth-century frontier, it is no wonder that the settlers placed great emphasis on establishing the beliefs and institutions, spiritual as well as secular, that they brought west with them.

"These are a long-suffering people out here," said the Reverend Clarence Swihart, who was the Reverend G. H. Moyer's predecessor at the Federated Church from 1953 to 1979 and is still active as assistant pastor for senior citizens and fills in for ministers in neighboring towns. "We had a teacher here in McDonald who now teaches in a town near Topeka who returned for a visit and told me that he learned true Christian love in McDonald. It's in the way people act toward each other here. This is a caring community. That's one reason Eleanor and I came back after an eight-year absence." With a touch of civic pride, he observed, "I would also note that McDonald has the best musicians and potluck dinners of any community I've been in. I spent four years in Bailey, Colorado, and filled in at about forty-five churches in the Denver area and none of them could match what we have here."

Although technology has made life on the High Plains much easier physically, living there can still take a mental toll, as it did during the farm recession of the 1980s. The knowledge that bad times are always lurking just over the horizon is one reason why the people hold tight to their faith.

"When I moved here in 1979, the agriculture community was doing very well and people were excited about their prospects," recalled the Reverend Mr. Moyer. "Then came the hard times in the mid-eighties and people were really down. We didn't know how many were going to make it and were surprised at how many did. Some were thinking of suicide and I tried to help them in any way I could, to get counseling, whatever they needed. I brought some farmers over from Quinter to tell those in my congregation who had lost farm equipment to repossession to pool what they had left so they could keep on operating. Some flirted with Posse Comitatus [a radical, often armed, survivalist libertarian movement]. You could sense how down people were at the foreclosure auctions, that many were thinking that this could soon be happening to them and they wouldn't be getting much for their property, either. Things are better now, but the people are still down somewhat." He estimated that about 10 percent of his parishioners sought counseling back in 1989.

This can make people theologically conservative, which is how the Reverend Mr. Moyer describes his congregation. In that case, they have the minister to match. He is a handsome, dark-haired man in his late forties, a brawny one-time football lineman whose experience under fire with an Army assault helicopter unit in Vietnam was a catalyst in his spiritual life. "I went to church every Sunday before I went into the Army, but my experiences in Vietnam made me recognize that I had a spiritual need. I became a Christian." A native of Prince Georges County, Maryland, a suburb of Washington, D.C., he is a nondenominational graduate of the Dallas Theological Seminary. He is guided by the independent Bible church movement espoused by Dwight Moody, the nineteenth-century evangelist and religious educator, which holds that each church should be autonomous and independent of any governing theocratic hierarchy. The Reverend Mr. Moyer's ministry draws a number of worshipers of several denominations from neighboring towns who believe their churches have become too liberal.

The winds of modernism are always gusting around the corners, however. "We've been affected by the church/state and prayer-in-school issue," the Reverend Mr. Moyer said. "The school board did away with the baccalaureate service for the high school graduating class years ago, just before I got here, because of a Supreme Court decision. However, we had a prayer before the graduation service each year and a benediction afterwards with a minister from Bird City and one from McDonald participating and everyone seemed happy with that. But that was disallowed for the '93 class graduation because of a Supreme Court decision that arose from a rabbi's prayer at a graduation exercise, which prompted a suit by a girl who was an atheist. So, the school board decided that there would be no prayer at graduation because it feared a lawsuit. Then they got a letter from Pat Robertson's legal counsel saying that prayer at graduation was okay and they should go ahead, but that was followed by a letter from the ACLU to school superintendents nationwide threatening a suit if they did. The kids in the class of '93 wanted a prayer at their graduation, so the board decided to reinstate baccalaureate and held it an hour and a half before the graduation exercise. Reverend Swihart spoke and I offered a prayer. More than two hundred people came to it. It was terrific."

This is to be expected in a society whose founders in the nineteenth century brought a devout faith west with them from their homes back east or directly from the old country and which has remained culturally very conservative. "I've been here fifteen years and for the first ten I was the 'new pastor' in town." The Reverend Mr. Moyer laughed. "That's how people introduced me."

Religious practices in Kansas were colored by two major national movements, abolition and temperance. With the passage of the Kansas-Nebraska Act in 1854, churches in New England and other northern states cooperated with the New England Emigrant Aid Company in organizing emigration to the Kansas Territory. They founded the first city in the territory, Lawrence, now the site of the University of Kansas, and established abolitionist colonies in Ottawa, Topeka, Big Springs, Osawatomie, Manhattan, and other towns. Congregationalist churches, including Henry Ward Beecher's, supplied the founders of the Beecher Bible and Rifle Church in Wabaunsee with Bibles and Sharps rifles; a few months after its establishment in 1856, Wabaunsee became a station on the "Underground Railroad" and the Sharps were used to drive off slave owners who had tracked their fugitives into Kansas.

After the Civil War, the churches, particularly the Methodist, Baptist, and Presbyterian, turned their attention to prohibition. They were instrumental in passage of the state's constitutional prohibition amendment, which was ratified in the general election of 1880, and were the shock troops in the assault on the saloons, brothels, and gambling dens of the boisterous cow towns made famous by Carrie Nation and her hatchet. Kansas was a leader in the national prohibition movement. The state remained dry until 1948, when package sales of wine and hard liquor were allowed by county option; Rawlins County narrowly voted "wet" on that but was "dry" in 1986 on a county option amendment on liquor by the drink.

As noted earlier, many settlers emigrated to the New World, and Kansas, in search of religious freedom. About 400 Mennonite families, totaling about 1,000 people, left the Ukraine, and German Russians who were Catholic fled the southern Volga area in the early 1870s to escape religious persecution. As the tide of settlement moved west after the Civil War, churches became the centers of town development and community life. Where there was no minister, residents gathered in sod houses, in barns, and on the open prairie to read the Bible and sing hymns; on isolated claims, homestead families would set the Sabbath aside as a day of observance.

The first church in Rawlins County, which was erected several years before my family moved there, is a remarkably apt symbol of the settling of the frontier and the faith behind it. It was built of limestone from a nearby outcrop by its parishioners in 1891–92, a time of horrendous drought that scorched and shriveled the soul as it did the crops and land. The only crop any of them was able to raise in the summer of 1891 was a few acres of sorghum by one James P. "Uncle Dick" Stevens, which was converted into a few barrels of molasses. The molasses became a security deposit for materials used in the construction of what was named "Stevens Chapel" on its completion.

The early newspapers in the area reflected the religiosity of their time. An editorial in the *McDonald News* of October 4, 1907, reported that a reader had asked, "Can I dance, play cards, and go to the theatre and be a church member?" The editor concluded that the correspondent hadn't phrased the question correctly and proceeded to set him straight:

> We believe a man can turn handsprings, play golf, and attend ball games, and be a good American citizen; that he can pitch horseshoes, play mumblety-peg, and attend pink tea, and be a Republican; or that he can eat huckleberry pie, drink soda pop, and go to church Sundays and be a Democrat. . . . We think a man can be anything he wants to and be a member of a church, but being a Christian is a different proposition.

In an item in the December 13, 1907, issue, headed "News from Oak Ranch," the correspondent asks: "Have we all lived as near to God as we should? No, I fear not but let us try harder in this month than ever for we shall never see 1907 again and if we see 1908, let us try harder than ever before." The same edition quoted a minister who denounced the "desecration of the Sabbath by young girls practicing shorthand while taking in his sermons."

⚜

My family's recollections and obituaries stress the devoutness of my grandparents' generation and their forebears. The Phipps family, which migrated to Indiana in the early nineteenth century from North Carolina, a heavily Baptist state, was and is primarily Baptist. The obituary of my great-grandmother Margaret Ann Holbert Phipps noted that "she was converted at the age of 33 years [in 1870] and united with the Baptist church in Freedom, Indiana. . . . She has always been a most earnest christian [sic], always at her place." She was a midwife and nurse who spent a lot of time sitting up with the ill and dying. After the family moved from Indiana to a farm near the town of Long Island in western Kansas, she was in frequent contact with a Dr. Benny, who was described by one family member as "our town's strongest and best-educated infidel" and with whom she debated frequently and at great length. "He preached it [his case] like a true evangelist," the account continued, "but he did finally pat her on the back and say, 'Grandmother, if you are right, you have something. If I am wrong, I have nothing.'" This is a frontier version of Pascal's famous "wager."* Margaret Phipps was taught to read and write by my great-grandfather, Tolliver Phipps, after they were married and Dr. Benny referred to her as "the best-educated uneducated woman" he ever knew.

The evidence indicates that Tolliver Phipps was somewhat less rigid in his faith than his wife. He was converted about fifteen years after she was and the family accounts bespeak a tolerant man who betrayed more signs of the nature lover than the dedicated soldier of the Lord his wife was. He was a cattle breeder renowned for the quality of his animals, for his gardens and orchards, and for his concern about soil erosion a half century before the Dust Bowl; some of his contemporaries thought he was a bit "touched" on this subject, as one account put it, because they thought it didn't rain enough in western Kansas to wash the ground away. They also had yet to experience the serious wind erosion that would come in the great "Dustbowl" of the 1930s after most of the native sod was turned under and which was the darkest chapter in the state's history.

Grandmother Phipps's mother, Sarah Matilda Kauffman Duling, was described in her obituary as one who was "converted early in life and always kept the faith." Grandfather and Grandmother Phipps themselves were baptized in 1896, partly as the result of being favorably impressed by the Democratic presidential candidate, William Jennings Bryan; Grandpa was a leader in founding the Federated Church, served for years as the Sunday school superintendent, and was described in his obituary as "a man who lived his religion."

Over the years, church activities constituted a large part of my grand-

---

*Blaise Pascal, a seventeenth-century French scientist and religious philosopher, argued the need for mystic faith to comprehend the universe. Probably his most famous debating point, which became known as "Pascal's wager," was that accepting Christianity was in effect a safe bet because if you were wrong, there was nothing to lose, but if you were right, you would be rewarded with life everlasting in Heaven. He also founded the modern theory of probability and was a factor in the development of differential calculus, and his experiments with the equilibrium of fluids contributed to the invention of the hydraulic press.

parents' life. They often attended Baptist meetings and conclaves at the Clough Valley Baptist Church, a country congregation near St. Francis, a town about twenty miles west of their farm. They also attended church in McDonald, making the three-mile journey in a buggy or spring wagon twice on Sunday, once in the morning and again in the evening. Morning church services were followed by dinner with friends in the congregation, either as hosts or as guests. They were also frequent hosts of evening prayer meetings of ten or twenty people during the week, both on the farm and in town when they moved there in 1920. "Much of the conversation in the house revolved around the church," Uncle Wayne recalled. "It was the most important thing in their lives. They didn't want anything to interfere with their religion."

Uncle Charlie, who lived to be just a few days shy of 100, didn't share his sister and brother-in-law's piety and observed the passing scene with a certain bemusement. To the best of my knowledge, he enjoyed a touch of Old Crow, a chew of Beechnut tobacco, drew constant amusement from the human comedy, and went through life with an irrepressible and irreverent gleam in his bright blue eyes.

One bright summer Sunday afternoon when I was nine or ten, he was teaching me to chew tobacco in Grandmother's backyard. He assumed that in the course of growing up, a taste for "eatin' tabacca," as he called it, would come to every man and as part of this particular rite of passage, he threw in some theological observations to boot. I enjoyed my sessions with Uncle Charlie, mostly because he was one of the most entertaining characters I'd ever known, but also because Beechnut, at least, tasted good.

"The thing about Jim and Lizzie and their friends in church," he observed, referring to my grandparents, "is that they don't believe in smoking, drinking, chewing, playing cards, fast dancing, or making a little noise late at night because they think Jesus didn't do any of those things. I sure do admire them for it." That he envied them seemed to be a different matter. He thoughtfully aimed a stream of Beechnut juice at the hapless denizens of an anthill and concluded: "Sure seems to me they miss out on a lot, though." This came as no surprise. I had observed that Uncle Charlie's "not feeling up to" going to church services, which he pleaded on many Sunday mornings, didn't noticeably diminish his appetite for Grandmother's fried chicken or roast beef Sunday dinners or any other of his normal activities of the day such as listening to the baseball game on the radio.

In those days, Sunday was indeed a day of rest because the King James

Version of the Bible, which was the Word people took literally, recounted that after his six days of Creation, God rested on the seventh; the exception was wheat harvest. All the businesses in town were closed on Sunday except for the drugstore, which was open in the morning so we could pick up the Sunday *Denver Post* and *Omaha World-Herald,* and, in the evening, the movie theater. Even at picnics in the summertime, the menfolk, Uncle Charlie included, spent Sunday afternoons sitting around stiffly in their unaccustomed white shirts and neckties (remaining dressed for church apparently was part of the ritual). If there was one thing that convinced me early on that I would have to make my life somewhere other than in a small rural hamlet, which I otherwise loved, it was those empty Sunday afternoons, which seemed to get longer as I got older.

One of the hardest sells I ever made was badgering my mother into letting me go to a movie on a Sunday night—*Gulliver's Travels*—when I was about ten. She put no restrictions on music and dancing or movies or theater or culture of any sort, including card playing of the nongambling variety. In fact, she had no proscriptions on Sunday movies per se. She and her sisters went to Atwood one Sunday afternoon in 1940 to see *Gone With the Wind* and they came home titillated beyond measure, giggling guiltily after hearing Clark Gable's soon-to-be-immortal line to Scarlett O'Hara, "Frankly, my dear, I don't give a damn," out loud in a moving picture. They could scarcely bring themselves to repeat it for the edification of their curious mother, who was more amused by her daughters than scandalized by the rakish Rhett Butler. (As a rake, I always thought that Rhett, in fact, could have taken lessons from Uncle Charlie. On the occasions that I happened to overhear their conversations, I was struck by the amusement Grandmother derived from Uncle Charlie's repertoire of barnyard jokes and droll, sometimes mildly risqué, observations; she thought her brother was one of the funniest men on the face of the earth, as did the rest of us.)

As a matter of fact, I had already seen *Gulliver's Travels* in Atwood on a Sunday afternoon two or three weeks before. The problem was that Mother didn't want movies interfering with important matters, so when she finally capitulated, I still had to go to Christian Endeavor that historic night. That meant that I missed the first five minutes or so of the movie, which started at eight, but it was a small price for breaking the Sunday night taboo on movies.

I wasn't the first in the family to undergo that struggle. Aunt Fern, the youngest of Mother's family, was under the same no-Sunday-movies dictum laid down by her father and finally coaxed him out of it as I did with

Mother. "I can remember my first Sunday movie," Fern recalled. "I was in hog heaven. I had a date with either Claude or Clarence Bell [Claude's brother], I can't remember which, and we went to Bird City because McDonald didn't have a movie theater yet. I can't remember what the movie was. I didn't care at the time."*

Although religion was a major factor in my grandparents' lives, for some reason this wasn't passed down to all of their children. One exception was my mother, a devout and demanding Southern Baptist who was a throwback to my great-grandmother Margaret Ann Holbert Phipps. Mother was the only child in her family for whom religion appeared to be more than a social or business convenience. In my mother's uncompromising Baptist view, religious belief was all or nothing at all, a 100 percent commitment. She forbade the use of "Xmas" for Christmas on the grounds that "X" was a totally unsuitable substitution for Christ's name and I was so strongly conditioned on the matter that this dictum has stuck with me to this day; even though haste and expediency often tempt me to use it, I seldom give in to it. Mother put her money where her mouth was on religion, as she did in everything else. For thirty of the thirty-five years they were married, she and my stepfather tithed to the First Southern Baptist Church of Lemon Grove, California—10 percent off the top, 10 percent of gross income, not adjusted gross or after-tax income (he occasionally grumbled about it to me privately, but he wisely kept quiet on the subject when she was around).

After they moved to San Diego, she was a leader in the Lemon Grove Baptist church and was instrumental in its impressive evolution from a ragtag group that started up right after World War II meeting on the second floor of the Lemon Grove volunteer fire department building, a modest, two-story white frame building, to a solid, broad-based institution that now occupies a complex of buildings. There was no big money involved; it was done on the tithing of modest, hard-working people like my parents.

Mother treasured the little pins and certificates I accumulated for years of perfect attendance in Sunday school and church, along with Christian Endeavor on Sunday evening. I think she was disappointed that I didn't get the call to the ministry, but she was pleased that I followed her brother, Wayne, into journalism. However, she could take satisfaction in that I internalized and lived by the Christian ethic. I also shared her view that

---

*My uncle Vic Ritter and his brother, Ernest, built three brick buildings adjacent to each other on Main Street, one of which was the movie theater. One is now the McDonald Grocery, the other two, including the old theater, are vacant.

religious beliefs should be a total, all-out commitment and admired her for hers.

✳

The preachers and traveling evangelists of my youth didn't make it easy for their congregations to withhold commitment. A common tactic in trying to persuade one of the unwashed to witness for Christ was simply to scare him or her into it. The preacher would note how suddenly and unexpectedly the life of a heedless youth could be snuffed out in an auto accident, which certainly was true enough; we all had tragic firsthand experience with that. Then the preacher would dwell on the question of where such a youth would spend eternity, roasting in anguish in the fire and brimstone of Hell, or in paradise with Jesus.

When I was seventeen or eighteen, one revivalist in particular got my attention on the matter of just how long eternity is. It sometimes seemed to me in those days that the hour-long church service was a pretty good start on it, but this evangelist put it into its true perspective: If a tiny sparrow, he said, were to take a grain of sand from a California beach and fly all the way to the Atlantic coast and deposit it there, and then fly all the way back to California and get another grain of sand, and were to continue that process until it had moved *all* the grains of sand on all the California beaches to the East Coast, and then moved every grain of sand from the Atlantic beaches back to California, *you still would not have put even a dent in eternity!**

It didn't take any particular genius to grasp that the preacher was talking about a very substantial passage of time! I was shaken enough that I seriously considered going forward to be washed in the "blood of the Lamb" right then and there. What restrained me was that I had been well taught that for salvation to really work and save you from Hell, your conversion had to be *sincere*. You had to truly believe and accept Christ as your savior. I thought maybe the preacher was cheating a little, although, beleaguered as I was, it certainly didn't occur to me to make an issue of it. I was more impressed by the feeling that not only could my fear-driven conversion not fool God, it would render me guilty of the additional sin of hypocrisy, which would land me in worse trouble than I already was. That may have been my first experience on the horns of a serious dilemma. In any event, I made it through the service and a few minutes in the bright

---

*The last stanza of "Amazing Grace" refers to eternity, but doesn't poleax the sinner the way that preacher did: "When we've been there ten thousand years/Bright shining as the sun/We've no less days to sing God's praise/Than when we'd first begun."

summer sunshine pretty well restored me to normal, but the preacher had made an indelible impression. In the short run, I thought a lot more about the possibility of a head-on collision at seventy or eighty miles per hour or more out on the highway, and in the long run, I started thinking seriously about eternity. My baptism came a bit later.

I was always interested in the number of missionaries to China who passed through town, several each year, while on home leave in the States. Their purpose was to solicit contributions and report on the eagerness of the "heathen" Chinese, as some called them, to embrace Christianity. They described in glowing terms the happy Chinese who had been cleaned up, clad in chaste white uniforms, taught English, instructed in the Gospel, put to work in the missionary compounds, and otherwise "civilized," i.e., rescued from their pagan lives and spared the fate of not knowing Christ as their savior and its consequence, burning in Hell throughout eternity.

I recall little suggestion that out in that howling wilderness of heathenism the Chinese had any history, culture, or religion of their own. I wondered at first at the ability of my small church to support so many Baptist and Methodist missionaries but soon grasped the fact that a multitude of such churches supported them. It wasn't until I got to college that I learned that in this there was a connection between my small town and the larger world. Many American Christians, Protestant and Catholic alike, had a dream of converting China to Christianity, which had a secular, political side; this included Henry R. Luce, the founder of *Time* and *Life* magazines and the son of Presbyterian missionaries, who himself was born in China. This dream was that the United States and a converted China together would constitute a dominant global Christian political power. It was not a modest dream and it was no wonder the faithful contributed so willingly.*

This dream had profound political ramifications, however. Conservatives, particularly in the isolationist Midwest and West, opposed the Allies' original strategy in World War II of giving first priority to defeating Germany and then turning their attention to the Japanese. The Anglophile liberals back east, including Franklin Roosevelt, were more inclined to be oriented toward Europe. As a result, political pressures forced the United States to put more resources into the Pacific war than the

---

*Nor was it a monolithic dream. The Reverend Clarence Swihart expressed skepticism that it was a major factor with American Christians at the time and its importance is debated by historians.

beat-Germany-first strategy originally envisioned. The dream also fueled the fury of some conservatives over the Communist takeover of China in 1949, which became a factor in McCarthyism.

McDonald originally had both a Baptist and a Methodist church, but in 1915 the two small congregations decided to merge into the Federated Church. Grandfather Phipps was a leader in this, although giving up the separate Baptist church was not easy for him and Grandmother. In my grade school years, the Federated Church minister was a Baptist, the Reverend J. W. Coppoc, and I remember him as a forceful, unyielding evangelistic orator of the old school. He had little tolerance for those in the community who in his eyes fell short of their religious commitments. He had particular scorn for the unfortunates who regularly attended church once a year, on Easter Sunday, and was no shrinking violet in voicing his opinions. In his weekly church notes, a regular front-page feature in the *McDonald Standard,* the weekly newspaper Uncle Wayne owned and edited at the time, the Reverend Mr. Coppoc would voice a few well-chosen words about poor attendance during harvest:

> Sunday was a red-letter day for the wheat grower but it was not so good for public gathering in the morning. We couldn't hold Sunday School officers' elections due to small attendance.

Nor did he confine himself to spiritual matters. Contemplating reports of a possible major labor strike in October 1945, the Reverend Mr. Coppoc observed in his weekly note:

> There seems to be someone who wants war all the time. As soon as we have disposed of the Japs and Germans, the labor unions get more aggressive. It is a sorry commentary on Democracy when a few hundred thousand of the people can put 135 million of the people to so great an inconvenience.

The pastor's wife, an equally formidable person, taught the youth and teenage Christian Endeavor class, of which I was a member. The ordeal of facing a scurvy band of heathens like us every Sunday night in the classroom in the church basement must have sorely tried even that stout heart and sturdy faith. I sometimes wondered if she ever harbored the un-Christian thought that trying to bring the Gospel to such a pack of infidels was truly a case of casting pearls before swine, but if she ever shrank from the prospect, she never betrayed it. One of her inspirations, when I was nine or ten, was to have us answer roll call by reciting a Bible verse. Her logical assumption was that it would motivate us—force us, actually—to begin learning at least some of the Bible. Ah, but, as Bobby Burns so aptly said, "the best laid schemes o' mice an' men/Gang aft a-gley." It was entirely predictable that the first thing someone would discover would be that the shortest verse in the Bible is "Jesus wept" (John 11:35). The first roll call under this regimen went like this: "John Cole." ... "'Jesus wept.'" "Marshall Confer." ... "'Jesus wept.'" "Keith Davis." ... "'Jesus wept.'" "Vernon Davis." ... "'Jesus wept.'" "Dick Dickenson." ... "'Jesus wept.'" "Bob Johnson." ... "'Jesus wept.'" And so on, to the accompaniment of rising snickers and a corresponding elevation of Mrs. Coppoc's temperature.

The only break in this fiasco was Lela Rose Halligan. Her mother was almost as fiercely devout as Mrs. Coppoc, and her father was the grade school janitor and dealt on the side in scrap metal. Lela Rose invariably recited John 3:16, which is the very core of Christianity, the belief in the divinity of Christ. She ran through it so fast, as though she might somehow forget it if she paused for breath, that the verse came out as one long word: "'ForGodsolovedtheworldthatHegaveHisonlybegottensonthatwhosoever-believethinHimshouldnotperishbuthaveeverlastinglifeAmen.'"

After this debacle, we were given the word that since we'd obviously mastered John 11:35, it was time to expand our repertoire. Mother also handed the word down that she had better not hear of my pulling that caper or anything like it ever again. Knowing her son, she didn't leave it to chance, which wasn't her style in any event; she had the Bible in my hands every Sunday afternoon and I had to recite a verse other than "Jesus wept" before I got out the door. Unfortunately, many in the class didn't enjoy that quality of moral and intellectual support and forgot to memorize anything until the last minute. The result was variations of this theological debacle: "John Cole." ... "Uh, 'The Lord is my shepherd, I,' uh, 'I shall not want. He,' uh, 'He maketh me to lie down in,' ah, 'green pastures. He,' um, 'He restoreth my soul.' Uh . . ."

A stricken silence, and then the sufferer sometimes would make a desperate break for the safety net, "Jesus wept," which drew the reaction it deserved. I don't recall that anyone even considered using John 3:16. That was Lela Rose's private preserve and she hauled it out every Sunday evening, with no recorded objection by Mrs. Coppoc. At that point, I suppose the last thing she wanted was a hassle with Lela Rose, who at least was good for more than two words and was on the soundest of doctrinal grounds.

My account of that first night of roll call amused Grandmother greatly, as I knew it would, and we enjoyed the memory of it throughout the rest of her life; it took Mother a little longer to put it in the same perspective. Mother gave a 110 percent commitment to everything, including being a parent and her religious beliefs. I admired her enormously for it; even at that age, I understood the benefit I realized from her unselfishness.

As amusing as I find this story (and it is not an isolated example, many, like the Reverend Mr. and Mrs. Swihart, are familiar with the phenomenon), it is more interesting that many of the youngsters in that class grew up to be as devout and observing as their parents. Religious beliefs fill a profound need in people everywhere and at all times. Faith is always a great comfort to those who hold it. It is never more so, of course, than in times of great stress and my experience is that the more constant the faith in good times the more strength it provides in time of need. In a period of just a few years, the Phipps and Dickenson families experienced tragedies that put their faith to the test and demonstrated how valuable it was to them.

C H A P T E R   S E V E N

THE TRAGEDIES

AS WE HAVE SEEN, THE EARLY YEARS OF THE TWENTIETH CENTURY were a period of prosperity and tranquillity for the American farmer thanks to good crops and fair prices for agricultural products. Unfortunately, however, life is not always fair and the Phipps and Dickenson families experienced their full share of tragedy and heartbreak in the first decades of the century. They suffered the deaths of three of their sons, young men taken tragically and unexpectedly while in the prime of life. My uncles Blaine and Asa, Grandfather and Grandmother Phipps's second and third sons, respectively, died within a little more than a year of each other, in 1917 and 1918. My father died in 1934 at the age of thirty-three when I was two and a half.

These deaths were part of the family lore and in later years whenever those tragic events were recounted to us kids—my cousins and me—always in hushed tones, I listened with horrified fascination and regret. They profoundly shaped our attitudes toward Grandmother Phipps and my mother because of the feeling that they had suffered so tragically, above and beyond the normal hard life on the frontier. Due to the intimacy of small towns, a death in any family is an immediate, personal event because everyone knows everyone else. Children in those societies have to come to terms with death as grim, hard reality, not as a dramatic device on television or in the movies in which everyone understands that the deceased are resurrected and go on their lunch break after the scene is shot. Even before they experience death in their own families, the children learn that in real life there is no return and that the loss is permanent and profound.

🙰

In the spring of 1916, Uncle Blaine was a student at the University of Illinois and a member of the ROTC, which was mandatory at land grant colleges and universities. In those days, this automatically made him a member of the Illinois National Guard as well, and he was mobilized in June 1916 as part of the expeditionary force that President Wilson dispatched to Mexico under the command of General John J. "Black Jack" Pershing, later commanding general of the World War I American Expeditionary Force in France. Pancho Villa, a revolutionary hero to many Mexicans but a bandit in American eyes, was blamed for a border clash at Columbus, New Mexico (now the site of the Pancho Villa State Park), in which several Americans were killed, and Pershing's force spent eleven months in Mexico unsuccessfully pursuing him.

In early July, Blaine was sent with Troop B, First Illinois Cavalry, to Brownsville, Texas, where he was billeted in a muggy, hot camp. He never got south of Brownsville, however. One day, Grandfather and Grandmother Phipps got a telegram informing them that Blaine had contracted tuberculosis. Grandfather Phipps took the train to Brownsville and brought his second son home.

"We were shocked by how he looked, how gaunt and exhausted he was," Blaine's youngest brother, my uncle Wayne, recalled. "After he was home a while, the folks sent him to California, to the desert for several months, the way people did in those days, in the hope it would help." It didn't, and Blaine came back to the farm in western Kansas to die. Because TB is infectious, the family put up a muslin tent for him in the backyard, in which he lived until just before he died on the hot summer night of July 25, 1917, at the age of twenty-four.

"I heard Mother talking to the doctor that evening and the doctor said he wouldn't last the night," Wayne recalled. "It was so hot that Mother went in with a fan to cool him and be with him when he died." The funeral was held on the front porch of the house.

"We didn't think it was the military that killed him," Wayne said. "He probably wore himself out at the university. He worked eight hours a day plus going to school and probably didn't get enough sleep and was rundown by the time he got to Brownsville. There was no resentment of his military service. We accepted it, expected it. My grandfather was in the Civil War and for years we had his army rifle around the house along with a cavalry saber he'd picked up on a battlefield and sent home."

This tragedy was to be played out again just fourteen months later, when Asa, the third son, enlisted in the Army. In many ways, Asa and Blaine were 180-degree opposites. Blaine was tall, reserved, scholarly—a brilliant student. Asa was stocky, a cheerful extrovert who, in Wayne's words, "was everybody's friend, he liked everybody," and an eighth-grade dropout. He entertained his friends—and anyone else within hearing—doing impersonations of people who amused him, mostly figures of authority such as the town fathers and schoolteachers. One notable exception was a teacher named Grace Kennedy, who taught in the Mc-Donald Grade School from 1917 to 1920 and whom he was dating seriously when he left for the Army.*

From the day of America's entry into World War I, Asa yearned to get to the war, but his father kept talking him out of it. At one point, Grandfather Phipps bought a new tractor, as Wayne recounted, "in the hope that it would take Asa's mind off the war and he'd stay home. I never understood why he wanted to go to war. It didn't sound like a very good place to me." These efforts were to no avail. When the government announced an extension of the draft, Asa went to his father and argued that since he probably was going to be drafted anyway, he might as well enlist. Grandpa reluctantly assented and Asa and two neighboring young farmers, Harry Archer and George Calnon, enlisted and departed together.

Young men went off to war in some style in those days. "The custom was for the people to go to the depot to see them off on the train, and the whole town turned out," Wayne recalled. "I remember the crowd and the three of them standing on the rear platform of the train and the people cheering and waving good-bye as it pulled away."

Asa was typical of many young men at the time. About 83,000 Kansans served in World War I, some with the British, French, and Canadian armies prior to America's entry into the war, and about 2,680 were killed or wounded. Two won the Congressional Medal of Honor, one posthumously, and 176 received the Distinguished Service Cross, the nation's second highest decoration, 37 posthumously. Most Kansans served in France in the Thirty-fifth Infantry Division, a Kansas-Missouri National Guard unit, the Eighty-ninth Infantry Division, and the Forty-second Infantry Division. The Thirty-fifth and the Eighty-ninth fought at St.-Mihiel and the Argonne. The state had little trouble meeting its

*Grandmother Phipps stayed in touch with Grace Kennedy Morris even after she married and the family still has some of their letters. In 1976, Grace and her husband stopped in McDonald over the annual alumni and Memorial Day weekend and visited with one of Asa's sisters, my aunt Margaret Ritter, and her husband, Vic.

enlistment quotas; it also exceeded its quota in every war-savings-stamp and Liberty Bond drive during the war.

Asa's enthusiasm was by no means unanimous, however, and the young men of the state occasionally were prodded by some of their elders. "About 90 percent of the young men of this county who are being conscripted express their opinion of that law by claiming exemption and the reason of a good portion who are not doing so is because they can figure no legal grounds whereby they are allowed to," sniffed the editor of the *Atwood Citizen-Patriot* on August 9, 1917. He concluded that these individuals "will be the least missed when they're gone."

As in every war, the reality often didn't square with the romantic fervor that many such as Asa brought to it. The tragic and needless deaths of millions of young men like Asa plus the other victims of the war were the most obvious instance. The trampling of civil liberties and the perfervid cruelty that so often is perpetuated in the name of patriotic zeal was another dreadful downside to the war effort as the Wilson administration made strenuous efforts to unite the people in the cause.

In Kansas, as in the rest of the country, the administration's intensive domestic propaganda campaign led to ugly acts of xenophobic and patriotic hysteria. In Kensington, Kansas, a German Lutheran church was burned by a mob of "patriots" celebrating what turned out to be a premature peace announcement. In several towns, the houses and businesses of citizens were streaked with yellow paint for a variety of reasons—because they hadn't purchased their quota of Liberty Bonds, were suspected of hoarding food, or were of German background. A bank president in Wamego was removed by the state bank commissioner on charges of refusing to subscribe to Liberty Bond and Red Cross drives and for allegedly encouraging his son to evade conscription. Sauerkraut was renamed "liberty cabbage," Spanish was substituted for German in several high schools, and a secret organization called the "Night Riders" circulated leaflets warning of neighborhoods suspected of being pro-German.

Asa, George, and Harry went through basic training at Camp Funston, which was set up near what is now Fort Riley, a few miles west of Manhattan, the site of Kansas State University. Funston became one of the Army's major training centers. After he completed training in October 1918, Asa was ordered to Camp Kilmer, New Jersey, for transit to France. He never got to the war he wanted so much to be a part of, however.

Before he left Funston, Asa came down with the "Spanish" influenza, which swept much of the globe that autumn. It was the most lethal and fast-moving epidemic in history, including the Black Death, which ravaged Europe and parts of Asia in the fourteenth century and killed as much as three-fourths of the population in those areas. The 1918 flu epidemic was one of the great disasters of history. The most recent estimate is that more than 30 million died worldwide in it, including about 550,000 Americans. Ten times as many Americans died of the flu as were killed in action in France, and more American soldiers died from disease than gunshot in the war. Ironically, the epidemic appears to have broken out at Camp Funston in March 1918 and was spread to Europe on American troop ships. From there it went on to ravage nearly every corner of the globe.

By October 12, 1918, the day Asa died, more than 7,000 cases of Spanish flu had been reported in Kansas, 500 at Camp Funston alone. Governor Arthur Capper issued a statewide order closing all public facilities for a week in an effort to stem the epidemic. By October 22, the number of cases reported in Kansas exceeded 20,000 and the state board of health estimated the actual number at twice that.

Wayne remembered it all vividly. "We were told later that the doctors at Funston told him there wasn't any room in the hospital because of the flu epidemic but that if he'd just go to his tent or barracks or whatever they were living in and go to bed, he'd be all right. But he didn't do it. He got on the train to New Jersey, rode three nights and days sitting up in a chair car, and was in bad shape when he arrived. If he'd just stayed in bed in his tent, he'd have been all right. But he wanted to get to that war.

"The first word the family got was a telegram that said their son 'was seriously ill but we have hopes.' Then they got a collect call from the telegrapher in town informing them that there was another telegram. Chet drove Father to town and when they got back Father didn't say a word. He just put his arm around Mother and walked her into the house. I just ran upstairs to the bedroom. He was my hero, my big brother. He was awfully good to me. I thought the sun rose and set on him. Dad needed him there on the farm, needed him bad. And he lost him." Asa was twenty-one, Wayne was ten.

Sixty-seven years later, Wayne could not recount that tragic episode without breaking down. "It just seemed more than Mother could bear," one of Asa's sisters, Margaret, recalled. "She broke down when she heard of his death and she was broken up when the casket came back on the train. Dad never showed much emotion. Men weren't supposed to in those days."

Asa came home by train in a casket on October 29, 1918, and once again the town turned out. "A large number of people met the body of Asa Phipps at the depot Monday afternoon," the *Atwood Citizen-Patriot* reported. "The stores were closed in tribute to the noble boy who met death in the service of his country." The Boy Scout troop formed an honor guard for the funeral procession, which moved from the train station down main street and then out to the farm, where the service was held, once again on the front porch. The mourners sang the hymn "Open mine eyes that I may see visions of those who died for me." The funeral was outdoors in the front yard partly to accommodate the crowd, partly because of fear of the disease's contagion. "People were afraid to be in crowds indoors," Margaret recalled. "They associated contagion and epidemics with lack of ventilation."

It's not certain that if Asa had stayed in his bunk at Camp Funston he would have been all right. George Calnon, like Asa, a big, strapping farm boy, who had enlisted with him, died of the flu on the same day Asa did— at Camp Funston. Harry Archer survived the war and lived into his nineties. The deaths of Blaine and Asa, along with the service-connected disability of their grandfather Tolliver Phipps from the scarlet fever he contracted after he enlisted in the Union army, illustrated once again that men may go off to war in a blaze of glory, but that there is very little romantic heroism in proportion to the tragedy, grief, and suffering once they get there. World War II was the first war in history in which more men died from enemy gunfire than disease.

✒

The deaths of Uncle Blaine and Uncle Asa were part of the family lore and in later years whenever those tragic events were recounted to us kids—my cousins and me—always in hushed tones, I listened with horrified fascination and regret. We also had to endure the relatively less traumatic but still powerfully saddening death of Grandfather Phipps, of heart and respiratory complications, in July, 1936, at the age of seventy-eight. It was in the depth of the Great Depression and the Dust Bowl, a time that seemed unbearable enough.

I well remember the hot, blinding summer of 1936. For a week or so during Grandpa's illness, the farm was unnaturally hushed and we children were cautioned to be quiet at our play. I made my own contribution to the family's collectively frayed nerves, particularly my mother's, during that time when I decided to climb the ladder up to the top of the windmill, which was twenty-five or thirty feet high. I had gotten about halfway up when Mother spotted me out of one of the windows and came charging out the door with a shriek of alarm that I thought might have been heard all the way to town and which almost startled me off the ladder. Even at that age, I didn't have to be told that I had done a very dumb thing at a very bad time and fortunately Mother understood how I felt.

At the end, Grandpa's grandchildren were taken one by one into the darkened sickroom and allowed to climb up on the bed beside him for a final hug and good-bye to Grandfather Phipps. I remember feeling then, even at age four, a powerful sense of loss because of the realization that, like Dad and Blaine and Asa, I'd never get to know him.

⚔️

Much more immediate to me, however, for obvious reasons, was the death of my father, Richard Doak Dickenson, two years before, in July, 1934, when I was two and a half. This tragedy was a palpable presence in the family as I was growing up.

Like Blaine and Asa, Dad also was young—less than a month shy of his thirty-third birthday—and like Asa's his death was completely unexpected. Except for a tendency to being slightly overweight, he was the picture of health. He was on the Rolla City Council and was running unopposed in the Democratic primary for county clerk.

Mom and Dad were married in McDonald on December 28, 1930. She was just six days shy of her thirtieth birthday, seven months older than Dad. After graduating from Ottawa (Kansas) University in 1926, Mother was hired as a high school teacher in southwest Kansas, first in the little town of Rolla, in the very southwest corner of the state, where she met my father. Three years later, she accepted a similar job, teaching English in the high school in Plains, about sixty-five miles east of Rolla. To get to Plains to continue his courtship, Dad had to drive his brown Model A Ford coupe through the town of Kismet. "It was fate that sent her there, and fate that makes me follow," he joked of his weekly commute.

Dad died on July 5, 1934, the day before he was scheduled to be released from the hospital in Liberal, a town fifty miles southeast of Rolla, four days after what had appeared to be a routine and successful appendectomy. For years, I thought the cause of death was peritonitis, but it was a staph infection, which was lethal in those days before penicillin and other antibiotics.

While he was recuperating from the operation, Mother rented a room across the street from the hospital. Because many of the nurses were off for the Fourth of July holiday, she volunteered to sit with him that day and was making arrangements to take him home the next day. One of her instructions was to give him only tepid water to drink even though he craved cold water and talked about the cool well water he had enjoyed all his life.* But when she returned to the hospital the morning of the fifth, the doctors told her that Dad had had a difficult time during the night and that he had a fever and was delirious. They let her see him briefly and told her to come back in two or three hours. When she did, he was gone.

My aunt Opal contends that part of the problem was that Dad's intestines had been jiggled out of their normal alignment because of years of rough riding on a tractor and that as a result the risk of infection had been increased because the doctors had had to search for the appendix during the operation. One of Dad's brothers, Uncle Dean, a blithe bachelor who had been particularly close to Dad, was moving around the country at the time, looking for work here and there, and had been out of touch with the family for several weeks. When he drove back into town unannounced a couple of weeks after Dad's death and unaware of the tragedy, he stopped by the barbershop to ask Dad's whereabouts. That sad afternoon when he got the stunning news haunted him the rest of his life.

I was fortunate that Dad had five brothers, all admirable men who went out of their way to look after their brother's boy and whom I had every reason to love and admire. Except for Uncle Wilbur, who moved to Belton, Texas, they all farmed in southwest Kansas and as a teenager I felt privileged to work summers for them. As I grew up, they told me about Dad and with their caring and good humor they did a remarkable job of filling at least part of the vacuum. I remember them with love and deep gratitude.

One evening when I was about seven or eight, Uncle Vernie and I were standing by the stock tank in his barnyard while the windmill was filling it and he asked me what I wanted to be when I grew up. I answered, "Oh, a farmer, I suppose, or maybe a sailor, or something like that." He put his hand on my shoulder and responded, "Well, whatever you decide, I know you'll be good at it." I was so gratified that my immediate thought was that I would never let Uncle Vernie down.

---

*A half century later, when Mother began to suffer from senility due to hardening of the cerebral arteries before she died at the age of eighty-nine, she had a recurring paranoiac fantasy that she *had* given him cold water and that if she ever returned to Rolla, she would be indicted for murder, if, indeed, she wasn't lynched first. This was the first chilling signal of her condition.

I suspect that some of my uncles' stories about my dad were apocryphal, but they were good stories and it doesn't matter if some may have been made up.* My uncles led me to understand that my father had been one of the most respected and popular men in the community and there was ample evidence of this.

One summer when I was fifteen or sixteen, I was running Uncle Dean's John Deere tractor, cultivating a quarter we had planted to feed grain (milo and sorghum, although we called it "row crop" because we listed it in furrows that held the rain and acted as dikes against wind erosion). The field was four miles north of Rolla and across the road from the place of one of Dad's friends named Bob Chambers, who had been a pallbearer at Dad's funeral. I ran out of fuel shortly before noon and walked over to the road to wait for Dean to pick me up and take me to town for dinner. An elderly man I'd never met was replacing a strand of the barbed wire fence around the Chambers place and I walked over to say hello and pass the time.

He was Bob Chambers's father and he said he knew I must be a Dickenson boy because of the field I was working in, but he just couldn't place me. When I told him who I was, I was astonished by his reaction. His eyes lit up and he grasped my hand with both of his and said, "You're Doak Dickenson's boy? I always wondered what had become of you after you and your mama moved back up north with her folks!" He told me what a wonderful man my Dad had been and how much everyone thought of him. When Uncle Dean arrived, Mr. Chambers told him how nice and good-looking I was and how happy he was to have finally caught up with "Doak's boy."

My uncles generally responded to compliments directed at me and my cousins by joshingly countering that, homely, mentally deficient, and poorly behaved as we were, we were generally all-around embarrassments to the family. This was the family way of expressing their affection for us and I treasured those jocular insults, taking them in the spirit in which they were intended. However, when Uncle Dean arrived and heard Mr. Chambers's account of our meeting, this routine escaped him. He was so moved by this memory of his beloved lost brother that he was unable to speak on our drive into town. After that, I always made it a point to seek

---

*As an example of Dad's quick sense of humor, Uncle Dean told me when I was in my late teens that Dad was in the barbershop getting a shave one day, cranked back in the barber's chair with his face swathed in hot towels. A friend walked in and patted Dad, who was prematurely bald, on the top of his head. "Damn, Doak," he said. "Your head is as smooth as my wife's rear end." Dad, according to Uncle Dean, rubbed his head and responded, "Yep, damn if it isn't." I accepted this as evidence of a ready wit for a long time, but over the years I have heard the same story related in the context of other men. I accept it as symbolic, if not literal.

out Mr. Chambers when I was working that particular field and to give him a wave whenever I drove past the Chambers place.

Uncle Dean saw me through several rites of passage, one of which involved his Model G John Deere tractor. It didn't have a battery or starter, the ignition was from a magneto, and the engine was cranked by rotating the big flywheel on the left side of the engine. It took a certain amount of strength to turn the flywheel over fast enough to ignite the spark, and until I was big enough to do that, Uncle Dean had to come out each morning and start the tractor up for me. Finally, one morning, when I was fourteen, I was able to do it myself and after that could start the day without his help. He checked me a couple of mornings, but after that he didn't show up, which I took as a sign that I had taken a significant step into manhood.*

The editor of the Rolla newspaper, a man named A. B. Edson, was a good friend of Dad's and enjoyed twitting him in print. When my parents were married, the editor noted that mother had taught high school for three years at Rolla and that

> when she left the Rolla school to accept a position in the school at Plains there were expressions of regret from nearly every patron of the school who had a daughter in the school. She taught at Plains one year and had contracted again for this year when Mr. Dickenson calmly talked her into accepting his proposition here at Rolla, and the community is delighted to have her back, and they all agree that "Doak" has for once at least done something worthy of honorable mention for his community.

The editor went on to explain that

> Doak is a sort of special friend of the editor as we have tried every way we know how to make him mad and we never did succeed, and when we find a chap that we can't get on edge we call him a friend. For several years Doak has been a prominent figure in the athletic activities of this community and as a player in baseball or basketball he was always good—always played clean and in either defeat or victory he was always just "the same old Doak." A man who can play absolutely clean in ath-

---

*There was a petcock on each cylinder that the operator opened to reduce the compression enough that a human could turn the big engine over by hand. The operator had to open the petcock before cranking, then close it after the engine started so it would have full compression and full power. The petcock was right next to the spark plug and a careless, hasty teenager like me would invariably manage to touch the plug at some time or other. Those magnetos put out a powerful spark—touching one of those plugs would almost literally lift you off the ground, yet another rite of passage in learning to operate machinery.

letic contests can generally be relied upon to play clean in the game of life, and Doak begins his marital life with the complete confidence of all of his friends and associates.

Dad was born in Cross Timbers, Missouri, on July 31, 1901, the second youngest of six boys and two girls. In 1918, he followed his older brothers out to southwest Kansas, to Rolla, where he took up farming and in 1930 became the White Eagle (now Mobil) bulk fuel dealer, supplying and delivering gasoline, kerosene, and other fuels and lubricants to farmers. He was successful enough his first year with the dealership that he had to pay income tax—which required a minimum annual income of $3,000. This would be the equivalent of about $25,000 in 1994, with further adjustment for other "market basket" inflation in areas such as health care.

"Oh, he really bragged on himself when he had to pay income tax," Aunt Opal, Uncle Lawrence's wife, laughingly recalled. "It sure made him think he was one of the up-and-coming young men of the community. It also made him think he had enough to go courting that young gal that was teaching down at the high school. He also decided that he could afford to join the Masons. We'd all heard about the income tax, but none of us made enough to have to pay it. Doak was the first one in our family to have to pay it."

Mother and Dad met about four years before they were married, when she took the job of teaching high school English and music at Rolla. During her year at Plains, she accepted his proposal. With the obvious exception of the Great Depression and the Dust Bowl, the evidence is that they had a happy three and a half years together, surrounded by friends and family members and with Dad making a good living.

I was told that when Dad was stricken, a couple of his friends almost got into a fight over who would drive him to the hospital at Liberal. In his obituary, A. B. Edson reported:

> When he was taken ill and rushed to the hospital it seemed that everyone who knew him lost interest in current events and were interested chiefly in his well-being. Following a serious operation the news of his improvement was received with brightened countenances. . . . Then like a thunderbolt came the report of his death—a collapse—the end of his fight—a battle lost.

The editor also recorded the turnout for the funeral at the Methodist church in Rolla:

Never before has there been such a floral offering at a local funeral, and never before has there been so many assembled to pay their last respects to a departed friend. The church could accommodate but a minor part of those who came, not only from the home community but from neighboring towns and counties.

That was the easy part for A. B. Edson. Then he had to recount his friend's life in his front-page obituary:

It was with pleasure that we wrote of kindly humorous and odd incidents in the life of Doak Dickenson. It was a pleasure to tell the story of the incident five years ago when he ran a mile across the field to recover a little dog who had wandered away from a friend and bring it back to its owner here in town. It was a pleasure to chronicle his wedding to a young lady as dear to the hearts of the people of this community as was he; and then the birth of a little son, and so on.

But today we have come to the most difficult task. That of giving fit tribute to a departed friend, whose leaving has left sadness in the hearts of countless friends and loved ones. . . . To this task we give our best efforts, but such will be inadequate to truly describe the sterling qualities of the one man we knew who had high ambitions, unquestionable honor, the finest morals and ideals . . . a faculty of looking at the other fellow's problems as though they were his own but never bothering with the problems which confronted him. . . . With such a future before him, it seemed unkind that providence should alter his course—so strong had his influence become in his home community that it was becoming a power for good. . . ."

Nearly sixty years later, I am as moved by A. B. Edson's words as ever. They make me wonder about the man I never knew. The most poignant grief I felt, however, was after Mother's death in August of 1989, when I was going through her diary and a baby book she kept for me until his death, neither of which I recall seeing before she died. In the baby book, which she wrote as though I were the author, she related how Dad and I both loved it when he took me with him in his White Eagle tank truck to deliver fuel to the farmers in the country. The last ride I took in the truck with him was that summer of 1934, just a few days before he died, when the three of us, Mom and Dad and I, went to pick up a load of fuel in Elkhart. On the way, my cap blew out the window and we all enjoyed a short pleasant summer stroll back down the road to retrieve it.

The diary tells how excited I got when he came home from work and how cross I'd be if he'd had to leave before I woke up in the morning and could see him. On a trip to Dodge City not long before his death, he bought me a big blue toy McCormick-Deering tractor and could hardly wait for me to wake up the next morning so he could give it to me. For all the other toys I got, I always went back to "the tractor that Daddy bought." The last entry in the baby book follows the story of the tractor: "Nothing pleased him more than to do something that would make me or Mother happier. It hurt him to have anything happen that would sadden our day and he wanted to do everything he could to make us forget that little trouble of ours."

With those words, the baby book ends. His death made us forget, for a time at least, what "little troubles" were. Reading those loving and happy accounts for the first time, nearly sixty years after the fact and knowing the tragedy that shortly was to follow that last entry, was, and still is, almost more than I can bear.

Mother's diary entry for December 31, 1934, which recounts our return to Rolla from McDonald, where we had spent the holidays with her family and the celebration of my third birthday, six months after Dad died, concludes: "Dick asked for his Daddy." That powerful, simple declarative sentence induced a long-delayed grieving and still has the power to reduce me to tears. It was an enormous help to read subsequent diary entries and letters telling what a happy child I was and how much pleasure I got in the years immediately following Dad's death from my aunts and uncles and cousins and Grandmother Dickenson, who moved in with Mother and me until we moved up to McDonald three years later. The last thing I needed was to learn that I had been part of the problem.

⚊

Obviously, we all had cause over the years to ponder this particular cruelty of providence. As a child, I would occasionally think about the fact that my life wasn't "normal" because I had lost my father at such an early age and had never gotten to know him.* As an adult, I occasionally speculated about the direction my life might have taken had he lived, whether we would have remained in Rolla or if his budding political career might have taken us to Topeka or possibly Washington. Mostly, however, we didn't dwell on it. Life goes on and no one wanted to risk doing anything

---

*I have a very dim memory of getting a sandbur in one of my feet while playing in the yard one afternoon and waiting on the front porch for him to come home from work and remove it, which he did. I'm not sure whether it's a memory or a fantasy, however.

that might contribute more to Mother's grief; when I enlisted in the Marine Corps my apprehension about what lay ahead took the form of worrying about what the effect on Mother would be if anything happened to me. I increasingly regret that because of my reticence I didn't ask her more about him while she was still alive.

I am moved to ponder the societal changes A. B. Edson's journalism reflected—the binding sense of community and intimacy and the presence of a large extended family of the sort that was so supportive of Mother and me. We have traveled a long distance from that in the intervening decades. The changes in how our society is organized and alterations of our lifestyles entailed giving up community and family in exchange for mobility and privacy. Maybe they have been worth it—they were inevitable, in any event—but it's regrettable that so few today truly realize how much we've lost.

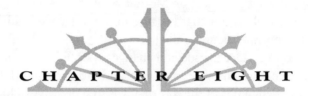

CHAPTER EIGHT

"FEAR ITSELF"—THE GREAT DEPRESSION AND THE DUST BOWL

On a small corner of the leeward side of a field, a particle of soil, broken loose by the wind, struck a cluster of soil particles like a cue ball striking the racked balls. The avalanching effect of soil erosion gathered force as it moved across the field. By the time the effects of one tiny wind-driven soil particle reached the opposite side of the field, a mighty force was assembled to assault the neighboring abandoned field. Soon a dirt storm was burning any living plant, while the soil around the plant's roots was joining the race across the stricken land.

—Historian Paul Bonnifield

If a man took a lot of machinery out into the middle of the Sahara Desert to start farming, we'd call him crazy and probably commit him to an asylum.
—Meade County (Kansas) farmer in 1937

THE MOST INFAMOUS DAY OF THE 1930S DUST BOWL WAS APRIL 15, 1935, the apocalyptic "Black Sunday." Driven by winds up to fifty miles an hour, the dust storms blew out of the southwest, the west, and the northwest in great black clouds that in the distance looked like massive thunderstorms. They struck with a primal force like tidal waves capable of carrying everything in their paths and inspired a sense of Judgment Day awe and doom. When they hit, they would turn the brightest day black as a moonless night. They were called "black blizzards" and people became accustomed to turning their lights on at midday when it became as dark as night. Farmers would become disoriented and lost on their own places in mid-afternoon because they literally couldn't see the radiator caps on their tractors. People would get lost on familiar roads, as they did in blizzards.

At the height of the Dust Bowl, these storms would often last for two or three days, and seem longer. Generally, a storm would blow for only a day or part of a day on its own, but the dirt it stirred up would blow again when the wind picked back up. The only outdoors work that could be done during the storms was emergency work, such as repairing power lines, and it had to be planned in advance before the men ventured out.

Although the High Plains bore the brunt of the Dust Bowl, it often shared its travails with the eastern half of the nation. In May of 1934, an estimated 12 million tons of High Plains topsoil dropped on Chicago. The historian William Leuchtenburg recounted that on Black Sunday "a dust cloud 7,000 feet thick darkened the city of Cleveland, yellow grit from Nebraska sifted through the White House doors, and bits of western plains came to rest on vessels in the Atlantic three hundred miles at sea. That winter, red snow [dirt, probably from Colorado or New Mexico] fell on New England."

Bad as that was, the folks back east were lucky. Black Sunday's "black blizzard" hit Rolla, Kansas, where my mother and I were living at the time, at about 4:00 P.M. Mother, preparing for the upcoming week, was grading papers at the high school, which was just across the street from our house. "An awful cloud from north," she noted in her diary. "Darkness came in an instant. I just beat the storm here . . . took up rug and covered things with sheets." My aunt Opal Dickenson was at the Methodist church practicing for the Easter sing. "Your mother thought the end of the world was coming," she recalled, laughing. "When I got home, I lit a coal oil lamp and it was so dark you could hardly see it, even though it was the middle of the afternoon. . . . Somebody was in a truck parked on the curb right in front of the drugstore downtown and the dust was so dark and thick they couldn't see the lights in the store from across the sidewalk." That infamous day was immortalized by Woody Guthrie's popular song written in Pampa, Texas, "So Long, It's Been Good to Know Ya."

⚔

In the late summer of 1936, nearly a year and a half after Black Sunday, Mother, Uncle Wayne, Grandmother Phipps, and I were at Grandmother's farmhouse three miles west of McDonald. The house didn't have running water or electricity, and the three adults were sitting around the dining room table by the light of a kerosene lamp. I, age four, sat nearby picking up occasional bits of the conversation while trying to decipher the farm machinery column in the agriculture newspaper, *Capper's Weekly.* This was a feature that always caught my attention because of its half-tone truck and tractor illustrations, which particularly interested me because I thought the tractor drawing might have been of our Model L Case, with which I was already fascinated.

Grandfather Phipps had died in July of that summer and the talk was about how Grandmother could keep the farm, given its debt load in those dark, seemingly hopeless years of the Great Depression and the Dust Bowl. She did manage to keep it, thanks to a long-term, low-interest New Deal loan, which she was able to pay off in just a few years, after the rain started falling again and crop prices were pushed up by the burgeoning demand of World War II. The war was an exhilarating period of sudden prosperity made even more dazzling by contrast to the bleak, despairing decade that preceded it, along with the drama and excitement of the war effort.

That Great Depression/Dust Bowl evening conversation was an experience common to many at the time: The realization that economic and natural forces beyond an individual's control could—and did—storm in and sweep everything away. Listening in on that meeting, I didn't feel any particular concern. I assumed, like all children that age, that the grown-ups would take care of things; it wasn't until I was an adult that I realized how indelibly marked the depression generations of my parents and grandparents were by the pessimism, fatalism, and resignation of the time and how much had brushed off onto my generation. This should come as no surprise when it's noted that an estimated half-million farmers were forced off the land in the 1930s by the catastrophic combination of the worst drought and worst depression in the nation's history.

It was a historic time in several ways. Grandmother Phipps was just one of thousands of Dust Bowl–area farmers whose farms were saved by the intervention of such government programs as the Agricultural Adjustment Act (AAA). That was the beginning of federal policies aimed at saving family farms on the High Plains and the changing of those farmers from independent, self-sustaining operators to wards, partially at least, of society as a whole, with the federal government as their agent. It was a tacit recognition that farming in that area of scanty rainfall was too risky to be sustained without outside help. If the nation wanted to be sure that its wheat belt breadbasket would do business as usual, the taxpayers were going to have to contribute; New Deal subsidy and acreage-reduction programs, beginning with the AAA in 1933, cost $2 billion in the 1930s alone. The economic and market forces that buffeted the farmers in the 1930s were the work of mostly unknown and unseen factors and manipulators, but the Dust Bowl was all too immediate and tangible. It compounded both the injury and the insult of the Great Depression.

In 1920, when he was sixty-two, Grandfather Phipps sold the farm that he and his family had lived on for fifteen years and moved into McDonald. He and Grandmother Phipps bought a big two-story frame house a block off Main Street. The property had a barn for the horses, a well, a windmill (the municipal water system was put in about ten years later), a well house, and a chicken house and yard in which Grandmother raised layers and fryers. She also put in a large garden every year.

Grandfather Phipps got $90 an acre for his farm (which had expanded to 310 acres), or about $28,000, which he earmarked as his retirement nest egg; he also got an unpleasant surprise when he learned he had to pay income taxes on it. In addition, he had the income from another half section (320 acres) of land he bought during World War I, which he didn't sell and which his oldest son, Chester, rented from him during the 1920s.* During the 1920s, he built a house and barn and other outbuildings on the half section.

As one of the town gentry, Grandfather Phipps managed to keep busy. He was on the school board, was a member of the board of directors of the cooperative that owned and operated a grain elevator, and served as mayor, church deacon, and Sunday school superintendent. In addition, he kept a cow in a lot and shed on the east end of town, which he milked and fed mornings and evenings with such regularity that the residents in the area joked that they could set their clocks by him.

At first, Grandmother Phipps missed the farm more than he did. "It was home," she told her children. Having gone through the trauma of the deaths of their two sons, the Phipps family had settled into the relative stability of the 1920s.

For farmers, it was a precarious stability, however. Farm prices slumped after World War I as the global economy adjusted from war to peace with the warring nations in Europe returning to normal production and

*The normal rental agreement was that the owner got a third of each crop and the renter got two-thirds. The renter paid the expenses, which generally took half of his share or one-third of the total crop value.

becoming competitive in the international markets again. This adjustment caused a farm depression in 1920–21, but there was some recovery as the decade progressed, although agricultural prices declined. Farmers maintained a precarious parity because prices of many of their necessities dropped as well.

Through most of the 1920s, after legislation that eased farm credit proved inadequate, farm-state organizations and politicians tried to enact the McNary-Haugen Act, which would have empowered the federal government to buy up farm crop surpluses to keep them off the market and from depressing prices. The Congress finally passed it in 1927, only to have Calvin Coolidge veto it. The Roaring Twenties, in western Kansas as in many other places, were more uneasy than noisy. The Stock Market crash of 1929, however, made all the noise anyone wanted, and economic unease changed to foreboding and terror. A year after the crash, the price of winter wheat in Chicago was more than halved, plummeting from $1.37 to $0.61 a bushel, a devastating blow to farmers already strapped by debt and low prices during much of the 1920s.

⚞

In 1933, when his youngest child, Fern, graduated from high school, Grandfather Phipps was ready to move back to the country. Grandmother Phipps and Fern didn't want to—they had gotten used to electricity and running water and the other amenities of town living and hated to give up "those sanitary facilities and other comforts," as Fern put it, by moving to a farmhouse that lacked them. But that's what he wanted to do, so they went along with him.

Periodic economic depressions are part of Kansas history; the state has filled up and emptied out three times, in the depressions of the 1870s, which also experienced a disastrous grasshopper infestation, and in the depressions of the 1890s and the 1930s. After the Civil War, Kansas attracted the greatest number of the settlers who migrated westward from Illinois, Indiana, Iowa, Missouri, and other points east of any western state—and had the most of whom the drought and depression of the 1890s forced to retreat to their homes back east. Drought is endemic to Kansas, particularly the western half of the state, which is on the subhumid and semiarid High Plains. Drought seems to come in tandem with depression—it is often a contributing factor to economic problems—but there has never been anything to match the length and severity of the Great Depression and the Dust Bowl of the 1930s.

In western Kansas the suffering of the Great Depression was compounded by the ferocious Dust Bowl. Because they had settled in the town of Rolla, in the far southwest corner of Kansas, the Dickenson family suffered more from the Dust Bowl than the Phippses, who were 200 miles north in the northwest corner of the state. Morton County was squarely in the middle of the Dust Bowl, an area that extended about 400 miles north to south and 300 miles east to west; the most intense Dust Bowl region was a 100-mile radius around Liberal, Kansas, 50 miles southeast of Rolla (Liberal is the town where my father died in July, 1934, in the midst of the depression and Dust Bowl).

The Dickensons managed to keep farming, however, although they had to take up sidelines from time to time to make ends meet. Uncle Dean augmented his income by clerking in the drugstore in Rolla. Uncle Lawrence at one time ran a school bus—his farm truck, on the bed of which he mounted a shell provided by the school district during the school year and which could be taken off and the grain bed replaced during the summer—for which he was paid sixty dollars a month and provided his own gasoline. He also operated the dray service, hauling and delivering goods, including freight and mail between the railroad depot and the post office. For a while, he worked on the new bridge the Works Progress Administration (WPA) built across the Cimarron River eight miles north of Rolla, a job he hated and considered demeaning. "We used to call the WPA, 'We Piddle Around,' and laugh about how they just stood around leaning on their shovels," his wife, Opal, recalled.

Most Americans came through the depression and Dust Bowl all right in the long run, but it was a time of fear and anxiety because no one knew at the time how things would turn out. When times are bad, it's easy to get the idea that they'll never improve and it was hard to see light at the end of the tunnel during most of the 1930s. Many lives *were* shattered by the depression and no one who suffered through it came out unmarked. An editorial cartoon of the time, referring to the bank and stock market failures, shows a worn-looking man sitting on a park bench wearing a shabby suit, which also had seen better days. A squirrel gathering nuts for the winter asks the man: "Why didn't you set something aside for hard times?" The man responds, "I did."

The rules had rudely been changed in the middle of the game. Actually, it sometimes seemed that the rules had been abolished and chaos held sway in their place. The old virtues of thrift and hard work appeared to count for nothing as failed banks swallowed up savings, jobs vanished, and plummeting agricultural prices and poor crops forced thousands of farmers into foreclosure. Many were marginal operators whose existence was precarious before the crash, which administered the coup de grâce to them; this has happened in every farm depression, including the most recent one, that of the 1980s. Many farms were too small and many farmers were trying to scratch a subsistence out of marginal land that should never have been cultivated in the first place or that had been exhausted by erosion and continuous cropping. In their desperate struggle to survive, these farmers couldn't or wouldn't protect their land from erosion or adopt conservation measures such as crop rotation that would have maintained its fertility.

There are about 423 million arable acres of cropland in the United States and in 1934 the National Resources Planning Board reported that 35 million acres of this had been completely destroyed for farming, that almost all the topsoil had been eroded from another 125 million acres, and that serious damage was in progress on another 100 million acres. All of this, of course, contributed to the disastrous Dust Bowl. Because Kansas, and my family, were at the epicenter of this catastrophe, they suffered the consequences of this monumental negligence as much as anyone.

Their hardship wasn't eased by the fact that greed, abetted by modern technology—particularly the tractors that plowed up the native grasslands during World War I and on into the 1920s—was a major factor in the Dust Bowl's severity. In the southwest corner of the state, including Morton County, where the Dickensons settled, farmers rushing to get in on the wartime bonanza broke out thousands of acres of sod. Uncle Dean recalled the long hours on the tractor and how he and others tied themselves to the tractor seat with a length of rope in case they dozed off.

In 1914, winter wheat was sold for an average of $0.87 a bushel. By 1917, the price was $2.74 a bushel (in June of 1993 it was less than $2.50). On May 10, 1918, the *Topeka Daily Capital* reported that gas tractors were "tearing the whole country upside down" in southwestern Kansas and that the native short-grass pasturage of that section would soon be gone. Trainloads of tractors had been shipped into the area. About 3,000 acres were being broken on one ranch in Morton County alone. Another had eleven outfits plowing. In Rice County, twenty tractors were plowing on the Sherman ranch. Ten tractor outfits were unloaded at Satanta in Haskell County within two days and five at Montezuma in Gray County in one day.

Mother Nature exacted a fearsome long-term payoff economically, emotionally, and ecologically, not only from the farmers of the High Plains but the entire nation, when the dirt began to blow. Millions of acres of marginal land that should have been left in grass literally blew halfway across the continent to the East Coast and on into the Atlantic in those bleak, desperate days of the 1930s.

During World War I, the federal government helped lead some farmers astray, not for the first time nor for the last, by encouraging them to break much of the remaining virgin sod on the High Plains to help meet the wartime food demand. Much of this land was adequate for grazing livestock but marginal for farming, which was why it hadn't been broken earlier, and should have remained in grass. About 13.5 million new acres, including 11 million acres of native grass, were plowed and planted to wheat on the High Plains between 1914 and 1919. This environmental rape was continued during the 1920s, with about 5.2 million acres of sod broken between 1925 and 1930, 1 million in southwest Kansas alone. Henry Wallace, Franklin Roosevelt's first secretary of agriculture, had it right, however, when he noted that everyone was complicit in helping create the Dust Bowl disaster—farmers, bankers, the government, land speculators, equipment dealers, agronomists, everyone.

Wheat production shot up by 300 percent during the 1920s, which resulted in a severe glut on the market by 1931. The reason for this increase was that the farmers in the area tried to compensate for the low prices in the 1920s by boosting production. They continued to break out marginal grassland, between 5 million and 6 million acres during the decade, and the wheat acreage in the heart of the Dust Bowl area doubled between 1925 and 1931. This practice continued during the 1930s, for the same reason—the farmers' standard response to stress and hard times is to increase production, either through larger acreage or through improved yields. This is true today and is the reason farm surpluses are so difficult to bring under control.

In 1931, Kansas farmers produced a record wheat crop, but the price sank to twenty-five cents per bushel and many productive fields were left abandoned in 1932, the first year of the drought and big dust storms. In Morton County, there were 113,000 acres in wheat in 1931 but only 59,000 in 1932. The parade of bankruptcies began.

Many farmers had borrowed heavily during the war and postwar years to buy land at inflated values and acquire expensive machinery. One student of the High Plains, John Opie, estimated that with an average price of $1.03 per bushel for wheat and average wheat yields of eight to ten bushels per acre during the 1920s, many Kansas farmers put as much as 40 percent of their gross incomes into mechanizing their operations with tractors, trucks, and combines.* The farmers were unable to accumulate financial reserves during the 1920s because of this debt load and the collapse of farm prices in the postwar recession. As a result, many were caught short when the great crash sent both farm prices and land values plummeting.

Another long-term consequence of this capital-intensive mechanization was to speed the radical alteration of the nature of farming from a mostly self-sufficient food-raising frontier outpost operation—with milk cows, chickens, eggs, garden produce, and hogs and cattle for slaughter, and producing relatively small cash crops of wheat and feed grains—to an agrarian form of industrial capitalism geared to producing ever-larger profit-making crops. The farmer lost the last vestige of independence as he became bound into the national economy and the international market system, forces over which he had no control, and then into the New Deal government support program. Mechanization, of course, also made possible the huge plow-ups of the first three decades of the century, which resulted both in crop surpluses and making the ground vulnerable to the drought. As John Opie noted, mechanization pushed "ordinary drought into the extraordinary Dust Bowl."

~※~

Drought and depression added up to economic disaster and hardship for many. A lot of people had to "go on the county," i.e., the county dole. This meant lining up once a week at the post office to receive commodities such as rice, beans, corn, flour, and peanut butter, which were distributed by the county government. It was a deep humiliation for people who prided themselves on self-reliance.

"You could get a balanced meal, but it sure wasn't anything fancy," Aunt Opal, a doughty, indomitable soul, recalled a half century later.[†] Aunt Fern also remembered that in high school during the depression there wasn't any money for the amenities. "We always had plenty to eat, with milk from the cow and meat from the animals. A lot of people would

---

*There were 3,000 tractors in Kansas in 1915, 17,000 by war's end, 66,000 in 1930, 95,000 by 1940; in 1925, there were 4,700 combines in the state, by 1930 this number had more than quadrupled to 24,000, and by 1940 there were 42,800.
[†]Although her hearing was failing when she was in her nineties, her mind hadn't slowed a bit. When I would call, sometimes as much as two or three months after our previous conversation, she would pick up right where we had left off. The reason I knew that was that I had my notes to refer to. She didn't need such aid, however.

sign a tab for their groceries during the year and settle up after [wheat] harvest, but we never had to do that. However, I never had a nickel for a Coke or ice-cream cone at the drugstore after school. One of my friends always had spending money and new clothes, but her dad worked for the post office and had one of the rural mail routes and got a regular government paycheck. Dad didn't have money for my high school graduation pictures [1933] until Miss Cole [a longtime family friend] stepped in and lent it to him, I guess is how it worked out. It was a beastly struggle in those days."

A guaranteed paycheck, however modest, seemed like wealth to many at the time. One of my grade school friends, Willard Edgett, whose family was on the dole for a time, vented his frustration and humiliation by once spitting out to me, referring to the fact that my mother was a teacher in the high school: "You're rich!" She also got a regular paycheck. The fact that my family, like most others, felt nothing but compassion for those unfortunates was probably unknown to Willard and the rest. It never occurred to us to feel smug in those days; we all knew the truth was that, but for the grace of God, there go I, and that any of us could be in that line at the post office the next week.

Women were given work in sewing rooms set up by the WPA making women's clothing, which was distributed free to the needy. "You couldn't get WPA clothing if you had an income of more than twenty-five hundred dollars a year," Aunt Opal recalled. "The dresses all looked the same. A lot of women who got them would crochet lace or something as trim to put on the dresses to try to hide the fact that they were from the WPA." Opal also remembered neighbor women who couldn't afford fuel in the winter. "They'd go over to the school building, where it was warm, and stay a while. Then they'd go out and pick up wood litter out of barns and build a smudge fire in someone's heating stove and all huddle around it."

The drought made gardens hard to grow, but people learned that one way or another they could find forage for milk cows. The hard times even disclosed virtue in the green Russian thistle, that stubborn and pesky bane of the farmer; matured and dried out, it's better known as the tumbleweed. People learned that they could cut the thistles in the spring, when they were green, and store them for cattle feed. Some thought they were almost as good as alfalfa. Many counties organized drives to hunt the area's numerous jackrabbits, driving them into pens, where they were shot by the thousands and butchered for their meat.

Opal recalled that there were no crops or gardens and all many people had was milk. A lot of people lived for a while on cottage cheese and cream. "Lawrence and I kept a cow or two all during the depression and when Terry was born [in 1932] the doctor bill came to the whole sum of twenty-five dollars. We paid it off by taking the doctor half a gallon of cream every week because he liked to churn his own butter. We lived twelve miles from town on a rough road and by the time we got there the cream was already pretty well churned."

Many families also fed a few pigs and the calves from their milk cows. "Each year, we'd butcher a hog for each member of the family that sat down at the dinner table," Opal said. Some smoke-cured their hams and bacons. Some, like Uncle Lawrence, used salt and brown sugar; others, like Uncle Vernie, cured them in brine. "In the winter, we'd butcher a steer and hoist a quarter of beef with a block and tackle up on the windmill, up higher than the flies would get, and the air would dry it kind of like jerky," Opal recalled. "When we needed some meat, we'd just lower it down with the pulleys, wash off the dust, and cut off what we needed. We didn't have any refrigeration in those days, but of course we butchered after the weather turned cold and we didn't have to worry about it spoiling."

Actually, they did have refrigeration. Townspeople had electricity and some had refrigerators. Others, including some farm families, could buy 50- and 100-pound blocks of ice to chill their iceboxes. Until the Rural Electrification Administration (REA) completed wiring the countryside for power after World War II, many farm families refrigerated in the summer by lowering milk and butter and other perishables down into the well or keeping them in an ice cellar, which was lined with straw for insulation and filled with huge blocks of ice cut from the lakes and rivers in the winter.

People helped each other with the farm work. Neighbors would help each other harvest and many brought their own lunches. "One man had nothing but fried egg sandwiches," Opal recalled. "I remember him telling me, 'I don't care for myself, but I sure do hate to have my family have to eat like this.'" Out of necessity, women pitched in with the work. In southwest Kansas, where many farmers raised broom corn (from which house brooms are made), which was cut by hand with knives in those days, women would often work in the fields alongside the men. They also contributed more than just labor.

Opal was a schoolteacher. She was also a liberated woman decades before the feminist movement came on the scene. From the very beginning, she was underwhelmed by the male chauvinism of her time. "It wasn't 'nice' for women to know too much about the family business; it wasn't 'ladylike,'" she recalled scornfully. "If you wanted something, you were supposed to say, 'I want it,' and the men would say, 'We haven't got it; you can't have it.' But one time I had saved eighty dollars from my teaching salary and that was what enabled us to buy seed so we could put in the wheat crop that year. In fact, I think the reason the bankers started Lawrence in farming was because we got married and I was getting a regular teacher's paycheck."

The depression brought out reserves of strength and generosity in people, but sometimes it summoned less admirable traits up from the vasty deep. One afternoon when I was about four or five, an elderly couple walked past the front yard while I was out playing and asked what I'd had for lunch that day. Macaroni and cheese, I responded, and was mildly interested that they informed me, with a tone of superiority, that *they* had had fried chicken. It didn't matter to me—I liked both—but it did to Mother, when I reported the exchange to her. In her day, she was capable of a fearsome temper, a strong tendency to be judgmental, and, as best I could tell, feared no one but God. Years later, I learned that when she caught up with those misguided souls, reports of that confrontation provided a break in the daily routine and a topic of conversation in our tiny town for some time. They obviously didn't know whom they were dealing with; none of Mother's family or friends would have tempted fate like that.

Entertainment, of a more conventional nature, was necessarily cheap and simple in those times. Married couples took turns hosting potluck suppers and card parties and would play rummy, pinochle, and Rook while the children played in the bedroom. School activities such as plays and musicals and basketball and baseball games were major social events. As the high school English and music teacher, Mother was involved in many of the events and her diary entries during the mid-thirties chronicle an incredible array of operettas, Girl Reserve and Hi-Y choruses, junior- and senior-class plays, choirs, trios, mixed choruses, girls' and boys' glee clubs, quartets, double trios, Christmas chapels, cantatas, and carnivals. The listing is even more imposing because the high school enrollment totaled only about sixty or seventy in the four grades. Mother and Fern were accomplished pianists and Fern taught music in the schools for several years. Mother hoped that I also would at least play the piano well enough for my own enjoyment, as she did, but the talent wasn't passed on. I dutifully butchered the trumpet and piano through grade school and high school, but my piano lessons with Hertha Benkleman were a tribulation as I would be called away from play at 1:30 every other Saturday afternoon to take a bath, get dressed up, and go try Hertha's vast store of patience.

Those little towns also fielded town teams in basketball and baseball. The players were the community's young farmers and businessmen and the teams were usually sponsored by organizations such as the Lions Club or the American Legion post. Dad and two of his brothers, Dean (who at one time held the Missouri high school single-game scoring record) and Lawrence, played on Rolla's baseball and basketball teams, and the games were a big part of Dad's courtship of Mother. Those and the high school teams' games were a major part of the social life of those towns; Mother, who played in high school and college, also coached the high school girls' basketball team.

In those hard times, there was a premium on inexpensive activities. Opal and Lawrence could cut costs with the best of them. "We'd double-date with my best friend and her beau and the four of us would walk down the railroad track out into the country together in the evening when the weather was nice or something like that," Opal recalled. "It certainly wasn't anything fancy." Radio was an increasingly popular medium and a common phrase of the times made a verb out of the noun, as in one of Mother's diary entries, "We radioed last night." Prior to electrification, radios out on the farm were powered by batteries, which were recharged by a wind charger, a miniature windmill mounted on the roof to catch the ubiquitous winds.

<hr />

For anyone who lived through the Dust Bowl, the opening scenes of *The Grapes of Wrath* is a nightmare revisited. The movie, appropriately in black and white, begins with a portrayal of a barren, lifeless, sand-blown Sahara in Oklahoma that once had been productive farmland. Tom Joad returns home from prison to find that his road gang hell has been replaced by a new one, a destructive, punishing dust storm pushed by a ferocious wind whose banshee howl is punctuated by the banging of the doors of the abandoned, desolate farm buildings being blown open and shut. The only other sound is the roar of the bulldozers that are knocking the buildings down.

It is almost more than one can bear just to read the account by Lawrence Svobida, a farmer in Meade County: He struggled to keep his land from blowing away and save his crops from the relentless drought, heat, and gales. Hopes are raised by a timely rain, only to be crushed; just as you think things have become unbearable, they get worse. Svobida's farm was near the town of Plains, where Mother taught high school in the 1920s when Dad was courting her.

When drought sets in, its victims begin to believe that it's never going to rain again, ever. The wind, blowing hot and dry, dusty and destructive, whiny and insinuating, is like Chinese water torture; February, March, and

April, the "blow months," were and are the worst. The wind suffuses the subconscious and when it suddenly stops the unanticipated quiet and relief leave its victims temporarily off balance and disoriented.

The worst of the drought was 1932 to 1936, but the period of misery was twice that long. There were good wheat crops in 1929 and 1931, the early years of the depression, but low prices precluded farmers from accumulating a reserve that would help them through the next disastrous years. The dust continued to blow for several years after 1936 and rainfall in parts of western Kansas as late as 1939 was 25 percent below normal.

The dust and drought went on, day in, day out, week in, week out, interminably and almost unbearably, parching the land and burning out pastures and crops, with the wind stripping the topsoil in some parts of a field and blowing it into dunes in others. Many areas lost as much as five or six inches of topsoil and much was stripped to the hardpan. Farmers helplessly watched their livestock die of thirst and starvation and many were forced to sell their herds at a loss in a glutted market. Many cattle died from ingesting dirt as they rooted for forage, and the dirt in their feed wore their teeth down to the gums.

Drought and depression, those relentless, pitiless horsemen of that particular Apocalypse, drove many to the limits of their emotional, physical, and financial resources and pushed some over the brink of despair. Drought and depression parched people's souls and blasted their hopes, in some cases permanently. "It wasn't unusual for people to just get up and walk away from their homes, furniture and everything, particularly since many were renting," Aunt Opal recalled. I remember my uncles expressing the wish that weeds would grow in the fields simply to help keep them from blowing away.

In one county in southwest Kansas, 109 people, members of 26 families, some of whom had been in the area since the 1880s and 1890s, had left or were packed to go by May of 1935. Some members of their families had died of dust pneumonia, a widespread ailment of the time. Steinbeck's Joads at least had vehicles in which to load their families and possessions; townspeople in western Kansas who wanted to leave often had to do it on foot and there are accounts of hundreds of people with their possessions on their backs out on the roads of western Kansas at the time.

In some areas in 1934, the temperatures topped 100 degrees for 35 straight days; on the 36th day in Vinita, Oklahoma, 30 miles south of the Kansas line, it rose to 117 degrees. With the heat and drought came the dust storms. Technicians at the Panhandle A&M Experiment Station in

Goodwell, Oklahoma, recorded 70 days of severe dust storms in 1933, only 22 in 1934, but 53 in 1935, 73 in 1936, and 134 in 1937.

A group of teenage boys out hunting arrowheads near Rolla one Sunday afternoon were caught in such a storm. "Their folks just worried and worried till the dust finally went down and they came home," Aunt Opal recalled. "After that, everyone was told to just get down and stay where they were when they got caught in a storm. You couldn't always find a fence line to follow and you could get lost just like in a blizzard."

That wasn't the only hazard of the Dust Bowl. Many people put Vaseline in their nostrils and tied handkerchiefs over their faces to protect them from the dust, but that was only partially effective. The dust caused and aggravated respiratory problems such as dust pneumonia, which could be fatal; when Eugene Sramek, the younger brother of one of my classmates in McDonald, was born in 1935, his father nailed wet burlap bags over the windows for fear the powdery dust would suffocate his infant son. This was by no means some wild imagining. Hundreds of people of all ages, infants, the elderly, young people in their prime, died of acute respiratory infection such as dust pneumonia and other ailments caused by dust that clogged the lungs, windpipe, intestines, and other internal organs. Farmers like Lawrence Svobida who spent their days on the tractor in the worst of the storms desperately plowing their fields to keep them from blowing were most vulnerable.* The dust made him too ill to get out of bed and go to the fields several times, which may have saved his life; he had a friend whose respiratory system was so clogged that when his doctor worked on his bronchial tubes he coughed up several slugs of solid dirt, three and four inches long and as big around as a lead pencil. Many contracted silicosis, a disease common to miners, in which the silica particles cause scar tissue on the lungs and makes the victim susceptible to tuberculosis.†

The dust was as destructive to machinery. When it got past an engine's air-cleaning system, or simply overwhelmed it, it quickly ate away pistons, valves, connecting rods, and crankshafts and scored cylinder walls beyond reboring. Svobida tells of a brand-new tractor at an implement dealer's in Meade that had to be left outside on the lot for a week before it was sold. When it came time to start it up, the inside of the engine was packed solid

---

*They would use a disk plow to form shallow ridges a foot or two apart to try to keep the wind from blowing unobstructed across the flat, dry crust.
†In the desert war in North Africa in 1941 and 1942, there are accounts of soldiers being "drowned"—suffocated—by sand blown into their mouths and nostrils with great force by nearby artillery explosions.

with dirt that had apparently been blown into the exhaust outlet with such force that it bypassed the valves and pistons and clogged the crankcase.

Static electricity generated by friction of the dust particles would short out engines' ignition systems, knock out radio and telephone communications, and make pumping gasoline a hazard. The electricity would burn plants, either damaging them severely or destroying them completely. Trains couldn't run and arrived hours late because the dirt destroyed locomotive bearings and made the tracks too slippery for traction. A conductor on the Santa Fe's *Navajo* reported: "Noon was like night. There was no sun and at times it was impossible to see [as much as] a yard. The engineer could not see the signal lights."

Farmers and their families caught in town by such dust storms would have to stay overnight with friends; school either was not convened or was let out early when a big one was known to be approaching. "We had to stay home and we learned we had to keep supplies on hand," Opal recalled. A storm that struck during the night would leave several inches of dust in houses to greet the inhabitants in the morning. Often the storms would be so bad and the dust so pervasive that in order to breathe and sleep comfortably a family would have to move to the opposite side of the house the wind was blowing from, setting up in the living room if the wind was from one direction, moving back to the bedrooms when it shifted.

The Dust Bowl may have been harder on the women than the men. The powder would sift into houses around doors and windows and cracks in the construction despite every effort to keep it out with rugs at the bottoms of doors and rags around the windows. To make matters worse, the dust didn't clean up easily because it was sticky and hard to remove.

Families would eat meals with damp sheets hung over the table like a tent to keep the dust out. Housewives would try to protect their furniture by covering it with sheets. A common practice was to soak old sheets or pieces of unbleached muslin in stiff laundry starch and paste them around the window frames, both inside and out. "When you got the cloth on, it stuck," Opal recalled. "I don't know how many years we left those windows pasted up. We'd kick an old pair of overalls or something like that up against the bottom of the doors, but you had to open them at some point and dust would get in then."

All the efforts were futile. When Opal and Lawrence redid the house on the farm they bought just after World War II, they removed the casements from the sides of an interior door and found about a quart of fine powdered dust that had sifted into each one. "And those were *inside* doors!" Opal recalled with amazement. Housewives were unable to hang newly washed clothes outdoors to dry because of the blowing dirt. Opal laughed at the memory. "All you would have had would have been a mud ball. I just left my wash clothes in the rinse water and I'd take a piece out when it was needed. We drove nails in the wall on either side of the stove and we'd hang a sheet of newspaper on the nail to protect the wall and then we'd put a piece of clothing on a hanger and hang it on the nail to dry by the stove in the winter. The men wore long underwear in those days and you'd have long underwear hanging here and long underwear hanging there. It made for a very interesting decor when someone dropped in unexpectedly."

The blowing dust scoured the paint off everything from auto license plates to buildings, but the likelihood of another imminent storm made it impractical to repaint even for those who could afford to. The feathers of white leghorn and white wyandotte chickens were stained as brown as Rhode Island Reds by the dust. Often, when a ferocious storm struck and obliterated the sun, the birds would head for the henhouses and roost for the night thinking it was nightfall; some, unable to find their sheds in the pitch darkness, would simply roost on the ground.

The dirt banked up against the fences and the sides of buildings. A person could walk up one side of the dirt slope that had blown up against both sides of a five- or six-foot solid board fence, step over the few inches of fence top that wasn't covered, if any, and walk down the other side. Children played games such as "King of the Mountain" on these dirt banks. "At the Stones' [abandoned] place north of town, you could step right out of the upstairs window and walk down the dust bank," Opal recalled. Dirt from different parts of the country was layered in the yards. Delving into it was something like an archaeological dig that revealed the different layers—reddish, sandy dirt from Oklahoma and Texas, blue clay, sandy loam, black loess—all from different directions. The blowing dust covered headstones and graves in the cemetery; the WPA moved it out with a bulldozer and keeping the cemeteries clear became a permanent WPA project during the Dust Bowl.

Some of the storms were terrifying. On one blindingly sunny, scalding summer afternoon in 1935 or 1936, three of my cousins and I were playing under the trees that shaded the livestock watering tank on Uncle Vernie's farm north of Rolla when one of those black monsters peeped over the northwest horizon and was soon bearing down on us like an express train. When we spotted it, we began the panicky race across the farmyard, a trek made difficult by the fact that the hot sandy soil burned our bare feet.

Shortly after we reached the house, the storm hit and the bright afternoon turned pitch black.

Uncle Vernie had been running his John Deere tractor in the field just east of the farm buildings. When he saw the storm coming, he unhitched his implement and made his own race for home on the tractor. He lost. When the storm struck and plunged his universe into sudden, total blackness, he couldn't see the front end of the tractor. He had made it into the barnyard, however, and ran the tractor into one of the trees by the stock tank, where we had been playing a few minutes before. This, on a farm that was his home for fifty years. The tank gave him an orientation point and he was able to follow the fence to the house, which in such storms was like a fort under siege.

Everyone—Mother, Aunt Fairy (Vernie's wife), Grandmother Dickenson, Uncle Vernie, and all the children—set to work by the light of kerosene lamps putting wet towels and cloths around the windows and under the doors. The afternoon wore on and the wind and dust and unnatural darkness continued unabated, stretching the nerves seemingly to the breaking point; the adults later speculated that it must have been something like being under bombardment in wartime. The women fixed supper, which was served under a tent of damp sheets, and the storm whistled on, unbroken and undiminished. The radio offered some relief, but the wind often interfered with reception and the only escape was sleep. At midmorning the next day, the storm suddenly and miraculously ended, with everyone thrown so off balance by the change that the sudden stillness and bright summer sunlight seemed strangely inappropriate, almost ludicrous.

There were hundreds of storms like that. Nearly every entry in Mother's diary and nearly every letter she wrote during the 1930s reflects the preoccupation and constant struggle with the dust. "Terrible day!" reads the entry of March 15, 1935. "So dusty now I can hardly breathe!" She noted that day that because the wind blew in from the northwest she had to move us from the living room to the kitchen and the back bedroom to avoid the worst of the dust. The next day the wind shifted to the southwest and everyone was back in the living room.

It seemed the dust would never stop. Her diary entry of April 9, 1935, five days before "Black Sunday," described the "worst storm we've had. School let out at 1:30. Wind and dust still going hard at 10:30." The storm lasted well into the following day. "Such a bad dust storm only 1 bus in so no school. Worked on music till noon. Home the rest of day in kitchen. Dust was terrific. Had to have light on. As dark as night at times. No train."

The dust not only blew around the clock, it blew around the calendar, heedless of season. In February 1935, Mother wrote of "terrible dust storms," then, "It snowed for a while and the dust was settled for the time being although the wind kept blowing. This afternoon the dust started again and the snow stopped. We cleaned house pretty well this morning but it looks just like it did before we started it now. If we don't get moisture here, I don't now what will happen."

A year later, February 7, 1936, her diary entry laments, "Oh, the dirt! A terrible dust storm today!" On Sunday, March 15, there was "a terrible storm. Almost as bad as April 14, 1935." The year after that, on February 7, 1937, she reported, "Our worst dust storm! Have used lights most of the day!" She referred to the "terrible red dust from the north" that was "inches thick in the living room. I am awfully tired. This dust is sickening!"

<hr/>

Some hard lessons were gleaned from the Dust Bowl disaster. A big area along the Cimarron River in southwest Kansas is now the Cimarron National Grasslands. It was principally farmland that was foreclosed during the depression, allowed to revert to its natural grass state, and never put back into cultivation. There are several such areas in the High Plains that never should have gone under the plow, including the Cimarron and the huge Pawnee National Grassland in northeast Colorado. In the 1980s, the federal government also began paying farmers in some areas of the High Plains to plant thirty-one acres of grass per quarter section. This had a dual purpose: to head off another dust bowl and reduce surpluses of both grain and beef, since the grassland couldn't be used as pasture.

By the end of the 1930s, many erosion-preventive farming techniques was being utilized on the High Plains. The Roosevelt administration created the Soil Erosion Service in the Interior Department in October 1933. It began subjecting public grazing land to national regulation in 1934 and got Congress to establish the Soil Conservation Service in the Department of Agriculture in 1935. The service aggressively pushed antierosion farming methods. One was offering to pay ten cents an acre for tractor fuel or feed for horses to farmers who would plow at least a quarter of their acreage on the contour lines, sideways to the downward slope. This slowed water runoff not only on hillsides but around the edges of flat fields as well, which conserved precious moisture as well as preventing water erosion.

Many federal farm-subsidy programs were predicated on farmers adopting conservation techniques. These included planting cover crops such as Sudan grass or sorghum or practicing "strip farming," strips of cropland separated by strips of fallow land, which reduced wind erosion. Summer fallowing, the practice of leaving land idle every other year to allow the replenishment of subsoil moisture, became widespread. Some hardheads, however, refused to go along with these programs and the drifting dirt from their fields and those that were abandoned often smothered the crops of neighbors who were trying to conserve.

New implements for working the summer fallow were developed. Prior to the Dust Bowl, many farmers turned their wheat stubble under with a regular moldboard plow and then worked the ground with a disk, which powdered the soil and made it vulnerable to blowing. One of the new machines, the "chisel" plow—called a "chisel" for short—which was invented by an Oklahoma farmer named Fred Hoeme, had teeth like a harrow, or rake, and broke the crust into lumps instead of powdering it. After wheat harvest in June and July, if a field was relatively free of weeds, the stubble was often left standing over the winter to hold the snow. When the stubble was first worked, either in the fall or the following spring, it was generally with a "one-way," formally known as the wheat-land disk plow, which chopped the straw up but left it lying on the surface to hold the moisture and prevent blowing. The stubble was broken down as the summer fallow was chiseled and weeded during the spring and summer to prepare it for planting in September. By the 1980s and 1990s, tillage methods evolved so that the stubble wasn't disked and chopped up but weeded with herbicides and allowed to stand intact to further save moisture and inhibit blowing.

In 1940, the McDonald Standard, the local weekly newspaper, reported that there was six times as much land in cover crops and strip farming and five times as much summer fallow in western Kansas as in 1936. It reported that in Greeley County 100 miles south the farmers had gotten together to adopt Agricultural Adjustment Act conservation methods and voted that no farmer should receive federal payments unless he followed the AAA program of cover crops and strip farming.

But after years of trauma in which millions of tons of western topsoil blew off to the east and out to the Atlantic or was carried down the rivers into the Gulf of Mexico, no one felt particularly comfortable. Kansas's public school textbooks in the late 1930s and early 1940s had graphics that illustrated the estimated amount and percentage of topsoil that had been destroyed in the "Dirty Thirties" and how few years there were left if the rate of erosion continued.

In 1940, the memories of the depression and Dust Bowl were indelibly imprinted on everyone's psyche. In September of that year, the McDonald

Standard noted that the wheat crop had been good, with yields between twenty-five and forty bushels per acre and that there had just been a good rain. Lest anyone become complacent, however, the editor reminded his readers of the "disastrous" autumn just the year before, when rainfall had only been 13.4 inches, 5 inches below normal.

As the Dust Bowl ruined crops in the early 1930s, wheat prices started inching up. In 1932, wheat was $0.30 to $0.35 per bushel. In 1934, it was up to $0.94, by 1935, $1.21. It plunged to $0.60 in 1938 and a grasshopper infestation exacerbated the misery in 1937–38, but after that, rainfall and wartime demand rescued the farmers who had survived the ordeal. Kansas farmers harvested large wheat crops in 1942, 1943, and 1944, with farm income rising 165 percent. Global demand for foodstuffs remained high after the end of the war, but this push for production weakened the conservation constraints of the 1930s and in the 1950s a new drought and dust bowl was in progress.

This demonstrated once again that dryland farming on the High Plains was still a risky proposition because of the area's scanty and unreliable rainfall. At the end of the "Dirty Thirties," however, relief from the Great Depression and the Dust Bowl came from across the seas. The rains returned and crops were good, but it was the demands of World War II and its aftermath that finally ended the depression in the United States and triggered a decade of sustained prosperity for the farmers in McDonald and the rest of the High Plains.

CHAPTER NINE

"A DATE WHICH WILL LIVE IN INFAMY"

SUNDAY, DECEMBER 7, 1941, "A DATE WHICH WILL LIVE IN INFAMY," as President Roosevelt termed it in his dramatic war message to Congress the following day, dawned bright and sunny in western Kansas.

For our family, the morning, as usual, was taken up with Sunday school and church, followed by the customary Sunday dinner of fried chicken, mashed potatoes and gravy, and pie. We had just finished dinner and the Sunday *Denver Post*, which we shared with Uncle Wayne and his family, who lived next door, an economy measure held over from the depression and Dust Bowl days. Over the radio came the message, electrifying and chilling: The Japanese had bombed the great U.S. Pacific naval base at Pearl Harbor, inflicting great loss of life and ships. Invasion of the West Coast appeared to be possible.

As distant as it was, we had an immediate concern about Pearl Harbor. Six young men from the town or related to townspeople were stationed there, including two of my cousins and their wives. One cousin, Chester Phipps, Jr. ("Little Chet," as he was known, to differentiate him from his father), was on a submarine, the USS *Pompano*; the other, Harley Duling, was on the USS *California*, one of the battleships sunk by the Japanese but later salvaged.

There was considerable irony in their experiences. Little Chet missed the attack entirely because the *Pompano* was out to sea on patrol at the time, but was killed a year and a half later when his boat struck a mine off the coast of Hokkaido. Harley was blown off his ship into the water and in the confusion the Navy notified the family on Christmas Day that he had been killed in action but that his body hadn't been recovered. A few days later, however, the authorities finally located him in a hospital at Pearl Harbor, recovering from minor burns and exposure. Harley was not to be the town's first gold star serviceman, after all.*

That was the only action Harley saw in the war; a yeoman (clerk-typist), he was soon returned to duty, spent the rest of the war at Pearl Harbor, and subsequently retired after twenty years' service. The state of communications was such that it was more than a week before Little Chet's wife, Irma, who was with him in Honolulu and was seven months pregnant, could get a cablegram to their families that they both were safe.

Another young man from McDonald was at Pearl on the USS *Seagull*, a submarine tender for Chet's squadron. One was on board the battleship USS *Pennsylvania*, which was damaged, another was an Army chaplain at Fort Weaver, and yet another was a captain in the Army. The December 18 issue of the *McDonald Standard* ran a letter from the chaplain to his family:

> The Japs had successfully carried Armageddon across 3,000 miles of ocean and launched it with terrific suddenness upon the "Paradise of the Pacific." As the clear, pure notes from the bugle sounded the call to Divine Worship, the first rumblings of heavy explosions were heard in the direction of Pearl Harbor.

In the same issue, the editor, my uncle Wayne Phipps, offered some rhetoric of his own. "It makes the American heart swell with pride to read about an American flyer shooting down two or three Japanese planes. Several boys at Pearl Harbor did all right against the Japanese planes."

In another piece, he continued in a stronger vein:

> American boys aren't robots or animals like the German and Japanese warriors who are taught to hate and kill. They have been brought up the American way with responsibility for the rights of their fellowmen. But when it comes to defending what they believe in, they can, man for man, whip the living daylights out of the highly trained murderers of the blood-thirsty Axis cutthroats.

---

*Households with loved ones in the service proclaimed it by hanging a flag with red and blue borders in a window. There was a blue star in the white field in the middle for each serviceman from the household. A gold star in the middle proclaimed the supreme sacrifice.

The paper also reported that Kansas governor Payne Ratner had declared Sunday, December 21, as a day of prayer in a proclamation that read:

> Hitlerism is anti-Christian and Japan with its pagan gods is anti-Christian. Christianity and democracy are inseparably and unalterably linked together in the fight for existence. They threatened democracy and they are attempting to destroy Christianity itself.

On a more secular note, the paper's rural audience was also informed that "the German invasion of the Channel Islands brought hoof and mouth disease to Jersey and Guernsey herds. The Russian invasion of Finland did the same." As part of the *Standard*'s war effort, the horizontal rules, or lines, that marked the end of a story in the newspaper had added to them in the middle the tiny capital letters BDB, for "Buy Defense Bonds." In the next two months, the initials were expanded to spell out the actual message, "Buy Defense Bonds," and then expanded again to "For Victory: Buy Bonds."*

The father of my fifth-grade teacher, Verna Moline, a pretty young woman whom I adored, was a civilian construction worker on Midway Island at the time. His family obviously had many anxious moments about him until the naval battle of Midway, a turning point in the war in the Pacific, ended the threat that Midway would suffer Wake Island's fate of invasion and occupation by the Japanese. He returned safely shortly thereafter. On days when the news was particularly dire, we kids would crowd around her desk before class to ask anxiously about him and voice our sympathies—probably seeking reassurance ourselves in those dark early days of defeat at the hands of the Japanese. However, as my mother, who was teaching English in the high school at the time, finally pointed out, our constant solicitude was something Miss Moline probably could have done without, although she was too gracious to show it.

The news continued to be chilling for the following year. The Germans seemed to be on the verge of conquering Russia, and the Japanese appeared unstoppable as they raced from conquest to conquest, inflicting one humiliating disaster after another on the Allies as they won control of

*After defense bonds and stamps went on sale at the post office on May 1, 1941, the *Standard* ran a "Defense Bond Quiz" each week answering such questions as the interest rate they bore (2½ percent simple interest annually) and the convertibility of stamps to bonds. One question asked why children should buy defense stamps: "In buying stamps they write their names on a Roll of Honor of Americans who are doing their part to show the dictators that united America will never flinch to preserve her sacred liberty."

the Pacific basin from the Asian continent all the way to Australia. Whatever strength isolationism had in our area was emphatically blown away by
the attack on Pearl Harbor and the national emergency. In outrage, everyone turned to the war effort.

Tiny farm hamlets all over the country, including ours, were encouraged to impose blackouts at night, as incredible as it seems in hindsight.
The rationale was obvious: We were the breadbasket of the nation and the
only way the Axis could win was to destroy our food supply. McDonald
was on one of the transportation lines between Denver and Kansas City—
and as far as we were concerned cities didn't get any more important or up
to date than those two—and by showing our lights at night we might as
well have marked those lifelines in neon signs to enemy aircraft. I still
clearly recall the embarrassment of my mother and grandmother the night
Alan Larson, who owned the filling station where we bought our farm fuel
and who was our block warden, tapped on the door to tell us that a sliver
of light was showing through one of the curtains. We felt like Axis collab-
orators.

That seems laughable now, but those were anxious times. A welcome
bit of rare good news came in April of 1942. Jimmy Doolittle and his Army
Air Corps aviators, flying B-25s off the aircraft carrier *Hornet*, had
bombed Tokyo and other Japanese cities, including Kobe. We must have
gotten the news on a Sunday afternoon because at Christian Endeavor
that evening, with a little mischief in mind, I asked a group of the kids, including one of my cousins, if they'd heard about the bombing of Kobe.
They all reacted with alarm and dismay, thinking that I meant Colby, a
town fifty miles southeast of us, as I anticipated they would. Two months
later, Chuck Treadwell, who had joined the Air Corps in 1941 and had
been out of communication for several weeks, came home on leave and
hinted that he had been on the *Hornet* with Doolittle and his aircrews.*

⚓

Pearl Harbor Day dawned on an American people uneasily at peace and still
divided between interventionists and isolationists. The Great Depression
had nearly run its course and had been succeeded by an even greater menace, the profound threat to civilization posed by Fascist totalitarianism.

As more and more of the Western world fell to Adolf Hitler, the de-

---

*Doolittle's raid was April 18. The April 9 issue of the *McDonald Standard* carried a report that a
farmer from nearby Goodland had offered $100 to the first American pilot who bombed Hirohito's
palace in Tokyo on the theory that the emperor was viewed as "some sort of god and this would really
shake morale" in Japan.

bate over the course the United States should take became increasingly acute. Interventionists argued that the longer the United States held aloof, the more difficult the task of defeating the Axis would be—if not ultimately impossible. Isolationists, disillusioned by the Great War of 1914–1918 and its outcome, cited George Washington and countered that the current trouble in Europe was just further proof that no good could ever come from U.S. involvement in the quarrels of the decadent Old World.

Although the isolationists made Franklin Roosevelt's attempts to prepare the nation for war extremely difficult right up to Pearl Harbor, the clear and present danger of the Axis had become increasingly apparent. A Gallup poll in 1941 showed that 68 percent thought defeating Germany was more important than staying out of the war, 64 percent supported the draft, and 85 percent thought that the United States would enter the war eventually. Fewer than 25 percent supported isolationism.

Isolationism's geographic base was in the Midwest and mountain West and had an intellectual and political base in Populism. The debate over U.S. intervention in World War II was marked by Roosevelt's "quarantine the aggressors" speech in 1937 and steadily intensified as Hitler's aggressions progressed with the annexation of Austria and Czechoslovakia and the invasion of Poland and Western Europe.

From the "quarantine" speech until Pearl Harbor, it is difficult to identify a political leadership as blindly isolationist as that of Kansas. In 1939, the U.S. House of Representatives appropriated $375 million to build military aircraft by a vote of 367 to 15, with 5 of the negative votes coming from Kansas; it would have included all six representatives if one hadn't been absent that day. Governor Alf Landon, the 1936 GOP presidential candidate, helped draft the isolationist plank in the 1940 Republican platform and former Kansas governor Harry Woodring was forced to resign as secretary of war because of his obstructionist isolationism. Senators Arthur Capper and Clyde Reed actively opposed the lend-lease bill, as did Landon. Governor Ratner, whose eyes finally were opened to the Axis threat to democracy and Christianity by the Japanese attack, denounced lend-lease prior to Pearl Harbor on the grounds that it would give Roosevelt "the same power over material supplies now exercised by Hitler, Mussolini, and Stalin" and warned that it would "bring dictatorship to the United States."

In the spring of 1940, Roosevelt asked William Allen White, the great Emporia newspaper editor and disciple of Theodore Roosevelt, to be chairman of the national Committee to Defend America by Aiding the

Allies, and White worked hard in this cause. He undercut his organization's efforts, however, with his partisan refusal to allow it to campaign for the defeat of the isolationist senators and congressmen, which included most of the GOP incumbents who stood for reelection in 1940.

Many of the people in Kansas were out in front of their leaders, however, and by the time of Pearl Harbor the people in northwest Kansas were as supportive of intervention as anyone else in the country. It certainly wasn't difficult to find reasons to support interventionism. I vividly remember the horrified fascination with which I read the excerpts of Jan Valtin's book *Out of the Night,* which was excerpted in *Life* magazine and the *Reader's Digest.* The book was Valtin's (a nom de plume) account of the brutal, violent ideological warfare between the Nazis and the Communists and Socialists in Germany between the two world wars and is a valuable historical document. The accounts of his interrogations and torture at the hands of the Gestapo and the SS, accompanied by graphic, horrifying artists' illustrations in both magazines, particularly *Life,* were my first exposure to such brutality. Along with the equally lurid accounts of the Japanese "Rape of Nanking," they undoubtedly did their share of persuading many Americans of the nature of the totalitarian Axis powers and the need to destroy them.

One reason the people were ahead of their leaders on intervention may have been the fact that the *McDonald Standard* regularly ran two pages of "boilerplate" features that included a weekly news digest and analysis that supported Roosevelt's efforts to prepare the nation for intervention in the European war and warned of the Japanese threat in Asia.*

There were news items in the *Standard* such as the one, in September 1940, quoting an American businessman and his wife who had lived for thirteen years in Britain and were visiting in northwest Kansas. "Don't wait to arm," they warned. "Don't depend on the ocean to protect you."

Of course these matters are never clear-cut and tidy. In November 1941, the paper reported that a Chinese American in Beaver City, Nebraska, named Gum Fong was being held for shooting a man named Erich Brunhow. Gum Fong was described as a World War I "machine gunner in the AEF [American Expeditionary Force] whose patriotism to America has never been questioned" and who reportedly did the shooting after Brunhow "told him what Hitler would do to him when he took over America." This caused Gum Fong "to lose his head" and the story con-

---

*The syndicated features cost the papers very little and came already impressed into mats from which the printing plates for the press could be cast, so there was no typesetting involved.

cluded that "it will be difficult to find a jury on these western prairies who'll hang much on Gum Fong. A nice collection could easily be raised to buy him a medal."

It certainly sounded as though Brunhow asked for it, but there were some ugly signs of the jingoism and anti-German hysteria that had marred the war effort in 1917 and 1918. There was a report in July 1940 that Jehovah's Witnesses in neighboring Goodland asked for protection from mob violence because they hadn't "shown loyalty to their country and flag." In the same month, there was a story that "there was a Nazi shadow over the Great Plains area" near Kit Carson, Colorado, because the 15-section (15-square-mile) Bowers ranch had been sold to a German citizen "of the Reich and of course that means Hitler. . . . People are worried and there are fears that the Germans may use this tract of land was a landing field and base for warcraft from which they could bomb military objectives in the vicinity." Kit Carson is a town of about 7,500 located about 150 miles southeast of Denver in one of the most sparsely populated areas of eastern Colorado and the possible "military objectives" were not listed.

🖎

For many in our area, the major immediate concern at the time of Pearl Harbor was recovery from the Great Depression and the Dust Bowl, but the onslaughts of the Nazis and the Japanese steadily became an increasing worry. There was general support for President Roosevelt's embargoes of scrap metal and oil to the Japanese—the United States shipped 200 million tons of scrap metal to Japan between 1935 and 1940—which reflected the growing conviction that those materials would be turned against America and Americans in the not-too-distant future.

The fall of France left us with the shocked realization that the beleaguered British on their "right little, tight little island" were all that were standing between the free world and the Nazi menace. The Battle of Britain dramatized the peril and we followed with fascination the newspaper, radio, and newsreel accounts of its progress, of the scores kept of friendly and enemy aircraft lost, civilians killed, and buildings and cities destroyed. There was something about aerial warfare, about being bombed, that we could imagine happening to us in a way that was impossible with the accounts of infantry and tank warfare.

In addition, the impending war had become personal and local well before Pearl Harbor. Young men from the area were drafted in 1940 and 1941 following enactment of the conscription law, effective October 16,

1940—18 from Rawlins County were in the first call; about 240,000 registered in Kansas and about 900,000 were called up nationwide. In January
1941, World War I veterans were instructed to register for possible service
in the defense program. The number of men from the county called up by
selective service grew as 1941 wore on, and the *Standard* began carrying
large Navy recruiting advertisements.* The Marine Corps, being more
frugal, provided weekly news features to small-town papers, such as accounts of Marines who won the Congressional Medal of Honor in World
War I and other lessons in the history of the corps. In mid-1941, these
features became graphic, featuring drawings and exploits of individual
Marines.

Many men in the county, including about two dozen from McDonald,
joined a county rifle club, and the *Standard*, which ran their shooting
scores, explained that the ammunition was provided by "the federal government, which wants to improve the shooting ability of its citizens."

Many Americans didn't wait for the nation to get involved. In August
1941, the *Standard* reported that "Everett Connor has joined the Royal
Canadian Air Force" and noted that "a great many Americans are flying
planes for England and from all reports are making things tough for Hitler. . . . We hope he [Everett] will take care of enough Messerschmitts to
be awarded all the medals in England." Another local boy, Don Gibbons,
also joined the RCAF.

There was no general rush to the colors before Pearl Harbor, however.
On December 4, 1941, the *Standard* reported that the selective service
system had ruled that recent marriages were not grounds for deferment.
This was the result of an appeal by a young man in our county who had
been deferred the previous summer to work in the wheat harvest and then
tried to extend his deferment by getting married. The Navy also announced that enlistments were down, but this was primarily because parents wouldn't give consent to their sons who were under twenty-one
because of the reports of Allied shipping losses to German submarines in
the North Atlantic.

That changed with the Japanese attack, however. Two weeks after Pearl
Harbor, in its December 18, 1941, edition, the *Standard* reported that the
"recruiting offices of both the Army and the Navy are swamped." An
Army recruiting ad in the December 11 edition is a reminder of the inno-

---

*The campaign included a "Popeye" comic strip in which Popeye cited all the advantages of becoming
a bluejacket: "In the Navy you get free uniforms, free food, and no doctors or dentists bills. In the
Navy your pay is gravy." In one, Popeye pointed out a sailor walking with a pretty girl to a prospective
recruit, who concluded that donning Navy blue could similarly benefit him.

cence of the time. It showed two cheery young soldiers marching at right shoulder arms down a country lane and waving at a farm boy standing next to a shock of wheat. The text extolled the wholesome benefits of Army life, quoting a World War I veteran: "He gains a broadening experience and advantage in friendship and learning which only service in a common cause can give."

The ad continued:

> Our Army affords new scenes and still more heartening adventures. He gains a strong physique, good health, and a clean mind. He comes home equipped for his life's work with a brighter outlook and renewed energy. Comradeship and knowing his fellow Americans better makes him a better American!

Reflecting the American penchant for pragmatism, the ad also noted that the World War II soldier could "develop skill in handling vehicles."

🐚

Little Chet, my cousin, was one of the town's World War II heroes. He enlisted in the Navy in 1937 and at the time of Pearl Harbor was a petty officer, a motor machinists mate, first class, responsible for the operation and maintenance of one of the submarine's two big 1,500-horsepower diesel engines. In addition, he was captain of the three-inch deck gun crew and when the submarine was attacking enemy shipping it was his duty to convert the captain's periscope findings into firing data for the torpedo room.

In October 1941, Chet came home on leave, which was cut short because of the diplomatic crisis. "When the boys get a chance at Japan, they are likely to remember that," my uncle Wayne editorialized. He also quoted Chet, who turned out to be an excellent spokesman for the Navy:

> The U.S. Navy is ready to fight Japan and would like to get it over with. The sailors are tired of the endless tension caused by the wavering Jap attitude. Reports of the Japanese Navy in action against China gives every indication that the U.S. sailors can beat them in every phase of the game.

After Pearl Harbor, Chet was promoted to chief petty officer. In August 1942, when the *Pompano* was off the coast of Honshu on its third wartime patrol, he won the Silver Star when a Japanese destroyer caught the *Pompano* on the surface. The deck gun crew damaged it and held it off long enough to allow the submarine to crash dive.

By the time the *Pompano* was brought back to San Francisco for repairs and refitting at the Mare Island Navy Yard in California in the fall of 1942, it had sunk nine Japanese ships. President Roosevelt, who was touring the Mare Island facility, happened to pass by the boat's dock and saw the nine Japanese flags and sinking ships painted on the submarine's conning tower. He stopped his motorcade and had the crew called out on deck to congratulate them on their record.

Chet came home on leave to a hero's reception that October. That early in the war, he was probably the town's first combat veteran to return home and our natural pride in his heroism combined with the patriotism that marked that war was almost explosive. It killed me to have to sit in class while he was moving around the town, speaking at the Lions Club, the YWCA, the Navy Day programs at the high school and grade school, and other events. I made a pathetic attempt to feign illness so I could stay out of school, which to my delight he recounted with some amusement at the grade school assembly later that day. On the weekend he was home, we had a big Sunday dinner and reunion of our extended family, nearly forty of us including Chet's in-laws, at Grandmother's house. And then he returned to the war.

We never saw him again. The following summer of 1943, the *Pompano* disappeared on its seventh combat patrol, northeast of Honshu in the North Pacific, sometime between August 20, when it left Midway, and October 5, when it was due back. There were heavily mined areas in the boat's patrol zone and the official Navy conclusion was that it was sunk when it hit a mine. Little Chet was the first of the three from the town and its surrounding farm area who were killed in action in World War II.

In its first six combat patrols, between late December 1941 and August 1943, the *Pompano* sank ten Japanese ships and damaged four others, including an aircraft carrier near the Japanese main islands. Japanese records indicate that it sank two more on its final, fatal mission.

The *Pompano* had a relatively short and hazardous war. On December 20, 1941, two days out of Pearl Harbor on its first wartime patrol, it was almost sunk by U.S. Navy planes that damaged one of its fuel tanks before they realized their error. Trailing oil from the ruptured tank, the *Pompano* proceeded to Wake Island and then the Marshall Islands, where it sank a 16,000-ton transport. And, when it was surprised on the surface by the Japanese destroyer in August 1942, the submarine nearly came to grief again despite successfully crash-diving. It was damaged by depth charges and ran aground in about 250 feet of water. The skipper seriously considered surfacing and scuttling the boat, but was talked out of it by the other officers and managed to outwait the Japanese and work it free. When they surfaced, the *Pompano* was just 1,000 yards off the Japanese coast but managed to clear the area and survive for another year.

⚓

For a ten-year-old boy, already conditioned by the drama of the Battle of Britain, the war's tragedies were obscured by the excitement and drama of America's entering it. Cowboys and Indians gave way to Rangers and Nazis, Marines and Japs. We cradled our BB guns in our arms the way the paratroopers did and practiced jumping off the chicken house in our back-yard, somersaulting when we hit the ground the way they showed it in the newsreels. This allegedly reduced the shock of landing, but it didn't seem to, particularly when we graduated to jumping off the railroad boxcars, which were about fifteen feet high and were real teeth rattlers. One of Little Chet's brothers-in-law, Wayne Harper, an NCO with the Eighty-second Airborne Division who fought in Sicily, Italy, and Normandy, watched our demonstration with great interest—and amusement, no doubt—when he was home on leave one summer.

We fought the battle of Guadalcanal, and made the raid on Dieppe. As the war progressed, we pint-sized, wannabe warriors fought through Sicily, Italy, and Normandy, and crossed the Rhine with one hand while dis-patching Iwo and Okinawa with the other. When it wasn't in use, we con-verted the blue 1942 Pontiac four-door sedan my mother, grandmother, and uncle jointly purchased right after Pearl Harbor—one of the last Pon-tiacs to roll off the assembly lines before they were converted to war pro-duction—into a B-17 that braved the flak and Messerschmitts over Germany. We built all the model airplanes. I got the full range of solid models offered by the Boy Scouts of America through their magazine, *Boys' Life*—a B-17, a B-24, an A-20, a P-40, a B-25. Not only did we know all the German and Japanese combat aircraft, but we could have identi-fied a Russian Yak fighter if one had appeared over the town.

The surest way to pick a fight with someone was to call him a German or a Jap. We had discussions about whether the Germans and Japanese could possibly beat any of us up badly enough to force us to spit on the American flag—the consensus was that there was no way—we'd spit in their faces instead. Since we all agreed on the Known Universal Truth that the cowboy-movie star Hopalong Cassidy was the toughest guy in the world, we had a simple plan for winning the war: just parachute "Hoppy" into Germany so he could get into a fistfight with Hitler and it would all be settled. Immediately! Or as one of our number contended, whose sister was a student at Fort Hays State Teachers College, it would be over "toot sweet," which, he informed us, was French for "pronto."

Hard on the heels of Pearl Harbor came the new comic books and comic strip heroes. "Wings Comics," about flyers, was a big favorite, particularly its mechanic hero, Greasemonkey Griffin; the comics introduced us to new words, including, in the early days of defeat, *evacuate*, which I persisted in pronouncing "eva-cute," and *Luftwaffe*, which came out "Luft-waif." Terry (and the Pirates) and his buddy, Hotshot Charlie, contributed their aviator's derring-do to the war effort. Ozark Ike, the big, genial Li'l Abner–type rube from Cider City, Arkansas ("Cider City Moon I Love Ya/Cider City Moon That's No Kid/Cider City Moon I Left Ya/And How I Wish I Never Did," he sang in the barracks), reported for basic training along with his fellow draftee and newfound buddy, Oinie Fer of Brooklyn ("Oinie Fer," the city sophisticate explained patiently to his bumpkin friend, "spelled just da way it sounds, E-r-n-i-e F-o-y."). Skeezix and Joe Palooka were drafted along with the other able-bodied males of their generation.

The comings and goings of the servicemen were a constant source of excitement. None made a more dramatic appearance than Ward Benkleman, a B-24 pilot who wound up with the Fifteenth Air Force in Italy. Ward and his brother Bobby, who also was in the Army Air Corps, were scions of a well-to-do family. They attended Kansas University before the war and returned to the KU campus on the GI bill after the war, Ward graduating from medical school and Bobby becoming a dentist.

Like many others, Ward and his crew got their combat training in the Big Sky Country of Montana. On his way east to the war, he drew up his flight plan to take him over northwest Kansas. We all were at the table having our midday dinner when we heard the sound of an approaching airplane. A very low flying airplane. A very big airplane. This was a time when airplanes were still a novelty and the sound of one at any time, even at mealtime, was justification for everyone to run outside and look.

What we saw was a four-engine, olive-drab monster circling so low—in memory it doesn't seem that it could have been more than 100 feet—that we could clearly see the waist gunners leaning out and waving at us. *A real B-24! A real Liberator!* None of us kids had any trouble making the identification of that airplane! It was just like in the newsreels and newspaper and magazine pictures and the models we built, only more overwhelming!

Then, one of the waist gunners dropped a little parachute, a piece of cloth with strings tied at the four corners with a note to Ward's folks wrapped around a weight. He dropped it after the plane had passed Ward's parents' house on the north side of town and it landed near U.S. Highway 36, which runs along the south edge. It couldn't have mattered less. Every kid in town took off at high port racing for the honor of retrieving it and delivering it to Charlie and Hertha Benkleman. My disappointment that one of the high school boys found the parachute didn't alter the fact that it was the most exciting moment of my life up to that time.

Another local boy, Herbie Madsen, also was commissioned as a B-24 pilot that same summer. A year later, word came that he had been shot down and was a POW in Stalag 1, one of the German camps for Allied airmen. Two years later, after V-E Day, Herbie was back home and on hand to celebrate V-J Day. A few months after Ward's sortie, Chuck Treadwell, also with the Fifteenth Air Force in Italy by then, gave the townspeople a thrill of recognition when he appeared on the cover of *Life* magazine in October of 1943 as a pallbearer for an Air Corps comrade who was killed on a mission over central Europe.

We kept up with the boys in the service pretty well through the *McDonald Standard*, which ran everything provided by proud families and the military's public relations officers. Many of our servicemen took up the editor's offer of a free subscription for the duration if they would write to the paper about their experiences, so we got news items such as, in Italy, "Elmer George looked up Elaine Sramek, who is a nurse in an Army hospital." Elaine was an indefatigable correspondent and many of the local boys in the European theater were able to keep track of her whereabouts and look her up. In November 1944, she wrote that she was at a field hospital in the town in France where Jack Boyle, the postmaster, had been hospitalized more than a quarter of a century before, after being wounded by shrapnel in World War I.

Chuck Treadwell, a gregarious man who always looked for the light side of life and a regular correspondent, took advantage of the opportunity to periodically say "Hello B," whoever "B" was, and urged her to write. Harlan Larson related his thrill at being in the same Army Air Corps aviation cadet training unit in Santa Ana, California, as one of his heroes, Michigan all-American tailback Tom Harmon.

Staff Sergeant Earl Edgett was awarded the Silver Star fighting with the infantry in France and Germany (and, warrior that he was, reported that he went deer hunting in France while on leave). As the fighting wore on, however, the news tended to get worse. Leland "Bud" Hastings lost an eye in January 1944 on New Britain on a day that units of the First Marine Division were trying to cross a strongly defended river that they dubbed "Suicide Creek." Harold Edgett was killed in Italy in March 1944. A year later, word came that Harry Mann was missing and feared killed in action with the Ninetieth Infantry Division in Germany; he turned up after V-E day in a POW camp. Captain Robert Urbom of the Seventh Armored Division was wounded at St.-Vith. Lieutenant Duane Urbom, a Marine fighter pilot with the "Black Cat" squadron, was killed while on the deck of the carrier the USS *Franklin*, when it was hit by Japanese bombs.

⊰⊱

The major sacrifice on the home front, of course, was the shortage of consumer goods because of the conversion to war production and the rationing of most everyday products, including gasoline and tires, cigarettes, meat, sugar, and shoes, all of which were regulated by a cumbersome system of ration stamps.

Four days after Pearl Harbor, Fran Miller, a merchant advertising passenger-car and light-truck tires in the December 11, 1941, issue of the *Standard*, warned the citizens that the Office of Price Administration had ordered the cessation of their manufacture for civilian use. The ad advised readers that "it will pay you to lay away some for future use if you don't need them now. This supply won't last long."

The following week, the government instituted a ban on the sale of tires until rationing could be instituted. On January 15, 1942, Rawlins County got its first wartime tire quota—twenty-five truck tires, twenty-one truck inner tubes, seven auto and pickup truck tires, and six auto/pickup tubes. Of the truck tires, ten were allocated for distribution county-wide, seven to Atwood, the county seat, and four each to the towns of McDonald and Herndon. The *Standard* began running a column entitled "Tires and the Farmer," which reported the monthly allotment of truck and tractor tires and inner tubes and news of such developments as the invention of wooden tractor tires (not as good as rubber but serviceable), which never appeared, and the suggestion that farmers revert to the steel tractor wheels with lugs that had mostly been replaced with rubber by 1940. Another column of news and advice on shortages and rationing was headed "Victory Digest."

Books of ration stamps appeared in May 1942 and each town had its own rationing board to administer them. In McDonald, that thankless task was given to the newspaper editor, Uncle Wayne; Dr. Lewis Leslie; and the banker, Ross Wingfield. The citizenry was also advised that anyone guilty of exceeding the 35-mph speed limit would not be allowed to buy gasoline after rationing went into effect. Lists of maximum allowable prices for grocery items were circulated with instructions to report all grocers who failed to correct their prices. A Gallup poll reported that price controls were supported by 90 percent of its respondents—many Americans recalled the inflation of more than 60 percent between 1914 and 1918.

In response to cigarette rationing, there were ads for Prince Albert "crimp cut" tobacco, which "shape[d] up full, firm 'machine' smokes" for those who rolled their own. During the war, the newspaper printed a letter by Alfred Buck, the owner of the drugstore, advising the town's servicemen to bring their own cigarettes when they came home on leave because of civilian rationing. It was difficult for civilians to get the popular brands, Luckies, Camels, Chesterfields, and they had to settle instead for such deservedly minor—and vile-tasting—brands as Spuds, Dominoes, and Wings.

In retrospect, the miracle of the rationing system was that it worked at all. One instance of the culture gap that yawned between the Office of Price Administration (OPA) in Washington and the hinterlands was the OPA's demand that Denver coal dealers file ceiling prices for buffalo "chips" (dried buffalo manure) on the understanding that they were "commonly used for fuel." That had been true in the early years of settlement, but the city slickers' gaffe gave a temporary boost to morale.

Of greater import was the grievance farm folks felt about those staples, bread and butter. Butter became a civilian scarcity because the military and lend-lease had priority on butterfat, the base of cheese and milk products, and oleomargarine emerged as a substitute. There was a ten-cent-per-pound tax on artificially colored margarine but only one-quarter of a cent on the uncolored, which was a white brick that looked unappetizingly like lard. A little packet of coloring powder came with the uncolored spread, which with a great deal of effort could be worked into it with a fork or tablespoon. We grumbled at this insult added to injury, but we had the dairy lobby on Capitol Hill to thank for the ten-cent tax because of its opposition to the introduction of oleo. And, in an effort to hold down bread prices, Secretary of Agriculture Claude Wickard ordered a ban on sliced bread. Actually, many farm wives were accustomed to slicing the bread they baked at home, but this order on store-bought bread seemed like an egregious example of bureaucratic niggling over a minor matter.

As the war rationing went on, the citizens' ingenuity in devising culinary supplements and substitutes began to emerge and were duly published in the *McDonald Standard*. One suggestion was to put meat leftovers in a piecrust, which had the virtue of energy value because of the shortening—"Use high quality shortening," the recipe advised. Another was "hamburger pie"—hamburger mixed with green beans, eggs, milk, and a can of tomato soup and baked with a mashed potato crust—which the British had long known as "shepherd's" or "cottage" pie. Other suggestions included waffles for supper and baked eggs on spaghetti. And, of course, there was the ubiquitous Spam, for which I developed a taste that I never lost and which my wife calls "standing roast of Spam."

Equally important was the advice to farmers on preparing for the anticipated wartime shortages. A front-page story in the January 8, 1942, issue of the *Standard* urged farmers not to "wait until just before [wheat] harvest [in July] to order repairs and machinery overhauls." Dairy farmers and beef cattlemen were counseled on how to get government protection against price hikes on feed grains. Hog farmers were advised that feeding hogs over 300 pounds was inefficient because the bigger a hog got, the more grain it took to add a pound of weight. Wheat farmers were informed that they could get additional food-ration stamps for harvest hands. On the basis of 100 meals, these included an extra two pounds of sugar, ten additional processed-food points, and seventeen more meat and fat points.

✄

Another way civilians participated in the war effort was through scrap drives. Housewives saved cooking fats for glycerin, which was used in the manufacture of explosives and for which they got additional meat-rationing points. The newspapers carried all the information contained in the government's sales pitch: It took one pound of glycerin for six 75-millimeter shells or fifty .30-caliber bullets; 2,300 pair of nylon stockings was the equivalent of one parachute; thirty lipstick tubes would make twenty cartridge cases. There was no end of these statistics: In defense of sugar rationing, the papers informed us that it took the distilled sugar of one-fifth of an acre of sugarcane to make the gunpowder for one 16-inch battleship shell, that it took two-thirds of a square mile of sugarcane for the powder of 1,000 field gun shells, and that it took nine-tenths of a pound of sugar for a pound of smokeless gunpowder. Citizens were urged to contribute their old phonograph records, which would be recycled into new ones for the boys in the service.

In September 1942, the governors of Kansas and Nebraska announced a scrap-gathering contest between the two states, to which both states turned with a vengeance. Throughout the war, there were periodic calls for old farm machinery and other junk, and by war's end both states—the entire country, for that matter—had been pretty well scoured for broken-down farm machinery, junked trucks and autos, and old bottles and papers and were as free of trash and junk as they had been for half a century. "There's a lot of scrap metal here," my uncle editorialized in the *Standard*. "Let's get it melted up and on its way to Hitler and his gang. It's sabotage to keep it here where it does no good rusting away to nothing when Uncle Sam needs it so badly."

By the end of November 1942, the 5,350 people in Rawlins County had collected 200 tons of scrap metal, with the town of McDonald accounting for a quarter of it. By Christmas Day, Walt Halligan, the grade school janitor who was also the town scrap dealer, reported that McDonald had turned in another 30 tons of scrap iron, which was half a boxcar load, and two boxcar loads of other metals. The going rate nationally for scrap metal was eight dollars a ton.

The churches, the Lions Club, the Boy Scouts, and other groups periodically organized weekend house-to-house scrap collections that took on something of a festival atmosphere, with a community lunch or supper at the end. It was easy for us kids to fantasize that such things as old rubber inner tubes or hot water bottles from the town might wind up as part of a life raft that would save the life of Little Chet or one of the other boys in the service.

On occasional weekends, in the spirit of hitching free enterprise to support of the war effort, we kids would pull our coaster wagons out to the town dump, which was a gully a mile west and a half mile south of town, and rifle it for anything Walt might conceivably pay a quarter or a half-dollar for. On the way back into town, the temptation to jump on top of the load and ride down the two gentle dips the highway took just outside of town was irresistible. My Montgomery Ward "Chore Truck," a big, heavy-duty wooden wagon, had dual back wheels and removable sideboards, which meant that I could put a pretty hefty load on it. By V-J Day, the wheels' roller bearings were worn down to about half their original diameter, so that the wheels wobbled crazily and the wagon, otherwise perfectly sound, wasn't good for the heavy hauling it once was. That was a significant part of my personal sacrifice in the war against Fascism.

We contributed in other ways as well. In the "Third War Loan Drive," in the fall of 1943, our county was the fourth in the state to exceed its quota of $460,000. Two townships met their quotas two days before the drive officially began. In the "Sixth War Loan Drive," in the winter of 1944–45, Rawlins County raised $407,288, more than $70,000 over its quota. We also gave to the "War Fund Drive," which provided food and medical supplies and other "comfort and entertainments of the troops, Chinese orphans, and Polish refugees." And, we responded to the call of the general secretary of the American Bible Association for 490,000 Bibles for prisoners of war and refugees in Europe.

Some measures were spiritual rather than tangible—for the duration, the church bell was rung daily at 10:00 A.M. to summon the citizenry to "prayer for the boys in the war zone."

☙☙

All in all, World War II wasn't all that bad for most Americans who didn't have to go into the service. For many, in fact, it was a very good time. Suffering was nonexistent compared to the other combatant nations and in many cases the benefits offset the inconveniences. Wartime prosperity, with its immediate and dramatic contrast with the Great Depression and Dust Bowl years, came to rural Kansas as it did to nearly every other part of the country.

The drought began to break in the late 1930s and along with good crops came good prices because of wartime demand. The December 25, 1941, issue of the *Standard* gave farmers some good advice that if followed would have helped their sons and grandsons in the agricultural crisis forty years later.

> The outlook for farm prices is bright. Livestock production is more favorable possibly than wheat. With prices following the same trend as in World War I, the farmer's best insurance against post-war hard-times is to avoid loading up with debt during a period of high prices.

In 1943, northwest Kansas produced its biggest wheat crop to date, with many farmers reporting bumper crops of forty to fifty bushels per acre and a county-wide average of about twenty-five bushels per acre. Several servicemen still in the States training for combat, including Wayne Harper, the Eighty-second Airborne Division paratrooper, were given leave in the summer to come home and help with the harvest.

The war ended, of course, with a bang—the enormous detonation of the atomic bombs over Hiroshima and Nagasaki. At first, few of us could grasp the concept of "that big bomb," as many, including Chester Marshall, the farmer I worked for in the summer of 1945, called it.

Mr. Marshall's youngest son and I were classmates and his second son had been one of my mother's best—and favorite—high school students. The day we got the news of Hiroshima, the four of us had finished the milking and were running the milk through the cream separator in the separator room in the barn. Archer, my mother's student, had taken physics in high school and tried to explain the power of the atom to us. He started out by telling us that atoms were the building blocks of every form of matter, "of the wood in these walls and the metal in this separator," he pointed out. We all looked at the barn walls and the separator and wondered if they were going to explode on us. We listened intently and tried to grasp the concept, but finally Mr. Marshall shook his head and allowed as how it was beyond him. On that occasion at least, he was visibly impressed by his son's education. We all knew what he meant. It was some time before I had even the most rudimentary idea of what nuclear fission and nuclear fusion were about.

As every other town did, McDonald celebrated V-J Day with a bang of its own. At least some of the men did, including most of the servicemen who had returned home by then. It was easily the most spectacular—the only one, actually—mass public drunk I ever witnessed in the town. The drinkers flowed in and out of the pool hall to their cars and pickups, strolled up and down Main Street cheering and hollering, honked their horns, and made refueling runs to the bootlegger's house (Kansas was still legally dry except for 3.2 beer). There were even fireworks around, stored up possibly with the war's end in mind.

The town marshal, a position that looked to me at the time like a sinecure, was a hulking, good-natured man named John Johnson. John's contribution to the V-J Day celebration was to blow the fire siren every hour on the hour rather than his normal schedule of the dinner and supper times of noon and 6:00 P.M. (and, of course, when there was a fire). The button that turned the siren on was in a small, square wooden box mounted right next to the front door of the city building, which housed the jail and the fire engine. The box was kept locked, but John opened it, wedged a stick against the button to hold it down, and let the siren run for three or four minutes every hour.

As John's 8:00 P.M. siren was blowing, I happened to be strolling past, peeked into the box, and without giving it much thought pulled the stick loose. Just as it came free and the siren's wail began descending, I saw, with an electric shock of fright, John's gargoyle-like face staring down at me through the window in the door. I took off at high port with the law just a step behind me. That's the fastest half mile I've ever run and I escaped only because of my youth, adrenaline, and the fact that John was near the age of eligibility for Social Security. Of course, everyone knew everyone else in a town that small, and I knew that my escape was only temporary. A short time later, I came skulking back downtown, unable to resist the pull of the revelry, but when John saw me he only grinned. Who could be mad at anyone in the euphoria of that day? It became a private joke between John and me and he confided that scaring the hell out of a smart-aleck kid was just a little extra icing on what was already a very sweet cake.

And, how sweet it was. The war, of course, had been good economically for our area, just as it had been for most of the rest of the country, and we were full of the relief and pride of victory as well. The nation's war casualties had been comparatively light and most of McDonald's young servicemen returned home having seen parts of the world and undergoing experiences they would never have dreamed of otherwise. The European theater veterans were full of stories about the young women of England and France, and nearly everyone had encountered attractive and exciting girls in the cities of both coasts of the United States and the regions in between.

The Navy veterans of the Pacific, particularly, were replete with tales of lovely young southern California blondes in cream-colored Buick convertibles (it always seemed to be a cream-colored Buick convertible in those fantasies), all dead ringers for Betty Grable and all apparently half-crazed by patriotic fervor and the sight of bell-bottomed trousers. By implication, of course, they all were movie starlets. I avidly eavesdropped on these pool hall and street corner conversations, but even at that tender age I was struck by the fact that the girls all had apparently somehow managed to obtain identical brand-new automobiles even in wartime. For some reason, it was much easier to credit our returning warriors with the conquest of Nazi Germany and imperial Japan than of would-be Betty Grables.

Those young rural Ozark Ikes who hiked off to the war against Fascism from their depression-era farms and Main streets returned to postwar America older, smarter, and far more worldly, however. Towns like McDonald, and American society as a whole, could take enormous pride in the courageous, gallant performance of their young men in World War II. Indeed, the towns and society in general could take pride in themselves.

In his history/memoir *Goodbye Darkness*, William Manchester, a Marine veteran of Okinawa, remarked on what a "tightly disciplined society" the country was and how this contributed to the implacable and victorious war his comrades "in green camouflaged helmets" waged against the Japanese, who entered the war contemptuous of American fighting qualities. The war effort revealed how closely assimilated the often resented and reviled immigrants of the late nineteenth and early twentieth centuries had become. This was true particularly in comparison to the ambiguity in World War I of some groups such as the Germans and the Irish whose loyalties to their homelands still rivaled those to the New World; it is not to ignore, of course, the disgraceful segregation of blacks and discrimination against other groups, including women and Jews. In *A Democracy at War*, William L. O'Neill, a historian at Rutgers University, agreed with Manchester's point, noting also that "the mighty weapon" into which the 12 million citizen-soldiers of the U.S. armed forces were forged was due in part to the fact that the country had "the best educated men of any army" in history:

> The combination of courage and quality displayed by its young fighters was America's secret weapon. . . . The contribution of public schools cannot be overestimated. . . . At much expense, and as a rite not only of passage but almost of citizenship, few school districts failed to ensure that every able-bodied young male had the chance to play football and basketball—and usually other sports also. As a result, the young Americans of that era were team players and fierce competitors, their discipline and will to win having deep community roots. Localism, the curse of effective national government, was at the same time not only intrinsic to American democracy, but a superb maker of men.

That can be said of towns like McDonald to this day. They produced their share of warriors for the Korean and Vietnam conflicts and their community cohesion and discipline are as evident in the 1990s as they were a half century ago.

☙

In America, wars produce social revolution; the bigger the war, the bigger the revolution. Those returning servicemen may still have looked and talked like farm boys, but they had been substantially changed. They had seen a lot of the world for their tender years. Because of this and the GI bill, their expectations had been raised to a degree of which no one had the slightest inkling at the time. The GI bill enabled many who would never have dreamed of it in their wildest prewar imaginings to go off to college in 1946 and 1947 and its revolutionary consequences wouldn't be understood or appreciated until decades later. Those World War II GIs may have exaggerated their exploits ashore on liberty, but there was no exaggerating their impact on postwar America.

The social revolution that followed V-J Day was as profound in its own way as the one after Appomattox. It was to greatly change the nature of the nation, including rural areas such as western Kansas.

CHAPTER TEN

THE POSTWAR PERIOD—TRIUMPH AND TRAVAIL

IN THE MONTHS FOLLOWING V-J DAY, THE PEOPLE OF MCDONALD, Kansas, might have entertained some thought that it was they who had won World War II, with, of course, a little help from the rest of the nation and the Allies. Ebullient over victory in history's greatest war and the emergence of the United States as the number-one global power and reenergized by wartime prosperity, the people of the little town shared the conviction along with the rest of the nation that there was nothing the United States couldn't do.

The aftermath of World War II would have its dark side, of course, with the Cold War and the lethal menace of the nuclear age. The onset of peace, however, also unleashed enormous energies in the U.S. economy and society. In 1946, Uncle Wayne bought a new tractor to replace our Model L Case, a rugged, dependable machine that was about fifteen years old and had served us well during the war. He got a McCormick W9, the biggest tractor in International Harvester's line at the time. He may have chosen it because it was the first one he could get his hands on, which was the basis for many such purchases at that time after four years of wartime shortages. In any event, Wayne, like other farmers embarking on their postwar shopping sprees, was as proud of that tractor as a teenager with his first car. For that matter, like nearly everyone else, he also bought a new car, a Plymouth four-door sedan, as soon as one was available—at that point the Plymouth-Dodge dealer was the only auto agency in town.

Wayne was typical of the rest of the country. Four years of pent-up consumer demand and accumulated buying power ignited an economic boom that, except for occasional short-lived recessions, was unprecedented in its length. It contributed mightily to more than twenty years of national unity that weathered the McCarthy era and the Korean War and was finally ruptured by the Vietnam War. New autos, trucks, tractors, combines, and other machines and appliances were snapped up as fast as they came on the market. The wartime prosperity on the High Plains carried on into the postwar years, fueled by the demand for food in a war-ravaged world.*

The manufacturers eagerly swung back into peacetime production—but there was a period of adjustment. Henry Kaiser, the industrial genius who mass-produced the wartime military cargo transports known as "Liberty Ships," and his partner, Joseph Frazer, introduced two new makes of automobiles, the Kaiser and the Frazer, and typically they beat most of the others to the draw. Materials such as chrome for bumpers, radiator grilles, and trim were still in short supply, however, and for several months a number of brand-new cars, including Kaisers and Frazers, were running around the area sans bumpers and grilles.

⚜

World War II was a cataclysmic event that, among other things, set in motion forces that revolutionized life in the postwar United States, including the High Plains. Among them was the long period of economic growth and prosperity that began with wartime prosperity, abetted by social policy decisions that profoundly widened higher education and home ownership.

Because of the overriding drama of the military and diplomatic action, it is easy to lose sight of domestic policy decisions made during such major wars as World War II and the Civil War. In 1862, the Congress passed two landmark bills, the Homestead and the Morrill acts. The Homestead Act made federal lands in the West available free or at low cost to settlers. With the creation of the land grant system, the Morrill Act gave federal land to states on which to establish colleges and universities to teach agriculture, engineering, and home economics. Their research and educational programs have contributed enormously to the country's agricultural and industrial productivity, and their mandatory ROTC programs have trained a large number of junior officers for the military. The marriage of public policy and dammed-up economic energies was a major contributor to the post–Civil War settling of the continent and the con-

---

*Worry that the country might relapse into another peacetime depression under a Republican president was a major factor in Harry S Truman's stunning reelection victory over Thomas E. Dewey in the 1948 presidential election. This fear was underlined by slumping corn prices, and Truman's winning the farm vote, particularly Iowa, Illinois, Wisconsin, and Minnesota, was a major factor in his triumph.

version of the nation from a rural to an urban, industrialized society in a relatively short time.

The Congress enacted a much more revolutionary program during World War II, the Serviceman's Readjustment Act of 1944, better known as the GI Bill of Rights. The GI bill had a far greater impact on society than the Homestead and Morrill acts, as important as they were. The Homestead Act, as we have seen, never had the impact its backers hoped for because the 160-acre tracts it provided weren't large enough on the High Plains.

The GI bill was enacted partly as a measure of gratitude to the young men and women who went off to the service in World War II and partly to keep them from flooding the job market on demobilization. Whatever the reason, it turned out to be one of the most revolutionary measures in American history, along with the Declaration of Independence, the Constitution, and the Bill of Rights. With its low-interest, no-down-payment housing loans, the GI bill, along with low-interest FHA loans, helped transform the United States from a nation of renters to one of home owners; prior to World War II, only about 20 percent of American families owned their homes. Equally important were the educational benefits— the bill paid a seventy-five-dollar-per-month cash stipend and all costs, including tuition, books, and laboratory fees—which encouraged more than 8 million of the nearly 13 million veterans to either enter or finish college or get some other form of postsecondary schooling.

This demolished the most visible manifestation of class society in this country. Prior to World War II, college for the most part was the province of a relatively narrow, well-to-do segment of society, but the GI bill helped break down that barrier. The wall had already been seriously breached when collective participation in the common war effort, most particularly military service by millions of young Americans from all areas of society, blurred civilian socioeconomic and other class distinctions. In addition, the accumulated buying power stored up during World War II—in 1943, the Treasury Department estimated that Americans had about $70 billion in cash, war bonds, and savings accounts, with very little to spend it on— made postwar consumer goods, including houses and autos, available to nearly everyone. The GI bill gave an enormous boost to this economic egalitarianism by making higher education and its concomitant purchasing power available to all classes.

All over the nation, young men and women who prior to Pearl Harbor wouldn't have dreamed of going to college went trooping off to Harvard, UCLA, Kenyon, and Oklahoma A&M. In McDonald, young men just back from Europe and the Pacific, for whom higher education until then had been nearly as remote a prospect as flying to the moon, packed off to Kansas State University or the University of Kansas instead of settling down as they had expected in a job or on the family farm.

They became doctors, electrical engineers, sales managers, and school-teachers. One of my cousins, James D. Dickenson, attended Kansas State, and another, Billy Dickenson, went to Texas A&M on the GI bill, both getting engineering degrees. Many farm boys got degrees in agriculture at schools like Kansas State and Iowa State, which along with advancements in technology and the land grant colleges' research were factors in the ever-increasing productivity of the farm sector.

Obviously, nothing enlarges the middle class and strengthens society more than education and home ownership. Never has a social investment paid off so handsomely. The World War II GI bill cost an estimated $14.5 billion and the total cost of the program with Korea and Vietnam veterans added was $53 billion through 1982. The resulting increase in productivity in the economy through the upgrading of skills of these millions of young men and women is incalculable. It is difficult to think of an area of the society or the economy whose productivity and effectiveness wasn't boosted substantially.

The enormous social and economic changes wrought by the postwar affluence, which the GI bill helped fuel, made their impact on the High Plains. This affluence, along with technology—particularly the automobile, around which postwar society was formed—radically reshaped the nation. Beginning in 1945, with the end of gasoline and tire rationing, families such as mine could afford to drive the 225 miles west to the Rocky Mountains, where we'd rent a mountain cabin 30 or 40 miles northwest of Denver for a week in August after the wheat harvest and then spend a couple of days in the great metropolis itself. The women would buy school clothes and shop for themselves, and the kids would explore the exotic city—the hotel elevators, streetcars, tall buildings, and waitresses in the hotel coffee shop, who spoke a strange and exotic argot that we never heard from May Heer, owner, cook, and waitress of the City Cafe back home. An order of pancakes was "Stacks!" Two orders with sausage was "Stacks, a pair, with Porky Pig." Two poached eggs on toast was "Adam and Eve on a raft," which titillated us as being slightly risqué and blasphemous. We quickly would descend into such a case of the giggles that we'd have to leave to compose ourselves.

It didn't take much to dazzle a bunch of naive, artless farm kids in those days, but that didn't matter—like the rest of the country we would change. Millions of Americans were seeing new parts of the country as the new affluence and opportunity led to greater mobility and personal freedom. This allowed many to slip the gravitational pull of family, neighbors, friends, and church in their small towns and ethnic neighborhoods and flee the unrelenting scrutiny of their daily lives by the people they knew and loved best. Affluence and the automobile collaborated in the suburbanization of the nation, drawing millions from both the inner cities and the rural countryside.*

⁂

The automobile has been a major part of the revolutionary postwar change. It was a major factor in reshaping the social structure of the United States in the twentieth century and it has had a profound impact on the society of the High Plains as well, not necessarily all to the good. The auto, and then the interstate highways, were instrumental in the pull to the suburbs and their shopping centers. In 1945, there were 25 million automobiles and eight shopping centers in the United States; in 1994, there were nearly 200 million autos and 39,633 shopping centers, the vast majority of which were in suburban areas. Businesses, industries, educational institutions, the increasingly ubiquitous and popular discount stores, all have been drawn to communities on the interstate and other major transportation arteries.

"Industry wants the interstate and an airport," said Henry Cahoj, who farms south of McDonald, has an insurance agency in the county-seat town of Atwood, and served sixteen years as a Rawlins County commissioner. "Interstate 70 [which runs thirty miles south of McDonald and Atwood] is killing the Highway 36 towns." Laverne Goltl also farms south of McDonald and offered a different perspective. "It's fun for the women to shop in Colby at the big discount stores like Wal-Mart," he observed. "My wife likes to go even if she isn't looking for anything in particular." Colby is fifty miles southeast of McDonald, less than an hour's drive even for those who observe the speed limit.

One of the staples of American folklore is that the initial response to the first autos was skepticism and hoots of "Get a horse!" That may have been true in some places, but there is little evidence that it was the case in

---

*It has been argued that the World War II generation's determination that their children would have different experiences than they was a major factor in the counterculture revolution of the 1960s. These parents, particularly, tried to ensure that their children would be shielded from the economic hardships they experienced during the depression and this caused many of the "baby boomer" generation to rebel against the order, affluence—and boredom—of their suburban upbringing.

western Kansas. People who had lived in sod houses, who had plowed, sowed, harvested, and threshed by hand and with horses, and who had spent a good part of a day making the run to town in a horse-drawn buggy didn't have to have a roof fall in on them to comprehend the benefits of the internal-combustion engine. Needless to say, few if any had any notion of the change in their world the auto would cause.

In 1907, the Howard Auto Company in Atwood ran ads pointing out that the Ford automobile was not a will-o'-the-wisp and that there were 16,000 of them in operation in Kansas, whose owners were quite happy with them. This may have been the understatement of the century—the love affair of Americans with their automobiles is not only a staple of the nation's mythology, but a central fact of its history.

The automobile helped enrich the social and cultural life on the High Plains in many ways. With towns now just minutes rather than hours away for farm families, they developed burgeoning cultural and social lives as well as increased commerce. Many built a flourishing theater or theaters, often an opera house that presented light operas (Gilbert and Sullivan were big favorites). Other forms of entertainment included debates, lectures, elocution recitals, concerts, home talent plays, musical recitals, barbershop quartets, minstrel shows, magicians, and basket suppers for which young ladies contributed the dinners and their admirers bid for them. The proceeds went for such worthy causes as the town concert band.

The automobile also became a major source of recreation for young people in an area where entertainment opportunities were relatively scarce. It made movies, dances, athletic events in towns fifty miles away an easy evening's ride; one summer when I was working for my uncles in Rolla, my cousin, Terry Dickenson, and I dated two girls in Liberal, fifty miles distant, which didn't take much more transit time than my current daily commute does. Saturday nights in western Kansas featured a procession of carloads of young people slowly parading up one side of Main Street and down the other with individuals often jumping out of one car to get into another in order to talk to someone; this sort of Main Street parade was the central scene of the movie *American Graffiti,* made, if I understand correctly, in Stockton, California, and I have seen the same phenomenon in downtown Portland, Oregon. Driving to other towns to check out dances and parties was a major staple of entertainment; we also took our dates about three miles south of town where the atmospherics enabled us to pick up WSM, the 50,000-watt clear-channel radio station in Nashville that carried *The Grand Old Opry* on Saturday nights.

The auto became a mobile drinking and talking club and, of course, a bedroom for young lovers.

In the long term, however, the automobile, along with the other technological developments that made life and farming easier and more productive on the High Plains, had a profound downside.

"The slow, lingering, painful demise of Main Street began in the 1920s" and the smallest "never recovered from the setback they suffered in this decade," according to John Fraser Hart and Tanya Bendiksen of the University of Minnesota. "Main Street was the creature of the horse and buggy, and it has been mortally wounded by the automobile. The retail and service functions once performed on Main Street have been shifting up the urban hierarchy to larger and larger places, and especially to the malls and shopping strips that festoon them." Hart and Bendiksen noted that the prairies were penetrated by railroads that depended on the grain trade and that too many small railroad towns were founded. "Their spacing was appropriate for horse-drawn wagons loaded with grain, but they were too close to their competitors when automobiles and trucks replaced horses."

The automobile meant that people in towns like McDonald could shop for groceries, clothing, and other staples not only in the nearby county-seat towns of Atwood and St. Francis, but in larger regional centers such as Goodland, Colby, and McCook, Nebraska, as well. And, as roads and highways improved, the auto connected even the most remote farm family with such distant cities as Denver, Wichita, and Kansas City.

The automobile was introduced on the High Plains with a level of excitement appropriate to its ultimate impact. Accounts at the time indicated that the owner of the first auto seen in McDonald was an entrepreneur who charged the citizens twenty-five cents each for a short excursion around a nearby pasture. Such rides were the first exposure to the auto for many people and one editorial writer concluded that they succeeded in giving "people the auto fever." For most Americans, their first automobile ride was a major adventure. The editorial writer for the Rawlins County *Republican Citizen*, reporting on a trip in June 1910, commented that "at that speed the passengers were principally concerned in [sic] holding the hair on their heads. Just excuse us, about twenty miles an hour is all the swiftness we care for in an auto."

The first automobile in Rawlins County, a ten-horsepower Cadillac, appeared in Atwood, the county seat, in 1904. The first autos purchased in McDonald were bought in 1909 by two leading businessmen, the afore-mentioned Edwin Lyman, who made a fortune as a farmer-rancher and land agent, and E. L. Dobbs, who started out as a clerk and then became owner of the general store and a major landowner. With his son-in-law, Harry Harrison, a like-minded soul, Ed Dobbs made a fortune buying and selling farmland and became a High Plains merchant-prince.

Dealers included a driving lesson in the sale price. The lesson consisted of a few minutes of instruction in a nearby pasture on starting, stopping, and steering. When these basics appeared to have been mastered, the new owner dropped the salesman off at the agency and was on his own. Kansas required auto registration in 1913, with a $5 annual fee, $4.25 of which was earmarked for improving county roads. Driver's licenses were man-dated in 1931, $0.25 for a regular license, $2 for a chauffeur's license (trucks, buses, and other heavy vehicles); like many other farm states, Kansas still issues a restricted license at age fourteen for farm youngsters and a regular, unrestricted license at sixteen.

The first year of auto registration turned up 34,550 autos in the state. With farmers getting good crops and prices, the number of cars in the state increased steadily. In 1914, 49,374 autos were registered; in 1915, there were 72,520, an auto for one in every six families; and in 1916, it jumped to 116,122, one for every four families, with the newspapers re-porting that most farm families in Rawlins County owned an automobile by then. By 1925, 457,033 autos were registered in Kansas and a gasoline tax was enacted to help finance road construction and repair.

In December 1913, American and British teams played a series of auto polo games in Topeka. The newspapers also reported that in the same year the members of the county chapters of the Kansas Anti-Horse Thief As-sociation drove to their county picnics in automobiles and in 1915 the or-ganization voted to extend its protective services to auto owners.

From the beginning, the automobile was news. The McDonald News of December 13, 1907, carried this item: "Allen Shaffer's new auto is laid up in Atwood for repairs. A cylinder was broken, presumably from being froze [sic] up." It was still news a quarter of a century later. The editor of the McDonald Standard of June 1, 1933, reported that he was "privileged to drive a new Chevy, courtesy of Claude Chessmore [the Chevrolet dealer], and the way that baby eats up the roads and hills is nobody's business." The July 4, 1940, edition of the Standard carried a front-page report that "Elmer Halligan has resigned his position at Gustafson's [grocery store] to engage in wheat hauling with a new pickup purchased from the Chessmore Chevrolet Company." Another front-page article began, "Claude Chessmore announces the sale of a new Chevrolet town sedan to Roger Pemberton."

My grandparents bought their first auto, a Dort, in 1913 and the family was never without one thereafter. Their three-mile drive to town, which took twenty minutes or so by horse-drawn buggy or spring wagon, was a matter of five minutes by auto and the twenty-mile ride to the county seat took only a half hour or less.

This, however, is not to say that Grandfather and Grandmother Phipps took easily and naturally to the Age of Henry Ford; their children, in fact, did most of the driving. Shortly after the purchase of the Dort, Grandpa and his four sons, Chet, Asa, Blaine, and Wayne, drove into town, and the boys persuaded Grandpa to drive on the way back. He quickly lost control, however, and the car wound up in a ditch, which fortunately was shallow enough that they could drive out of it. Grandpa explained that the reason for his mishap was the difference between steering the auto and a horse-drawn "header," which was used to cut wheat before combines came into use. The header was steered the way a boat is. It had two main wheels up front and was steered with a single small third wheel that was under the operator's seat at the rear of the machine. The operator turned the header by swinging the rear end in the opposite direction of the turn, the way a boat is steered with a rudder. So, when the car started heading for the side of the road, Grandpa's instinct was to turn the steering wheel in the direction opposite to the way he wanted to go and drove it into the ditch.

Wayne, the youngest, who was only seven at the time, recalled years later how excited and amused he was by his father's mishap. "I couldn't wait to get home and tell mother and the girls about it," he recalled. "I jumped out of the car to go run in the house, but fortunately Blaine grabbed me before I could get started and told me that if I knew what was good for me, I'd keep my mouth shut! That was good advice and I took it."

Grandpa never did master the automobile and his forays brought a whole new dimension of adventure into his family's lives. "Whenever he drove, he scared us all to death," Fern, the youngest of the children, recalled. "I remember one time he and Mother and I drove to Ottawa (Kansas) to visit Anna [my mother, who graduated from Ottawa University in 1926]. I was in the backseat and so scared that I had a blanket over my head and Mother was up front riding with one hand on the emergency brake. And, Dad managed to slide us off the road and into a little streambed which, thank goodness, was empty. It was muddy because there weren't any paved roads in those days, and we were pulled out by a farmer with a team of horses who came along shortly after. Mother was standing by the car lamenting, 'And to think this is my birthday [October 12]!'"

Grandmother fared no better. For all her accomplishments, she never really learned to drive. The only time I ever knew her to even try—I was four or five at the time—was when she had to take a number of her grand-children, including me, into town in the family Terraplane because none of her children, all of whom were grown and out of the house by then, was available. I recall that she agreed reluctantly, only because for some reason we had to get into town and there was no one else.

She took a dirt back road in order to avoid the traffic on U.S. Highway 36, which turned out to be providential. We made it most of the way, but the big machine finally panicked her and we all wound up bumping across a shallow ditch and came to a sudden halt in the field at the side of the road. As a result of the braking, one of my cousins hit his head on the dashboard, and with the kids crying and shrieking loud enough to raise the dead, Grandmother was as distraught as I ever saw her. She somehow managed to maneuver the car the remaining mile and a half or so to town, but she took the pledge on driving right there on the spot. And a fervent pledge it was, too, as that loving soul contemplated the horrible notion that she might somehow inadvertently do harm to one of her brood.

The subsequent generations, however, took to the horseless carriage like ice cream to apple pie. Wayne and Fern learned to drive when they were ten or eleven and had misadventures of their own. "I'd put the car in low gear and drive around the farm," Wayne recalled. "Shifting from low to second worried me because I thought you had to do it real fast. One time when I was about eleven, the car was in town for Perry Reneau to fix, and I went by the shop after school out of curiosity to see if it was ready, which it was. Since no one else in the family was in town, I told Perry that if he could get me started and into second gear, I could take it home. He shifted from low into second, then jumped out, and I moved into the dri-ver's seat, pulled it into high, and headed for home. Well, about half a mile from the farm, two farmers in their wagons had stopped to talk and I had to go into the ditch to get around them. I killed the engine, but started it back up and drove the rest of the way home in low gear."

"We had to learn young," Fern said. "Wayne taught me and we drove Mom and Dad everyplace. I drove them to Rolla [where my mother was teaching school] and out to the farm and everyplace."

So did I. I was nearly crazy with the desire to drive even before I was big enough to see over the steering wheel. During the 1930s and through World War II, we had a series of family cars that Grandmother, Mother, Wayne, and Fern shared—a Hudson Terraplane, a 1940 Chevy coupe, and a 1942 four-door Pontiac, a luxury car, it seemed, purchased just before Pearl Harbor, which served them well through the war. The Terraplane was known as the "Terrible Terraplane." It was prone to "vapor lock," because the hot air from the exhaust manifold heated the fuel line, which caused the gasoline to boil and turn to vapor, blocking the flow of fuel to the carburetor. This always seemed to happen when the women were shopping in St. Francis or some other neighboring town and they'd have to ask some complete stranger for help. With my youthful sensitivities, I cringed with embarrassment and tried to hide on the floor in the backseat.

We also had a farm truck and a pickup. I spent hours sitting in the pickup when it was parked in the backyard, shifting gears, pretending to start and stop and steer and imagining that I was fulfilling my highest ambition—to haul wheat to town. When my cousin Terry Dickenson and I finally realized that ambition a few years later at age fifteen, we wheeled those trucks into town and onto the elevators' weighing scales feeling as dashing as fighter pilots. I'm not sure that if his dad and the rest of my uncles realized that in our minds we were emulating Hotshot Charlie, the fighter jock in "Terry and the Pirates," they would have entrusted us with those 120-bushel loads.

Nor would they have been reassured if they knew how we used our autos for recreation. One bright, moonlit winter night when I was a freshman in high school at McDonald, three or four carloads of us came up with the brilliant idea of playing auto hide-and-seek out on the dirt back roads southeast of town, with the headlights off, of course. Two of us narrowly missed a head-on collision when we saw the moonlight glint off the windshield of the approaching car, which provided me, at least, with the fright of that particular academic year.

Terry was born to be a fighter pilot and as a teenager seemed to regard driving at less than 85 mph as some sort of venial sin. It didn't take us long to get to our dates in Liberal that summer when we were eighteen, particularly since he had a 1950 Oldsmobile 88 two-door Rocket sedan, which was aptly named. It had the justly famed Olds V-8 engine, which he'd modified to boost its compression ratio and performance. One day when we'd been rained out of the fields, we set out to Guyman, Oklahoma, which is thirty-five or forty miles south of Rolla. He'd heard about a guy who had a Buick Roadmaster that was supposed to be hot stuff. We found him and had a two-car drag race on a paved back road south of Guyman. We were ahead up to 110 mph, but the Buick took us at 115. As copilot, my duty was to push down on Terry's right knee to keep the pressure on the accelerator when his leg began quivering with the tension. The race was mutually judged a draw.*

We were imbued with our love of the auto from childhood. In 1943, the summer I was eleven, I "helped" a friend, Russell Briney, drive his dad's GMC pickup to their farm near Goodland, fifty miles to the southwest, part of it on U.S. Highway 36, which was the autobahn of our time and place. Russell didn't need any help in the least and I wouldn't bet the rent that he particularly wanted my company, but I was not deterred. My mother was out of town at the time and I managed to persuade Grandmother to let me visit him for a couple of days. The Brineys were too polite to demur, but it meant that either they or someone in my family would have to drive me the fifty miles back to McDonald. I remember feeling a twinge of guilt about this while I was cooking up the deal, but I was not to be denied: *I wanted to drive that truck!* The siren song of powerful machinery, the tractors, trucks, and combines, kept me coming back to work for my uncles summer after summer despite the hard work, discomfort of heat and dust, and boredom of long, long hours in the field.

Along with most others, however, I had no inkling of the change the internal-combustion engine and these machines that so fascinated me was wreaking on our familiar and seemingly immutable lives.

✻

Kansas shared proportionally more in the postwar affluence because its per-capita income lagged well behind the national average all through the Great Depression and the Dust Bowl. The insatiable wartime demand for food products combined with bumper crops helped close this gap during World War II and the worldwide demand for food continued unabated after the war. In April 1946, citing the "desperate need to keep starvation at a minimum" in war-devastated Europe, the federal government offered a thirty-cent-per-bushel subsidy to farmers who would deliver their wheat to the elevators by May 25, 1946. In May of 1947, citizens were asked to donate to a food collection to meet "grave world problems" of starvation;

---

*More than twenty-five years later, I wrote a column about this in the *Washington Star* and Aunt Opal, Terry's mother, visited my mother shortly after it appeared. Mother told me that they looked at each other and shook their heads and agreed that it probably was just as well that they didn't know everything their idiot sons had been up to. At the time I wrote the article, I had suspicions along that line of activity about my teenage stepson, John Lerch, who in later years confirmed them.

crops in northern Europe had suffered winterkill, and rice production in Asia was still lagging. Rawlins County farmers responded by donating a boxcar load of wheat, 1,120 bushels.

This demand was matched by good crops and good weather. The 1947 wheat crop in Kansas was the largest until then, 286.7 million bushels, 14 percent larger than the previous high in 1931, and the 1946 crop was the third largest. The western one-third of Kansas got more than twenty-five inches of rainfall in 1946, the fourth largest ever recorded. The towns shared in this prosperity; McDonald's population grew from 377 in 1946 to 411 the following year, and the town had a housing shortage.

Few understood it at the time, but all these factors were inexorably speeding the alteration if not destruction of the social fabric of rural areas such as ours because of population loss or, in some cases, slower growth. The postwar prosperity lasted for about five years and the population spurt proved to be short-lived.

From 1945 to 1990, the nation's population grew from about 140 million to nearly 250 million, an increase of about 75 percent. During the same time, the population of Kansas increased from about 1.79 million to about 2.36 million, or 32 percent. Most of this increase was in the eastern one-third of the 105 counties; the population of Johnson County, a Kansas City suburb, increased fourfold between 1950 and 1970 and alone accounted for more than half the statewide increase in that period.

Many business and civic leaders in western Kansas were rightly apprehensive about what the future held in store for their region. In November 1946, the towns of northwest Kansas sent representatives to a statewide conference on the issues and problems of growth and development in the area's future. Two months later, the *McDonald Standard* had a front-page cartoon showing young men and women boarding a train and carrying their suitcases, one of which was labeled "Kansas' Ablest Youth Seeking Opportunity Elsewhere." The line at the top of the cartoon was the World War II slogan "Is This Trip Really Necessary?"

The populations of sixty-four counties, mostly those in the western two-thirds of the state, declined significantly after the war, however. The population of Rawlins County, an area of 1,080 square miles, declined from 6,618 in 1940 to 3,404 in 1990, a loss of 23 percent, and that of Mc-Donald dwindled from more than 400 to less than 200. In 1946, there were eleven implement dealers in Rawlins County; in 1991, forty-five years later, there were only two, and by 1994, there was just one. In 1946, McDonald had four gasoline stations (and three that had closed down), three grocery stores, a drugstore, a clothing store, a hardware store, a movie theater, a barbershop, three implement dealers, an auto dealer, a pool hall and card room, and three restaurants. Now there is one filling station, out on the highway, one grocery store, and one combination restaurant–bar–pool hall.

In addition, the average age for those living in both the state and county rose steadily because young people were forced to migrate in search of economic opportunity as the size of farms grew inexorably and their numbers contracted. This pattern of small towns dying, the number of farms decreasing, and the larger towns consolidating and growing is ongoing throughout the country's farm regions, and it accelerated during the agricultural depression of the 1980s.

Each summer after the war when I returned to western Kansas to work on my uncles' farms, there would be the news that two or three farmers who had been born and raised in the area and had survived the depression and Dust Bowl had been forced to sell out and move, most often to Denver or Boulder or Fort Collins or somewhere along the front range of the Rocky Mountains in Colorado. Many took jobs as welders, mechanics, auto parts salesmen, and the like, and entered into completely different lives.

In 1945, more than 20 percent of the nation's population still lived on farms. The farm population of America had begun shrinking around the turn of the century, however. In 1900, 30 million people, 42 percent of the population, lived on 5.7 million farms with an average size of 147 acres (from 1905 to 1920, my grandparents prospered on a 310-acre farm to which they added 160 acres in 1915). This number steadily dwindled, however, and the trend was greatly accelerated during the 1930s by the Great Depression and the Dust Bowl. After World War II, the contraction of the farm population quickened. More than a million farmers a year moved to town during the 1950s and by the 1960s more than 17 million had moved off the farm in the postwar era.

By 1982, the number of farms nationally had declined to 2.2 million with an average of 440 acres and only 2.2 percent of the population; 5.4 million people lived on them. After the farm depression of the 1980s, this number had dropped to fewer than 5 million people. In Rawlins County, the number of farms in 1989 was 540 compared to 866 in 1946, a decline of nearly 40 percent. By the end of the 1980s, however, about three-quarters of the survivors were in good financial shape with a good debt-to-asset ratio.

As always, the major factor was technology and increased productivity that outstripped population growth and domestic demand. This phenomenon dates back to the post–Civil War period when the amount of land in agriculture and farm output more than doubled, but the population increased at less than half that rate. Production of crops such as corn and wheat also rose after the turn of the century because the replacement of the horse by the internal-combustion engine eventually freed up about 65 million acres that had been planted to fodder for the animals, primarily oats. Despite some periods of prosperity, particularly in the first two decades of the twentieth century just prior to and during World War I and in the 1940s, during and after World War II, American farmers generally suffered more bad times than good.

⚜︎

It was World War II rather than the New Deal that pulled the economy, including the farm sector, out of the Great Depression, but the high wartime and postwar prices declined in the 1950s. This prompted the reactivation of acreage-control programs that were still on the books but had been unused because of the demand created by the war effort. The debate on whether to allow farm prices to be set by the open market or to involve government support ended with the passage of the Food and Agriculture Act of 1965, a part of the blizzard of Great Society legislation, which made price supports contingent on acreage restrictions.

The attempt to stabilize prices and reduce surpluses by restricting production failed because farmers consistently managed to offset their acreage reductions by increasing production through the use of improved machinery, fertilizers, herbicides, and pesticides, and the development of improved strains of corn and wheat. Average per-acre production of small grains and soybeans increased by as much as 50 percent. Farmers also took their least productive ground out of production.

In addition to the steady postwar attrition of the numbers of farmers in western Kansas, there was an additional shakeout because of the drought years of 1956–57. It was in the 1950s that towns like McDonald began noticeably declining.

"With the population of 1947–'48," recalled Owen Wingfield, the president of the Peoples State Bank, "Chet's Cafe was so packed for mid-morning and mid-afternoon coffee and at lunchtime that people were waiting to get in. We had a housing shortage and moved old one-room schoolhouses and farmhouses in from the country. But after 1950, we started declining. In the mid-fifties, a reporter from the McCook Gazette came over and wrote a story that we were a dying town. Everyone was furious about it, but unfortunately it looks as though he knew what he was talking about."

There was an even bigger decrease in the 1980s. The 1960s and 1970s were years of good crops, prosperity, and rising land prices. Many young men all over the Midwest were getting started, replacing older farmers. Unfortunately, they were buying in at a time of peak prices for land, live-stock, machinery, and other capital investments and astronomical interest rates. They then got sandbagged by the recession of the 1980s and the re-turn to normal of land prices, which had doubled and tripled in some areas. The number of farms in Rawlins County dropped by more than 14 percent during the decade, from 630 in 1979 to 540 in 1989, and McDon-ald lost a half-dozen businesses: Hattie West's notions and grocery store, Alfred Buck's drugstore, Fred Jenik's tractor-repair and John Deere–parts shop, the Copper Penny Cafe, Elsie Howard's clothing store, and the hardware and appliance store owned and operated by my uncle Vic and aunt Margaret Ritter. In addition to small-town businesses, many rural banks were forced to close.

"We lost a lot of people, particularly young people, during the 1980s," Owen Wingfield recalled in 1994. Somehow, the hard times never seem to let up. "And the last four years have been tough," he continued. "We had the late May freeze [a hard freeze on May 26, 1992, which devastated everything—wheat, corn, milo, sunflowers]. We had a dry year. Then there was the big hail in 1989." That hail was like nothing anyone had ever seen. It not only destroyed the fragile grain crops, but it killed hun-dreds of mature elm and cottonwood trees, stripping them of leaves, bark, and branches.

Developments in the 1970s and 1980s showed what a mockery the open market concept can be for farmers and how difficult it is for them to escape the cycle of boom and bust. Droughts and poor crops around the world and the purchase of large quantities of grain by the Soviet Union in the early 1970s boosted world market prices for farm products. At one giddy point, the price of wheat was a record five dollars a bushel. Inflation drove down the value of the dollar relative to other currencies, which made U.S. exports attractive. The Nixon and Carter administrations, eager to cut the trade deficit, encouraged farm production. Exports increased by more than 8 percent and the acreage planted to corn, wheat, and soy-beans rose by more than 50 percent during the 1970s. Agricultural land values soared in the Midwest and farm debt on land and machinery pur-chases, secured by these inflated values, tripled during the decade.

As sure as death and taxes, however, bust followed boom in the farm sector. The Federal Reserve Board's decision in 1979 to wring the infla-tion out of the economy by limiting credit drove up interest rates, which was disastrous for overextended farmers. U.S. exports suffered when President Carter cut off grain sales to the Soviet Union in retaliation for the invasion of Afghanistan. In addition, global production increased (the European Community countries also were overproducing because they heavily subsidized their farmers) and the increasingly large federal budget deficits of the Reagan administration helped drive the value of the dollar up, which made U.S. products more expensive and therefore less exportable. Hundreds of thousands of American farmers went bankrupt during the 1980s.

Large corporations such as farm implement manufacturers also suffered as machinery sales plummeted by nearly 90 percent in the 1980s. Tractor sales dropped by 40 percent, from 166,000 in 1980 to 95,000 in 1986, and the bottom fell out of combine sales, down by nearly 75 percent, from 25,760 to less than 7,000 during the same period. International Harvester and the J. I. Case Company were forced to merge and manufacturing centers such as the Quad Cities—Rock Island and Moline, Illinois, and Davenport and Bettendorf, Iowa (International Harvester)—and Waterloo, Iowa (John Deere and Caterpillar), were devastated. Once again, farmers were confronted with the reality that as much as they might prefer an open market, prices for their products stayed the same or declined on the world market while prices of their supplies, fuel, machinery, and fertilizer, steadily rose. Once again, American farmers found themselves pawns of political, economic, fiscal, and diplomatic policies over which they had no control.

CHAPTER ELEVEN

LIFE ON MAIN STREET

ALTHOUGH LIFE ON THE HIGH PLAINS HAS BEEN GREATLY CHANGED AND substantially enhanced in the twentieth century by technology such as the automobile, electricity, radio, and television, in many ways it has remained resistant to cultural changes. A small-town society is remarkably cohesive and mutually supportive. The rites of family gatherings, of church, of observance of holidays, and of socializing haven't changed a great deal in rural towns since the turn of the century.

Christmas, of course, is the most intense and anticipated of the nation's holidays and is the source of many activities in small towns during the season. Because the Fourth of July coincides with the wheat harvest in Kansas, the adults are absorbed by it and the observance of Independence Day is left to the young—and their firecrackers. Halloween has always been a favorite with young males because it provides a rationalization for antisocial, antiestablishment rebellion, all in the name of hallowed tradition, of course.

Drinking on the High Plains has its rites and ceremonies, as it does anyplace, and for some, unfortunately, represents a rite of passage. Kansas has an interesting history vis-à-vis drinking. Almost from the beginning it was a leader in prohibition, both statewide and nationally, and remained legally dry long after most other states had legalized and rationalized the sale of alcohol. As a frontier state, however, it also had a history of hard drinking in certain areas, particularly the cow towns and in the most sparsely populated regions. This was true on much of the High Plains, and I have always thought, after living in cities, that it had a great deal to do with the relative lack of other social opportunities.

"GOD BLESS US, EVERYONE!"

There is something about the intimacy of a small rural town that imparts a particular intensity to holidays; you can't escape the celebration of the holidays even if you want to. This intimacy magnifies an already intense holiday such as Christmas. To a great extent, it is the powerful bond of community and extended family, which enables us to share in each other's preparations and anticipations, that heightens the experience. When I was growing up, Christmas and Thanksgiving dinners with extended families and friends were major events of the year. Many were so large that there had to be a second "kids'" table for the youngsters; being relegated to this was like being exiled to Siberia for teenagers and preteens, and my cousins and I couldn't wait to be promoted to the "grown-ups'" table, which became a sort of rite of passage in itself.

At Christmas, the colored lights and decorations on the stores and homes contrasted dramatically with the bleak winter prairie landscape. There were parties, friends and family from out of town, charity bazaars, and the opportunity to join one of the caroling groups that trudged around town in the snow, pausing in front of each house to render a carol and solicit for some good cause or another. I remember being awakened at six or six-thirty one lovely, snowy Christmas morning when I was about eight or nine by a chorus of high school students singing "Angels We Have Heard on High." "Santa" (Mother and Grandmother Phipps), hearing me stirring, had to do a little last-minute stirring themselves to get the final, unwrapped gifts from the North Pole under the tree before I could get downstairs, knowing that the long-awaited day had started and there was no way to turn it back.

There were several school and church plays and musical programs, which gave everyone the opportunity to be a shepherd or a wise man or an angel. The teenage Sunday school classes one year put on a somewhat off-beat play for the season, entitled *Joseph and His Coat of Many Colors*, which was, in part, about the plot against him by his jealous brothers. There was a certain poignancy in the casting. Bruce Cole, the boy the teachers chose to play Joseph, had a stutter, which he subsequently overcame as an adult. As a child, however, this made him the victim of the teasing and cruelty of which children are so capable. The teachers weren't aware of this, but we kids were, and we watched with fascination as "Joseph's" tormentors acted out their real-life roles in the play. This one time, at least, Bruce prevailed, reminding us once again that there is a merciful God, after all.

My strongest and fondest memory of Christmas in Kansas, however, is

of the community production of *A Christmas Carol* we put on in 1942. I
don't know who came up with this inspired idea, but the high school English teacher produced and directed it.

One of the great benefits of a small-town community is the relative lack
of estrangement between adults and young people. This begins with the
need for children to help their parents with the work on the farm or in the
business, beginning at an early age, and the fact that by the time they're
teenagers rural youngsters are doing grown-ups' work. They want to become grown-ups and aren't as susceptible to the alienated and isolated
youth society that is the norm in so many areas elsewhere.

Recalling this production also is a reminder of what a pleasure it is to
put on a play, the satisfaction of seeing it come together as the cast settles
into their roles, and how the anticipation and excitement build as opening
night approaches. Putting on a play with adults obviously gave us youngsters a shared experience with them that we wouldn't have had otherwise
even in that community. Normally, we performed plays with our classmates; the high school juniors and seniors put on separate class plays and
never the twain did meet.

In *A Christmas Carol,* the youngest player was a fourth-grader, playing
one of the Cratchit children. I, as Tiny Tim, was in the sixth grade. The
oldest, in his sixties, was the Reverend J. W. Coppoc, who played Scrooge.

"Play" is hardly the word for the minister's rendition of the role. He was
a Baptist, a clergyman of no uncertain or tentative turn of mind. If you
liked your religion "with the bark on," as my great-uncle Charlie used to
put it, the Reverend J. W. Coppoc's was the pulpit for you. He knew that
Lucifer relentlessly stalked the streets of McDonald, Kansas, in a thousand guises and he shared this insight with everyone. No one ever had to
wonder what was on his mind; if he hadn't seen you in church in a while,
he wasn't bashful about mentioning it.

And, when as Scrooge, he pronounced Christmas a "humbug," the audience had no doubt that the spirit of the holiday was being sorely tested,
on that stage at least. There was no question that poor Bob Cratchit
would pay a fearsome price for using Christmas as a poor excuse to pick
that man's pocket every twenty-fifth of December. Nor did the Reverend
Mr. Coppoc need any coaching on how to deal with Scrooge's nephew,
Fred, played by Gus Hesselius, the International Harvester implement
dealer and hardware store owner, and his friends. These worthies, like Bob
Cratchit, also were soft on Christmas and had the temerity to approach
Scrooge on Christmas Eve to solicit him for charity. The minister treated

these interlopers the way he did the members of his congregation whom he saw in the pews just once a year, at Easter—with the contempt he felt they so richly deserved ("Are there no poorhouses" to which the needy could be dispatched? Scrooge responded angrily.)

But when he pleaded with Marley's ghost, "Mercy! Dreadful Apparition, why do you trouble me?" there was no question that this was a man sore afraid. And when the Ghost of Christmas Future showed Scrooge his newly placed, snow-swept tombstone, it occurred to me, watching from the wings in awe, that the Reverend Mr. Coppoc's roar of anguish and terror may have intruded on the profane pastimes of the denizens of the pool hall and beer joint all the way across town from the high school auditorium. On further reflection, I concluded that the minister may have conveyed as much about mortality and eternity to the audience in that scene as in all his sermons. That particular Scrooge's conversion to the Christmas spirit, of which in the Reverend Mr. Coppoc's rendition there was no doubt, probably was the best illustration of the Christian principle of redemption that any of us would be privileged to see.

The casting of Marley also was inspired. He was played by Harry Harrison, a town merchant prince, who probably died a millionaire but undoubtedly went to a better reward than Marley. "I wear the chain I forged in life," Harry intoned as he rattled Marley's chains. "I made it link by link and yard by yard. . . . In life my spirit never roved beyond the narrow limit of our money-changing hold." Some in the audience later sniffed that Harry didn't need a script for those lines, but even at the age of ten I knew envy when I saw it.

The rest of the cast included a high school teacher, my grade school teacher, a couple of farmers, several high school students, and a scattering of grade school kids. My uncle Wayne played Fezziwig, the youthful Scrooge's warmhearted and generous employer. A farmer and owner and editor of the local weekly newspaper, Wayne was not normally at a loss for words, but on opening night he suffered a classic case of stage fright and blew his lines spectacularly (due to popular demand the production ran two consecutive nights). When the Ghost of Christmas Past takes Scrooge back to his youth when he was in Fezziwig's employ and they revisit the scene of Fezziwig's annual Christmas Eve office party, Fezziwig is supposed to call on the musicians to strike up "Sir Roger de Coverly." At this point, Wayne lost it. Completely. A stricken look came over him as his mind went blank, and there was a long, expectant wait that in that packed high school auditorium seemed an eternity. Finally, in terminal desperation, Wayne managed to gasp out an ad lib from the mid– twentieth century: "Play something hot!"

Bob Cratchit was played by a high school senior, Gerald Mann, a tall, lanky youth who looked the way I imagined Cratchit did. A year later, Gerald was on his way to England and the Eighth Air Force. As Tiny Tim, it seemed clear to me that I was the star of the drama and I was a bit puzzled that I didn't have more speaking lines. "God bless us, everyone" didn't put an undue strain on even my mental resources and by way of compensation I hammed up the role unconscionably, waving my crutch with a vigor that belied Tim's feeble condition.

"TRICK OR TREAT!"

Each Halloween when I hand out candy to the costumed tots out trick-or-treating, generally accompanied at a discreet distance by their parents, I can't help thinking how things have changed. A lot of people consider it a nuisance, but I like it—the kids are cute in their enjoyment of their costumes and their ritual of pretending to terrorize the adults (they move past the pretending stage a few years later when they become teenagers) and by evening's end they've made me feel a little better about the world.

But I'm always tempted to respond, "Trick!" and see what they do. When I was a kid and we were too old to go out in costumes, generally as we entered our teens, "trick or treat" meant exactly that—it was a challenge that we hoped people would take. Some did because, at least back in those days, there was a percentage of grouches in the population who believed, with some justification, that the whole thing was a bit of nonsense they shouldn't have to put up with. Actually, in a town that small (about 400 population at the time) we knew who they were. Word got around. And, of course, they knew who we were.

In those days, the 1940s, there still were homes that had outhouses instead of indoor plumbing. They were always the first target and in our black little hearts there always lurked the hope that we'd tip one over that had some unfortunate soul in it. Every year there would be a couple of guys who reported that they'd caught someone that way, but like high school boasts of sexual conquests, I generally listened to them with skepticism but kept my mouth shut.

If there was no outhouse, we'd soap car and house windows, undo clotheslines, take gates off their hinges, and tip over mailboxes or fence sections (we never, or almost never, destroyed things, just moved them around a little). When I was in grade school, I heard the high school guys brag about hitting the teachers' and the principal's houses. Setting fire to some noxious substance—cow manure, for instance—on the front porch, then knocking on the front door and fleeing was regularly reported, but I never witnessed it. I also suspected that most of those reports were greatly exaggerated.

This harassment of innocent citizens was just the warm-up, however. The major Halloween night's work was rearranging the town. My first experience with this was the Halloween of 1945, when I was a freshman in high school. World War II had just ended and like the rest of the nation we were full of ourselves, flushed with victory and prosperity. Many veterans were back home, young and full of energy, many still celebrating the war's end and their safe return at every opportunity. Halloween obviously was as good an occasion as any.

At about 9:00 P.M., we all started coming in from our neighborhood forays and congregated on main street—high school boys, veterans, young farmers happy to have an excuse to come to town and socialize in the middle of the week. The first order of business was to organize a motorcade—a raiding party, actually—to Bird City, nine miles west on U.S. Highway 36. Bird was our archrival whom we were to encounter three weeks later in our annual season-ending Thanksgiving high school football game. We wanted the goalposts from the Bird City High School football field, which, for our purposes, was conveniently located on the edge of town, away from the lights and people on Main Street. The goalposts were made of wood and with a couple of ropes and pickups it was easy to snap them off at their concrete bases, load them up, and steal off into the night. Back home, we made a victory bonfire of them in the middle of our own football field, vowed to do terrible things to their football team three weeks hence (as it turned out, they did terrible things to us, cleaning our clocks by a score of 32 to 0), and then got down to serious Halloween business.

The railroad track and main street intersect on the south end of town right next to the highway, and one young vet, just back from Europe, who had been a leader of the Bird City foray, thought it would be a marvelous idea to move a boxcar so that it blocked entry to the town from the highway. One rationale, a spurious one of course, was that it would be protection against a retaliatory raid by Bird City because it blocked the main entrance into town.

Since the operators of the grain elevators had an old John Deere tractor to move boxcars around, this was easy. Fortunately for us, it didn't take a rocket scientist to crank up a John Deere. Main street runs north and south on the west part of town and our football field was on the east side. At some point, while we were engrossed with the boxcar, the boys from

Bird City, not surprisingly, sneaked in the east end of town, pulled down our goalposts, and had their own bonfire.

We, of course, had become too intent on moving everything that wasn't fastened down into the middle of main street to care about Bird City. The John Deere and International Harvester dealers parked their new implements on vacant lots on the east side of main street. It was child's play, appropriately enough, for a group to push each piece of machinery across the sidewalk and over the curb into the middle of the street, or to pull the larger ones with a pickup.

The implements were invariably joined by a couple of old outhouses from the alleys behind the stores, relics that no one had ever gotten around to removing. Then came a couple of tractors parked on the block behind the stores, which we towed with a pickup in the interest of stealth. By the time we had moved everything onto main street that wasn't anchored down, you could hardly walk down it, let alone drive a vehicle on it.

This didn't take long, either. And while the unsuspecting town fathers and the town marshal slept the sleep of the just and virtuous, we admired our handiwork, with the older members of our party drinking a toast to a good, dishonest day's (or night's) work. Then they toasted V-J Day. Then V-E Day. Then D-Day. When it looked as though they were going to make it all the way back to the Battle of Agincourt, I went home.

To my mother's chagrin, my uncle Vic Ritter, who was a partner in the International Harvester dealership, appeared at our back door about seven o'clock the next morning to conscript me for a work detail. The town merchants didn't know who all the guilty parties were, of course, but they figured correctly that if they rousted all the high school boys in town, including their own sons and nephews, it would be simple justice for most of them. Not all the high school guys dragooned into the press-gang were culpable, of course, and the town fathers couldn't finger the vets and young farmers—and wouldn't have, anyway—but as they succinctly noted, in response to protests, life sometimes is unfair.

It was worth every minute of it.

That night established a tradition that was carried on in the subsequent years and became more interesting. The town fathers sensibly concluded that an ounce of prevention was called for and had the town marshal swear in a number of temporary deputies to patrol the town, beginning at sunset. This didn't have the deterrent effect they'd hoped for, but it did result in a number of culprits spending the night in the town jail. This at least had the virtue of ensuring that the guilty parties got stuck with the cleanup detail. What took the steam out of Halloween in McDonald was the removal of all the outhouses when the sewer system was put in, in 1985.

Things just haven't been the same since.

THE GLORIOUS FOURTH?

The Fourth of July, truth be told, wasn't much of a commemoration in northwest Kansas. Not that we weren't patriotic, far from it, but it came right at the beginning of wheat harvest, which started about the first of July and crowded everything else out. The adults were too busy to indulge in the traditional parades and patriotic oratory.

So, it was left to the kids who were too small to work on the harvest crews to take up the slack, which they (we) did quite well, at least as far as creating noise was concerned. In the spirit that made America great, we made every effort to blow our fingers off with a variety of cherry bombs and cannon crackers. I came close a number of times because of my proclivity for absentmindedness. I would sometimes light a firecracker and then become so engrossed by the surrounding activities I'd almost forget to throw it. During World War II, we liked to pretend that they were hand grenades, and in our hands they certainly were potentially lethal, to ourselves at least.

If the town sounded a bit like World War II, we tried to make it look a little like it too. During the war, which everyone followed avidly, we built rubber band–powered model airplanes, mostly of Allied planes like the Mustang and the Spitfire but also Japanese Zeros and Messerschmitt 109s. At some point, we would get bored with putting cherry bombs under empty tin cans and blowing them into the air or dropping them into empty bottles and jars (this held our interest longer, since our parents specifically forbade it because the bottles could shatter and spread shrapnel, which stoked our parents' suspicions that we didn't have sense enough to come in out of the rain, let alone consider the idea that anything could ever happen to us with fireworks). At that point, it seemed like a terrific idea to glue the cherry bombs and cannon crackers to the model airplanes' bellies, wind up the propellers, light the fireworks, and launch the planes into their balsa and tissue paper Valhalla. Whatever value our destruction of our Zeros and Messerschmitts might have had to the war effort was offset by the fact that we invariably wound up destroying our P-51s, Corsairs, Spitfires, and P-40s as well.

"Vote Dry, Drink Wet!"

In the 1986 off-year election, the voters of Kansas, thinking of God-only-knows-what and obviously ignoring their state's history, passed a referendum legalizing liquor-by-the-drink in the Sunflower State.* It was county option, which meant that a lot of counties—including Rawlins—did not choose to be part of the debauchery.

At the time, I offered a silent prayer along the line of "Forgive them, Lord, for they know not what they do," because frankly, I didn't think the state was ready for liquor-by-the-drink. I thought that Carrie Nation, who I assumed was rotating furiously in her grave, knew what she was doing when she took the hatchet to the Kansas saloons in her famous late-nineteenth-century crusade against John Barleycorn.

As did the other frontier states, Kansas had its share of hard drinkers, in great part because often there was little else to do for recreation. Unlike most of its neighbors, however (Oklahoma being an exception), Kansas constantly attempted to thwart its tosspots. In 1881, Kansas voted itself dry with a state amendment that prohibited the manufacture, sale, and consumption of alcoholic spirits and then led the drive that resulted in national prohibition in 1919. When prohibition was repealed, Kansas allowed the sale of beer both across the bar and in package form, but not the hard stuff and not even wine.

Despite the state's history as a leader for prohibition, it wasn't evident to a lot of people that prohibition was any more successful in Kansas than elsewhere—Will Rogers's famous line was that "Kansans will vote dry as long as they can stagger to the polls."† The people of Kansas picked up on this and the widespread joke was that "Kansas votes dry and drinks wet."

Drinking in Kansas was not the type of social drinking associated with *The New Yorker* magazine, involving some lounge lizard with slicked-back hair holding a cocktail glass by the stem and trying to impress some Upper East Side socialite in a strapless evening gown with his chatter about the Riviera and his stock portfolio and coming up to see his etchings, although if we'd known what that meant, we could certainly have identified

---

*Liquor-by-the-drink refers to selling mixed drinks, such as highballs and cocktails, as well as beer and wine across the bar. Kansas already had enacted county option on package sales of bottles, six-packs, cases, and so forth in stores where consumption on the premises was not allowed. The distinction is sometimes referred to as "on-premise" and "off-premise" sales.

†Will, an Oklahoman, knew whereof he spoke. The Kansas Bar Association used to meet each May and when the county attorneys held their caucus it fell to the officers of their group to provide the refreshments. So, certain sheriffs would collar their local bootleggers in late April and turn the contraband over to their county attorneys for "disposal under the law." Their favorite speaker was a lawyer from Fort Scott whose topic, year in and year out, was "Confiscated Liquor. A Sacred Trust!"

with him on it. Drinking in rural Kansas involved a bunch of good old boys searching for an alternative to the usual Saturday night of watching the haircuts and snooker games in the pool hall. This frequently came down to chipping in to buy a jug.

Until 1948, when the state opened up somewhat by legalizing package sales of hard liquor, also county option, this meant going to the town bootlegger's house, generally waiting until after sundown to gain the cover of darkness. For people who really didn't want to be spotted going to the bootlegger's, getting supplied for Saturday night could be considerably more complicated than that, however.

One alternative system that worked for a while before World War II involved an agreement between a bootlegger and a consumer under which the goods were dropped in the weeds at the base of one of the telephone poles that ran along U.S. Highway 36. Each customer was assigned a pole (the third one east of Four Mile Road, for instance) and since there were hundreds of poles between towns, the bootleggers could accommodate a lot of customers. A farmer didn't have to drive all the way into town, just out to the highway. The problem was that these drop points soon became common knowledge and thieves and practical jokers got into the act. This eventually put an end to that particular distribution system, but not before causing strained relationships between several vendors and their customers.

Legalization of package sales of hard liquor, of course, rendered the entire question moot and made life for the thirsty somewhat simpler, if less colorful. Kansas didn't end its prohibition of liquor without a struggle, however. Glenn Cunningham, the great National Hall of Fame miler who was from Elkhart, just twenty miles west of Rolla, led a "Temperance Tornado" in an attempt to defeat the measure. Young people, mostly associated with church Sunday school classes, toured the state in trucks with their tents and bedrolls, holding temperance rallies. A couple of my cousins were part of it for a while, but at age sixteen I didn't have particularly strong views on temperance.

If the truth be told, I never thought the new law would make all that much difference. It didn't seem that it made drinking all that much easier than it had been with the bootleggers and it certainly didn't change the ritual of drinking. In the 1940s and 1950s when I was a teenager, such brand names as Four Roses and Three Feathers were favored, partly because they were cheap—very cheap, and deservedly so—partly because people didn't know any better. They drank those brands with Coca-Cola or 7UP and not with water or soda. For excellent reason.

I subsequently learned that these brands were known generically as "blends" and were distilled from the last of the sludge in the barrels, with some flavorings and other ingredients added. I was always curious as to what "flavorings" these might have been because the taste of these blends was so vile that it was impossible to drink them straight—a widespread joke was, "I was thirty years old before I learned that they made whiskey that you could drink straight without gagging." Four Roses and the like may actually have had some redemptive social value because anyone for whom they were the first exposure to the demon rum might well have considered that it was not a practice worth pursuing.

If someone wanted a shot of Four Roses, say, straight out of the bottle, he was well advised to have a bottle of pop as a chaser in hand to combat the whiskey's taste before his stomach turned over. This, however, was not considered suave.

Suave (pronounced "swa-vay" on the infrequent occasions the word was used) was driving down to the gas station on the highway, with each partyer hauling his soft drink, or "mixer," of choice out of the ice water in the red Coca-Cola cooler cabinet and buying a package of Planters salted peanuts to go with it. Suave was pouring half the pop out on the gravel driveway with a nonchalant flick of the wrist. Real suave was managing to empty about half the bottle without appearing to look or interrupting the conversation, which generally involved arguments over whether Ginger Rogers was better looking than Rita Hayworth, John Deere tractors were better than International Harvesters, Hank Williams was better than Hank Snow, or Billy Vessels of Oklahoma was better than Nebraska's Bobby Reynolds (either of whom was certainly better than anyone we had at the time at KU or K-State).

Then the drinker would fill the pop bottle up with the booze, pour half the peanuts in, shake the bottle vigorously using his thumb as a stopper, spritz the back of his throat with the carbonated fizz, and take his first drink, along with the peanuts. Cocktail hour in western Kansas, complete with hors d'oeuvres and the traffic whizzing by on U.S. Highway 36, was under way.

Actually, things may not have changed all that much. On a visit home in the 1960s, a cousin and I decided to visit my old friend, Ed Cahoj, out in the country and to take along a jug as an offering. Remembering the blends of my adolescence, I made a sincere—very sincere—effort to make the buy, but my cousin, Wally Ritter, had the angle on me and is bigger than I am.

To my astonishment, he bought a fifth of Wild Turkey, which is to Four

Roses what a Mercedes Benz is to a demolition derby. "Well," I thought, "we've come a long way, baby." Not that far, actually. When we got out to Cahoj's place, he broke out the Coke and 7UP. I asked for plain water and ice, a mixture Cahoj had apparently never heard of. He also seemed to take it as a slur on his hospitality, as he kept giving me curious looks during the evening and repeatedly assured me that he had plenty of pop on hand, to which I was more than welcome.

A few years later, I was covering the 1976 Democratic National Convention in New York City and was standing at the bar of the Pennsylvania Sheraton Hotel, which was the convention headquarters. A delegate next to me at the bar handed his drink back to the bartender, who took a sip of it.

"That's club soda," the bartender said, reassuringly.

"I know," the delegate responded. "I asked for sweet soda. You know, Seven-Up or ginger ale or something like that."

The bartender nodded, got a fresh glass, poured a shot of twelve-year-old Chivas Regal over the ice, and added ginger ale. The delegate sipped it and nodded his approval and I couldn't resist.

"I'll bet I know what state you're from," I said.

"How'd you know?" he inquired after I'd guessed.

"I don't know," I lied. "You just have that certain *je ne sais quoi.*"

✑

Like the old joke, "I didn't know he drank until I saw him sober," I never realized what a hard-drinking society western Kansas was until I moved away. In part, this was due to the popular culture, particularly Western movies and novels. In the movies, of course, the hero might knock a shot back, neat, and then get on with what was apparently the other major pastime, violence, either gunplay or fisticuffs.

The novels, in my case anyway, were primarily those by writers such as Luke Short and Borden Deal and serialized in the *Saturday Evening Post,* a major cultural vehicle in rural and small-town America until its death at the hands of national television, which stole its audience and advertisers. A typical scene would have the hero and his sidekick returning to the ranch after a long, hard ride in a cold, driving rain and downing a couple of shots of red-eye neat before tucking into the dinner prepared by the hero's wife, or the romantic interest who would wind up as his wife.

I didn't realize until later the extent to which many males there internalized these images and assumptions. When I started high school, right at the end of World War II, there was a sort of tacit assumption, passed down by the upperclassmen, that when a boy entered high school, he started drinking as part of the rite of passage to manhood. Most of us didn't, at least right away, because at the age of thirteen and fourteen most of us weren't interested and, in addition, many of us had grown up in tee-total households. But the implicit peer pressure was there and as you got older it became stronger because that's what a lot of the guys were doing on Saturday nights.

When I was a freshman in high school, I overheard a bunch of juniors and seniors talking about some guys who had already graduated who were comparing hangovers during halftime at a basketball game. Even at that tender age, I absorbed a lot of this sort of lore with silent skepticism. I was interested, therefore, to read forty years later in the McDonald Standard dated December 18, 1941 (when I was in fifth grade), an account of the previous week's high school basketball game, a loss for the McDonald Tigers. The reporter, a high school girl writing as a "stringer," or freelance correspondent, completed her account of the loss with this editorial note, of which Carrie Nation, my mother, Glenn Cunningham, and all the pro-hibitionists in the state before and since would certainly have approved: "One team member was heard to boast that he didn't get to bed until two o'clock the night before the game. In Friday's classes, it was quite appar-ent that this same person was not in his best humor. . . . Increasing regard for training rules will no doubt make the goal easier to hit."

After my family moved away from McDonald, it was a relief to be in a high school where drinking beer was unusual and not something that had to be done as a constant reaffirmation of manhood. In my new high school in Olathe, Kansas, a suburb of Kansas City, most of the students seemed to view drinking as daring and risky, shocking even, and most apparently dis-approved. Which was smart on their part because experience shows that the younger people are when they start drinking, or practicing any bad habit, the more likely they are to have trouble with it. I always thought the argument that if a young man is old enough to get drafted and die for his country at age eighteen, he is old enough to drink legally had it back-wards. I considered that a better argument for not drafting eighteen-year-olds rather than for lowering the legal drinking age.

CHAPTER TWELVE

"BRINGING IN THE SHEAVES"

IN THE OPENING OF HIS EPIC BOOK ROOTS, ALEX HALEY DESCRIBED
the fear and suffering in his ancestral African village each year as the
food supplies from the previous harvest dwindled and the tribe awaited
the ripening of the new crop. During that period, sickness and starvation afflicted the weak and elderly in the village's subsistence farming
society, particularly if the harvest was delayed or damaged by drought or
floods. The women dressed in traditional fertility costumes of large
green leaves and chanted ancestral prayers as they helped with the
planting and cultivation. The villagers danced the traditional rain dance
and sacrificed goats and bullocks so that Allah would send the rains before the dwindling supplies of rice and couscous were exhausted. However, no matter how bad things were, the elders could always remember
a time when they were worse. The harvest rite is the most basic that any
society observes because it commemorates the most fundamental issue
of all: survival.

Although life on the High Plains obviously doesn't get nearly as close
to the bone as in Haley's ancestral village, it can be harsh and insecure
enough. The wheat harvest has been the basis of economic survival for
most farmers there and thus is a time of more tension and graver import
than any other in the year. Ancient harvest and fertility rituals have been
transformed by Christian societies into festivals such as All Saints' and
Corpus Christi. As Christians, everyone in northwest Kansas accepted
without question that they would worship just one God, but I came to
suspect that if one of our farmers had ever stumbled onto the Roman

idea that a prayer or tribute to other gods—Demeter and Dionysus or Ceres and Bacchus, the Greek and Roman gods of fertility, say, or any other of the Romans' gods for that matter—could conceivably do him any good, he might well have offered it up. The citizens of Rome, operating under the same philosophy that prompts some men to wear a belt and suspenders at the same time, posted symbols of gods from all over the Empire above their doorways on the pragmatic grounds that there was safety in numbers and no harm could come from having spiritual backups.

As a child, however, I had the best of the harvest season: I was able to enjoy the tension and excitement without suffering the worry and stress of the adults. I was fascinated by the harvest and wild to be part of it. I drove my family to distraction with my insistence that I be taken out to the field and allowed to ride on the combine or in the truck, which is a terribly distracting—and dangerous—factor for men who have serious business on their minds. I would have spent the entire day, every day, out in the fields if the grown-ups had let me and whenever I first arrived in the field I'd throw dirt up in the air over my head in an attempt to get as dusty as the harvest crew.

Then came the time when I didn't have to resort to that. In the spring of 1945, I finished the eighth grade at the age of thirteen. After school let out in mid-May, I noticed that when I went downtown the streets were empty, as far as I was concerned—I was the only one my age around. All the others were working on their families' farms or had hired out to other farmers or had taken other jobs, with the town businesses, on construction crews, or the railroad section gang. I didn't have to have a roof fall in on me. Peer pressure worked its magic without a word being spoken. Out of boredom as much as anything, I took a variety of odd jobs during May and June, including helping to shingle a house, and by the first of July I was working on a wheat harvest crew. In all my 5-foot-5-inch, 115-pound glory, I was driving a McCormick-Deering tractor pulling a combine for Chester Marshall.

It meant twelve- and fourteen-hour days out in the baking Kansas sun and the dust and wheat chaff, but I was delighted to be there, particularly considering the alternative. Who wanted to be playing with the little kids when your friends were out working with the men, operating big machinery such as tractors, combines, and trucks? To me, wheat harvest, which in those days lasted two or three weeks, was the most exciting time of the year, almost as good as Christmas, and I wanted to be part of it. This isn't difficult to understand. Kansas was the twelfth-largest wheat producer in the world in 1992, with 363.8 million bushels.* At that time, wheat was the most important economic factor by far in the western half of the state and, like Grandmother Phipps, I think we all entertained a sort of glimmering notion that the universe revolved around us, at least at harvesttime.

When the state was first settled after the Civil War, wheat was a minor crop and corn was dominant. Wheat eventually supplanted corn as the state's major crop and winter wheat won out over spring wheat as the state's leading grain crop due to a couple of historic events. One was the great Rocky Mountain locust plague of the summer of 1874; the other was the emigration to Kansas of many Russian Germans who had been wheat farmers in southern Russia and the Ukraine and had been driven out in the late nineteenth century by the persecution of the czar.

Kansas suffered a serious drought in the summer of 1874, and by early August the farmers were anxiously scanning the skies for signs of rain clouds. At about 4:00 P.M. on August 6, a cloud *did* appear out of the northwest. The afternoon became so dark that according to one account the chickens "hastened to their roosts." The cloud, however, was accompanied by a dry rasping sound that turned out to be grasshoppers' wings. Instead of welcome, life-giving moisture, the cloud pelted insects on humans, animals, buildings, and the ground like hailstones. It proved, in fact, to be more destructive than even the worst of hailstorms. The cloud disappeared as the hoppers settled to the ground, and the hot August sun glinted off the backs of billions of grasshoppers that were feeding voraciously on every living plant from north central Nebraska south into the Indian territory of Oklahoma, from the Rocky Mountains east to Missouri. In some areas, the insects were three and four inches deep. Eyewitnesses reported that they lit in the cottonwood trees that lined the creek and river bottoms in such numbers that they broke off large branches.

They devoured leather harness and boots, and even wooden objects such as shovel and pitchfork handles that had absorbed perspiration ("They eet the fork handles," a shocked farmer relates in Hamlin Garlin's short story, "Under the Lion's Paw"). They stayed day after horrid day, eating grass, weeds, and gardens and leaving the revolting stench of their excrement. Trains were slowed and in some cases stopped because the locomotives' drive wheels couldn't gain traction on rails made slick by

---

*The leaders, in order, were the former Soviet Union, the United States, China, India, France, Canada, Turkey, Australia, Pakistan, the United Kingdom, and North Dakota. Kansas produced 15 percent of the United States total, North Dakota (469.8 million bushels) 19 percent.

crushed grasshoppers. Fires set by pouring kerosene on them made no impact on their numbers. They finally departed after they had devoured all the food. The farmers feared a similar plague the following summer because of the billions of eggs the grasshoppers deposited in the ground, but that crop of insects moved on after they hatched instead of staying put. Development of an effective poison subsequently helped keep them under control.

The one crop that escaped the grasshopper plague was winter wheat. It is planted in September, lies dormant over the winter, and in Kansas is harvested in June and July. Thus it had already been cut and had been spared the plague. Up to that point, Kansas farmers had been undecided on what to make their major crop. The choices were between corn and wheat and between winter wheat and spring wheat, which is planted in the early spring and harvested in late summer. Today, spring wheat is grown primarily in the northern High Plains states, where the winters are too severe for winter wheat. Winter wheat also won out over corn because western Kansas and the rest of the High Plains don't get enough rainfall to ensure good corn crops without irrigation. The grasshoppers, who were the harvesters of the corn and spring wheat crops of 1874, helped resolve this debate. It wasn't until 1914, however, that wheat acreage overtook corn, 9.1 million acres to 5.3 million acres.

The other major factor in this choice was the Russian Germans, including many Mennonites, who had migrated to the Ukraine in the eighteenth century to escape Prussian militarism when they were promised free farmland and exemption from taxes and conscription by Catherine the Great. There also were thousands of German Lutherans and Catholics, who became known as the "Volga Germans," who settled in the Russian provinces of Samara and Saratov along the Volga River. A century later, when Czar Alexander decreed universal military service and taxation, many of these Russian Germans packed off to the New World.

The Mennonites brought with them a hardy strain of winter wheat known as Turkey Red, which had evolved to withstand the harsh winters and scanty rainfall of the Ukraine and the steppes of Russia, where the climate is similar to that of the High Plains. Thus it was perfectly suited to the New World. The major varieties of red winter wheat grown in Kansas today are descendants of Turkey Red. The Russian Germans also brought dryland tillage methods that, like Turkey Red, traveled well to the Kansas soil and climate. Kansas farmers developed such techniques as "summer fallowing" their wheat, which is the practice of planting each field every other year to enable it to replenish the subsoil moisture. In addition to conserving the soil, summer fallow consistently produces twice the yield of continuously cropped fields and substantially reduces the fuel, labor, and other costs of continuous cropping.

This and constantly improving technology resulted in steadily increased production. Steel plowshares with better scouring capability than their iron predecessors made plowing faster and more efficient. Reapers were steadily improved and about the time of World War I, the reaper and the steam-powered threshing machine were merged into one machine, the "combine." It, in turn, was constantly improved and enlarged and evolved from the pull-type that was towed by horses or a tractor to the present self-propelled behemoth. Tractors evolved from clumsy, three-wheeled steam engines to the enormous machines of today, which can do the field work in a comparative twinkling. The internal-combustion engine revolutionized the preparation of the ground, the sowing, harvesting, transporting, and storing of the crops.*

It was the big tractors, combines, and trucks that fascinated me. In early June, several weeks before the wheat was ready to cut, the activity began to quicken. The farmers began fixing up their bins and elevators and overhauling their combines, from engines to V-belts, making all the adjustments in the big machines' complex, mazelike interiors to ensure that they worked properly. Business and other activities picked up as farmers laid in parts and supplies in advance. Itinerant harvest hands began to drift up from the south as they followed the ripening of the wheat, along with the "custom cutters," the entrepreneurs with combines and trucks whom many farmers hire to help cut their wheat; these often developed into regular year-after-year business relationships. The custom cutters start out in Texas in May and follow the ripening wheat north through Oklahoma, Kansas, Nebraska, the Dakotas, and Montana, winding up in Saskatchewan in September and October. Many custom cutters are farmers themselves who harvest their own fields as they pass through on their way north.

There was always a surge of excitement when the combines first went into the fields and the initial reports on the crop—estimated yield per acre, weight, weed and moisture content—came from the elevators where the grain was sampled and analyzed. The farmers swapped reports and information, some of which was reported in the local weekly newspaper:

---

*John Deere invented the steel moldboard plowshare. Cyrus McCormick didn't invent the very first reaper, but he patented one in 1834 that met the needs of farmers on the vast expanses of the Midwest prairies. J. I. Case was a leading manufacturer of steam engines and then tractors.

"Bill Payne reports starting to cut a stand three miles west of town that could make 45 bushels [per acre] and is testing at 61." (The standard weight of a bushel of wheat is sixty pounds).

Harvesttime is ulcer time for the farmer until the fragile wheat crop is safe from the not-so-tender mercies of wind and rain and hail. One of Grandmother Phipps's favorite hymns was "Bringing in the Sheaves," which was appropriate because the question of bringing in the sheaves on Sundays when the wheat was ripe and ready for the combines was a vexing one for devout churchgoers, given the plant's vulnerability to the elements. It caused considerable conflict and anxiety for Grandmother and many other of the faithful, a conflict that was aided and abetted by the aforementioned Reverend J. W. Coppoc, the tart-tongued pastor of the Federated Church in McDonald, who would remark in his "Church Notes" column in the weekly newspaper that "harvest is the hardest time in the year to keep your religion and save your wheat."

On the one hand, Grandmother and many others took seriously the commandment that the Sabbath was the Lord's day and was to be given over to him exclusively. On the other was the pressing economic need to get the harvest in with maximum possible dispatch in a fickle and hostile environment. Some shut down for the day and put their trust in God (Mr. Marshall, the farmer I worked for that first summer, was a Seventh-Day Adventist and he shut down from sundown Friday to sundown Saturday, no nonsense about it). Others, including my uncles, most of whom, truth to tell, were somewhat detached about religious strictures, chose to act on the principle that the Lord helps those who help themselves. They proceeded to render unto Caesar even on the Lord's day, with a minimum of discernible concern about divine retribution. Although it seemed that she had to fret about the question for a few minutes at the beginning of harvest each year, Grandmother Phipps always wound up concurring, and it never appeared to be a mortal struggle for her.*

For a kid, however, harvest was an exciting time, although I had sense enough to try to conceal this from my anxious elders. This was partly because of a teenager's enjoyment in doing a man's work, particularly if it involved driving a truck or a tractor pulling a combine. We also had the additional pleasure of working on harvest crews with veterans just back from World War II. For a teenager who had followed the war with fascina-

---

*She went through a similar exercise with the advent of the popular song "Praise the Lord and Pass the Ammunition" shortly after the Japanese attack on Pearl Harbor. She fretted that the song might be sacrilegious, but, in fact, she liked it and wound up deciding that it contributed to the cause of defeating the evil Axis enemy, who, after all, was the modern Antichrist.

tion, this was an embarrassment of riches. The GIs were full of war stories, women stories, travel stories, adventure and misadventure stories, some of which were probably true. One, a draftee who through wartime expansion had become the first sergeant of a rifle company in the First Infantry Division, recounted how a fellow NCO in Normandy raised his arm to wave his troops forward only to have it almost surgically amputated by a German eighty-eight (millimeter) artillery shell. This story was disputed by a couple of the vets, who contended that the shell would have exploded on contact and vaporized the victim, but the former topkick pulled rank, invoked superior knowledge of munitions, and never backed down (in fact, the eighty-eights were so flexible and accurate that when necessary the Germans did fire them point-blank at personnel). All the vets, of course, were experts who claimed vast empirical expertise on the sexual proclivities of English and French women, to say nothing of their American counterparts, and they naturally had an avid audience for their seminars.

In addition to providing worldly information and entertainment, the vets performed as medics on a number of occasions. In my second summer in the harvest, I came down with a malady we referred to as being "waterlogged." The sufferer would have a chronic thirst that no amount of water would relieve. I drank and drank and got absolutely no relief. I must have drunk two gallons of water, lemonade, and iced tea that hot, bright July day and literally sloshed when I walked. Keeping the one-gallon water jug I carried on the tractor full became an additional logistical burden as I spent the afternoon steering the tractor with one hand and hoisting the jug with the other. None of the civilians on the crew, including Floyd Andrews, the farmer we were working for, seemed to have a remedy—one did prescribe lemonade instead of water, which made absolutely no difference—but one of the vets recognized it immediately.

"You need salt," he said. "If we were in the Army, we'd give you a salt tablet." Sweating in the hot summer sun had apparently depleted my sodium level and my body's ability to retain water. Licking table salt off the back of my hand when we went to the farmhouse after shutting down that evening solved this problem just as the GI said it would and I had no more trouble with it.

The following summer, when I was fifteen, I suffered another malady, a strange one for a teenager. In retrospect, it sounds something like the prostate trouble of an older man. I felt the frequent urge to urinate but couldn't, although I could when it was necessary. The rest of the time, I had the discomfort of feeling the need to go to the bathroom without being able to relieve it. Another veteran, who had learned his medicine as a truck driver and mechanic with the *Red Ball Express* in France, as I recall, expertly diagnosed the problem. "Your kidneys are limed over" was the scientific diagnosis of the "doctor" and he prescribed the cure. "After supper, we'll go down to the pool hall and get a bottle of beer into you. That'll clear you up." Although I was well under the legal age of eighteen for buying beer, the primary vehicle for enforcing the drinking laws in those small towns was the discretion of the proprietors, who had a limited interest in sending the teenage sons of their friends and neighbors home drunk. Since I was in adult company and this was a medical case, Rex and Jake Confer, the pool hall proprietors, filled the prescription. While I was considerably more partial to Coca-Cola, I appreciated the Rx value of Budweiser, compared to most medicines I was familiar with. And, it must be said that all medicinal treatment should be so effective. For whatever reason, the symptom disappeared.

Harvest is a sensuous time. The memory of the season is one of vivid blues and golds: the blue of God's vast sky and the gold of His sun and bounteous wheat. The wind moves the grain in waves that ripple with a hypnotic rhythm like a great golden ocean stretching to the horizon in every direction. There also is a mesmerizing effect in the pace and cadence of a combine as it waddles majestically across the countryside like a great prehistoric mastodon. The header platform reel, which is something like a wide steamboat paddle wheel, forces the stalks into the teeth and sickles of the cutter bar. The wheat is mowed with a surgical precision and an auger or canvas conveyor belt relentlessly feeds the stalks into the combine's voracious maw, the heart of which is the awesome "separator," or "cylinder."

The cylinder is the major component of the threshing system. It is where the grain gets threshed. The cylinder is three or four feet long and a foot or two in diameter; on many combines, such as my family's International Harvester Model 11, the cylinder wasn't solid but made of steel bars with rasp teeth that looked like very coarse files; others had spikes instead of rasps. It rotated at about 800 revolutions per minute inside a round chamber formed by bolting together two semicircular solid walls known as the "concaves." The cylinder's action knocked the wheat grains out of the heads, and the rest of the machine's mechanism sifted out the straw and chaff, discharged it out the rear, and elevated the grain into a bin that was emptied into a wagon or truck when full. It always seemed a bit unbelievable to me that so much mechanical power and violence is needed to thresh something as fragile as a head of wheat. Woe betide any unfortunate living thing—rabbit, rodent, pheasant, or any other small creature—

that might somehow get caught up on the platform conveyor and fed into that remorseless, lethal, high-speed mechanism.

The muffled roar of the cylinder and the noise of the rhythmic march and shuffle of the elevator chains, sieves, raddles, and all the other elements of the big thresher's innards wraps it in a cocoon of sound and movement that makes it appear impervious to mere mortals. Conversation with the combine man required the participants to cup their hands and shout into each other's ears. An occasional shudder by the big machine and the thump of a heavy slug of straw hitting the system is the only sign of the inner struggle taking place in the combine's innards as it inexorably devours the grain, winding around the field in ever-diminishing circles.*

A number of things induce ulcers in farmers at harvesttime. The weather, obviously, is one. Harvest is one time rain isn't welcome. At best, it delays the process, increasing the potential exposure to damaging high winds and hail. Normally benign, rainfall itself can also damage the crop. Machinery breakdown is another. The combine is most prone to breakdowns because of its complexity. And because it is the prime player, it is the most critical—you could always rent or borrow a truck or tractor if necessary, but it is hard to find an idle combine. I recall Uncle Wayne's tense, high-speed runs to Colby, fifty miles away, to the regional International Harvester dealer when our local dealer didn't have the parts we needed. At first, I rather guiltily enjoyed the break in the heat and noise and dust when we had to shut down and could do some preventive maintenance on the equipment or just sit in the shade and talk, but getting the parts from Colby was a three- or four-hour hiatus and it wasn't long before we were chafing with boredom and apprehensively scanning the western skies for signs of menacing storm clouds.

The number of these traumatic episodes was reduced substantially when Wayne, who moved to Boulder, Colorado, to buy into the newspaper business there, hired Claude Pickett as the farm overseer and he was our combine man in harvest. Claude was good with machinery, electricity, plumbing, carpentry, and every other skill a farmer needs (he subsequently became the town's plumber and electrician) because he figured out how things were designed to work; he had also worked for implement dealers "tuning" combines—or setting their various parts and components to manufacturers' specifications, so that they operated as they should. He suggested to Wayne that some parts on the combine—certain bearings,

*Because my uncle Wayne also owned the local weekly newspaper, I was also exposed to the Mergenthaler Linotype and found its operation as mesmerizing as the combine's. They are two of the most fascinating machines I've ever encountered.

sprockets, drive chains, V-belts—failed more often than others because they were at the points of greatest stress in the operation. Since he knew what those stress points were, Claude made a list of parts to carry in the combine's toolbox. This thunderbolt of common sense undoubtedly added years to my uncle's life. The combine was an International Harvester Company Model 11, referred to as the "Number 11," as in "Let's fire up the Number 11 and get going." The manufacturer's logo, the initials "IHC," were printed in huge letters on the canvas hood that covered the straw spreader at the rear. This prompted Claude's often distraught predecessor as combine man, Arch Rummel, to dub the machine the "In Hell Continuously." As long as we had the necessary spare parts on hand, however, the old "In Hell Continuously" worked just fine. It also had another problem. It was originally built to cut a fourteen-foot swath, but International provided a kit that extended the header width to sixteen feet, which we did. This enabled us to cut a wider swath but put stress on a threshing mechanism designed for a smaller intake.

The old pull-type combines were replaced in the 1950s by self-propelled machines, and combine technology steadily improved. More powerful engines and increased threshing capacities made the self-propelled combines ever more efficient. Today's combine can move faster through the fields and cut larger swaths, as large as thirty feet, almost double the Number 11's sixteen-foot cut. Up to a point, they can also thresh damper straw. With the old pull-type combines, we had to shut down at dusk as the dew descended—even on the subhumid High Plains—and had to wait in the morning until the sun burned it off. Cloud cover delayed our start even more. The current machines can work at night if it's dry enough and three or four of them can cut the average farmer out in just a few days. This efficiency has greatly reduced a major source of stress for wheat farmers.

Another harvesttime hazard was what some farmers called "the operating handle retaining nut." This was the human operator, and we were all menaces at one time or another. Floyd Andrews had two pull-type Baldwin "Gleaners," an efficient and popular machine made of distinctive silver galvanized metal. These particular ones had a serious design flaw, however. The power plant, a Ford Model A automobile engine, was mounted sideways and protruded slightly out the side under the bin that held the threshed grain. This made the radiator vulnerable whenever a truck pulled under the bin to unload it. Floyd had a teenage truck driver, Gary Lebow, who made a sort of sub-career out of miscalculating his clearance as he pulled up alongside, with the result that he would snag the radiator with the truck bed. So Floyd carried spare radiator hoses and clamps on the combine, hoped that the radiator wouldn't be damaged too badly, and generally managed to keep the damage and delay to a minimum, although God knows what it did to his nervous system.

I made my own contributions to shredding Floyd's nerves. Easily my worst moment as a tractor man was when I fell into a reverie in the midst of turning a corner and failed to straighten out of it. The result was that the front end of the tractor turned right back into the combine's reel, breaking several of the wooden slats and bringing me, abruptly but too late, back into the real world; the tractor was an International Harvester Model M Farmall, which had rear-wheel brakes and could pivot in a circle on either rear wheel. Floyd and I worked replacing the slats, but that was a pretty silent job with none of the usual chitchat that helps pass the time for men working side by side with their hands. I suspect that Floyd, who for me was a pleasure to work for, spent some time reflecting on the farmer's need to hire half-baked teenagers and the near impossibility of firing them because of the intimacy of the community (his oldest daughter was a close friend of one of my cousins, and his son, Keith, and I were on the high school football team together).

The most demanding aspect of running the tractor was judging the heaviness of the wheat straw in relation to the combine's capacity and adjusting the speed accordingly. The heavier the stand, the slower the speed, of course. We obviously wanted to maintain maximum speed and sometimes we'd cross the line when we hit an unusually heavy or damp patch. This overload would "slug," or jam the combine's cylinder, killing the engine and bringing the whole apparatus to an abrupt halt. The tractor driver then had the sweaty, itchy pleasure of opening the hatches and digging the straw out of the cylinder compartment by hand while the combine man carefully smoked a cigarette and brooded on the lost time.

🌾

Food is a major factor at harvesttime. This is due in part to the companionship and camaraderie of the season. Most farmers in the years just after World War II ran at least two combine crews, each of which included the tractor man, the combine man, and a truck driver to haul the grain to the elevator. In addition, there often was a man or two running the portable, gasoline engine–powered augers that elevated the wheat into the farmer's granaries, plus someone working the summer fallow ground, getting it ready for planting in September. This meant that a farmer's wife often found herself cooking three times a day for ten or twelve people or more.

The meals were truly heroic. It was customary for a farm wife, her daughters, and/or a hired girl or two, often high school girls who lived in town, to produce for breakfast each morning several dozen fried eggs, bacon, ham, sausage, pancakes, potatoes, toast, and fruit, and some even offered an assortment of pies, including the usual apple and cherry plus rhubarb, apricot, plum, peach, coconut cream, chocolate, or lemon meringue as well. Dinner, as the noon meal was called, was generally fried chicken, roast beef, or ham with mashed potatoes and gravy, the usual assortment of vegetables and breads, and pies and cakes and ice cream for dessert. Even with all this, the women often provided sandwiches at mid-morning and mid-afternoon, and if the wheat was being hauled to town for sale or storage at the commercial elevators, the truck drivers got frequent orders for candy bars and cold pop, both of which were rich in sugar for instant energy as well as being refreshing. One of my favorite memories of those hot, blindingly bright Kansas summers is pulling one of those lovely thick-green-glass bottles that Coca-Cola used to come in out of the cold water in an insulated ice chest in one of the filling stations in town and chugalugging it, without stop, which stung the throat and made the eyes water and is still one of the most pleasurable experiences I've known.

The supper menu was the same as dinner. One rather avant-garde farm wife, a recent arrival from the city (any town over 5,000 population), offered cold cuts and potato salad in the evening on the unimpeachable grounds that they were cooler and lighter and thus more apropos to the furnacelike weather. She was duly informed by her husband that while they might be fine as hors d'oeuvres (although I don't recall anyone using that term), harvest hands still expected the main course. There also was the story, possibly apocryphal, of a young bride who didn't quite grasp the scope of harvest crew appetites and offered modest servings at her first noon dinner. This episode, so the story went, ended in disaster when the first hired hand served, with no apparent malice aforethought, emptied the entire meat platter onto his plate. The farmer had to take the crew to town to a restaurant and his bride had occasion to rethink her menu.

All these matters were larger than life during harvest because of its importance and tension. The excitement actually seemed to build on the final day as we finished cutting the last field. The rounds got smaller and smaller and soon we could gauge with the eye how many more it would be before we had finished up another year. Some farmers and crews celebrated the windup with a case of beer before getting on with the next cycle of work. But such celebrations were short-lived because Mother Nature never pauses, the sun was shining, the days were long, and the nights were short.

We quickly dispatched the anticlimactic task of putting the combine away for the winter. We stored the V-belts and the canvas conveyor belts in the toolshed, loosened the idler pulleys that kept the chain drives taut, greased the bearings against the winter moisture, drained the engine oil and radiator. Then we had to turn to and get the summer fallow ready for drilling in September, to get back to the grind of long days on the tractor to keep ahead of the weeds and race the season to planting time. For me, the end of harvest was a letdown, like the day after Christmas. For the adults, however, it was an enormous relief to be briefly savored before moving on in nature's inexorable cycle.

Celebrating the completion of the harvest is the true holiday in an agrarian society and is cause for profound relief. A successful harvest today means economic well-being for the farmer and low food prices for the consumer, but the emotion is still primal. It's rooted in the not-so-distant days of subsistence farming, when the stakes in villages like Alex Haley's were nothing less than starvation itself. For millions, possibly billions, of people, this is still a precarious, year-to-year, life and death proposition.

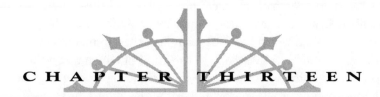

CHAPTER THIRTEEN

SHANK'S MARE TO SILICON VALLEY— THE MARCH OF TECHNOLOGY

THE SIREN SONG OF POWERFUL MACHINERY, THE TRUCKS AND TRACTORS and combines, collaborated to keep me coming back to western Kansas to work for my uncles summer after summer, despite the hard work, the heat and dust, and the monotony of the long hours in the field. Having control of all that power was irresistible. The adults must have had qualms about turning that equipment over to teenagers like me even though economics dictated that they bring us into the workforce, and if they had gotten an inkling of how much some of us romanticized operating that machinery, they might have had even longer thoughts.

During harvest, there was nothing I loved more than rolling down main street toward the Equity Co-op elevator at the wheel of a truckload of wheat. The first time I was ever entrusted with a fully loaded truck, at age fifteen, however, I nearly rode it to disaster when I underestimated the distance needed to stop a vehicle with the momentum of a three-and-a-half-ton load. I recall that I was under the misapprehension that the occasion called for me to make my appearance with a flourish. I almost did, all right. Good fortune averted catastrophe by a narrow margin, I didn't crash through the grain elevator, and I never came close to making that mistake again.

I also enjoyed hotdogging down main street on our International Harvester W9 tractor. I'd come in on U.S. Highway 36 from the west, slow down to turn left off the highway between the grain elevators onto main street. Then I'd open the throttle all the way up. The responding deep-throated bellow could be heard over in the next county when the big engine opened up and I barreled down main street in road gear, making enough noise to raise the dead and probably prompting some of the townspeople to wish I was with them.

⚞⚟

Technology—the railroad, the steel plow, the Colt six-shooter, the windmill, and barbed wire—made the relatively rapid settlement and transformation of Kansas and the High Plains in the nineteenth century possible. It could be said that the prairies were really settled by inventors, factory workers, and production managers on the assembly lines applying the techniques of the industrial revolution. Farming fell into the hands of the industrialists and financiers in the late nineteenth century. Newer technology—the internal-combustion engine, increasingly sophisticated machinery, electricity, irrigation, better methods of tillage and other agricultural techniques, improved strains of seeds and livestock, the computer, even improved retail-marketing methods—has continued relentlessly and radically to alter the area.

The railroad, of course, was crucial because it gave farmers a means of shipping their produce; without railroads, settling those vast, treeless prairies more than a few miles from navigable waterways would not have been possible. The steel plowshare speeded the process of converting the native grasslands to arable cropland because it scoured better than its wood and cast-iron predecessors.

The six-shooter enabled the white man to fight and defeat the Plains Indians on horseback, which was the first of many steps in vanquishing them and settling the plains. The mobility afforded by the horse had made it possible for the Indians to hunt efficiently on the semi-arid, treeless prairie and their accuracy with their light weapons, bows, and lances on horseback made them a formidable cavalry. The windmill enabled the white settler to harness the winds to draw water from wells.

Barbed wire was a cheap and efficient means of fencing in an area that didn't have rock or plentiful supplies of wood, the fencing materials in the east; it ended the days of the open range and by keeping the large ranchers' herds from overrunning farmers' crops made settlement of the range by thousands of small farmers and ranchers possible. The problem of fencing on the High Plains was illustrated by a Department of Agriculture survey in 1871 which showed that the nation's farm fencing had cost $2 billion and cost $2 million annually for upkeep. Barbed wire was invented in 1874 by a farmer near De Kalb, Illinois, named Joseph F. Glidden, who had the problem of enclosing his own prairie farm. He sold a half interest in his patent to a manufacturing company for $60,000 and a royalty of $0.25 per 100 pounds (cwt). They sold 145 million pounds of barbed wire between 1876 and 1880, which netted Glidden $362,500 in royalties, and by 1883 were manufacturing sixty miles of barbed wire an hour. With mass production, the price fell from $20 cwt in 1870 to $4 in 1890.

Technology made possible the rapid settlement and transformation of the entire United States. It took a millennium or two for Europeans to subdue their wilderness and bend nature to their bidding. In North America, it took less than a century. The steam engine and its successors enabled the American settlers to focus an almost infinite amount of energy on taming their vast wilderness—clearing the forests, plowing fields, building dams, and constructing a transportation system that brought the enormous continental distances under control.

As the historian John Steele Gordon noted, an area of eastern North America larger than all Europe was deforested in less than a single human lifetime. In 1850, Americans utilized an estimated 8 million horsepower, mechanical and animal; by 1900, it was 64 million, an eightfold increase. The settlement of the High Plains was no different.

Kansas—and the nation—enjoyed its peak rural population in the first two decades of the twentieth century, by which time the state had been settled to the Colorado line. The internal-combustion engine was just coming into wide use and would not completely displace the horse until the outbreak of World War II, and until it did, farming remained labor-intensive.

Technology made agriculture capital-intensive instead and in so doing radically altered the nature of farming. The family farm changed from being a self-sufficient operation from which the family realized most of its food and sustenance with some surplus to sell. It became one that was totally cash crop– and market-oriented and, to a great degree, dependent on government policies and price supports; the self-sufficient farm was the sort Grandmother Phipps grew up on and which formed her worldview.

There is a constantly enlarged and improved machine for every step of farm work from plowing and preparing the soil to seeding and harvesting. The reward for this easing of the farmer's physical burden is a steady and dramatic upsurge in productivity. In 1900, there were 173,000 farms in Kansas with an average size of 241 acres, the size of Grandfather and Grandmother Phipps's original farm near McDonald. By 1990, the census showed that the number of farms in the state was less than half that, about 73,000, with an average size of 642 acres. In 1900, one farmer produced food for 7 people; in 1940, with machinery replacing the last of the horses, a Kansas farmer fed 10.7 people; by the 1990s, it was estimated that one farmer raised food for more than 120 people. The reason for the nation's seemingly ever-present agricultural surpluses is that even with the nation's population more than tripling in the twentieth century, farm productivity has increased about 50 percent faster than demand, according to a study made for the National Governors' Association.

Rawlins County covers 1,080 square miles, or 691,200 acres, 650,000 of which are in farms. In the early years of the twentieth century, wheat yields in Kansas generally ranged from 12 to 15 bushels per acre (bpa), with an occasional bumper crop such as 1914, when it made 20 bpa. In 1915, Rawlins County farmers, most still operating primarily with horses, harvested 3 million bushels of wheat off more than 200,000 acres, an average of about 15 bpa. In 1985, the county's yield was 8,124,400 bushels off 142,000 acres, an average of 57 bpa. In the 1920s a good corn yield was 30 or 40 bpa; today, with irrigation, farmers can plant to 150 or 200 bpa. Acreage restrictions, an attempt to reduce wheat surpluses, have reduced the harvested acreage to about one-fifth the total farm area of the county, but technology has tripled and quadrupled yields. At the same time, the farm population of the county is only about a third of what it was at the turn of the century. The history of American agriculture is one of negating government policies aimed at limiting production, first through the farmers' increasing their acreage then through the use of technology.

⚜

And, the technological revolution proceeds unabated. There have been several major technological breakthroughs on the High Plains just since World War II. One was the completion of bringing electricity to farmsteads, which was begun in the 1930s by the New Deal's Rural Electrification Administration. The 1950s and 1960s also saw substantial improvements in wheat and corn hybrids, which produced ever-increasing yields and were hardier—more resistant to weather, disease, and insects—than their predecessors. The use of chemicals increased greatly, particularly herbicides and fertilizers such as nitrogen, phosphate, and anhydrous ammonia, a form of nitrogen. These, however, affect the water supply and are getting increased attention from the Environmental Protection Agency. Tillage methods have changed in order to reduce erosion and evaporation of moisture.

However, the biggest postwar technological advance was probably the ability to efficiently drill wells to underground water reservoirs such as the Ogallala Aquifer. It removed the risk of dryland farming to a degree that our forebears could not have imagined.

Many of the first settlers in the 1870s who made the long migration from Europe by ship, train, and wagon completed their odysseys by traveling the last few miles across the empty and seemingly endless prairie to their isolated homesteads on foot, or "shank's mare," as it was commonly called.

Like several other early Rawlins County farm wives in the 1870s and 1880s, Mrs. Joseph Dozbaba kept a diary. In it, she told of her weekly 14-mile walk to town and back to pick up mail and groceries and reported that her husband estimated that he walked 800 miles in their first few years on the High Plains looking for work, primarily on farms up in Nebraska, to help finance his homestead. Letters and reminiscences indicate that this was commonplace in the early days on the frontier.

In 1876, August Blume, the first homesteader in Rawlins County, walked to Crete, Nebraska, which is more than 250 miles to the east, to bring his family in a borrowed team and wagon to his homestead near what is now the town of Ludell. He guided five other homestead families to Rawlins County as well. He then drove the team and wagon back to Crete, worked there for a time to accumulate a stake, then walked the 250 miles back to his homestead in western Kansas. A Rawlins County homesteader named Gaines Constable walked from his farm to Sharon Springs, 100 miles southwest, to work for the princely wage of one dollar a day. At the end of his stint, he walked back to his farm, stayed overnight, then walked 30 miles east to the regional land office in Oberlin, where he made the final ten-dollar payment on his homestead, and returned home on foot carrying a fifty-pound sack of flour on his shoulder.

Shank's mare also powered much of the farm work at first. The history of farming in Kansas can be divided into four phases: foot and hand power, horse power, steam and gasoline engine power, and, finally, widespread irrigation and the use of chemicals, particularly fertilizer.

Many early settlers at first plowed, cultivated, and seeded their wheat and corn by hand, picked their corn by hand, reaped the wheat with hand scythes, and threshed it with flails; the Kisling family cut its first wheat crop in Rawlins County with butcher knives. The first Mennonites threshed their wheat by rolling cogged cylindrical stones over the bundles. Some farmers in eastern Kansas in the 1850s and 1860s planted corn by slitting the sod with axes, pushing the seeds into the slits, and closing the rows by stepping on them. By this method, one farmer consistently raised crops that made an astonishing 100 bushels to the acre, double the average for the time; not surprisingly, he became known as "Sodcorn" Jones.

The size of the holdings on the High Plains obviously made these practices impossible to continue, however. Horses quickly replaced shank's mare and in turn were supplanted by steam and gasoline engines.

A farmer with a single-share walking plow pulled by a team of horses could turn over an acre of prairie sod in a long day. Riding a two-wheeled horse-drawn plow with six bottoms, he increased this to five or six acres a day. The steel plowshare that John Deere invented in the 1830s helped the process substantially because it was more durable and scoured the rich, black High Plains soil much better than cast iron. Even with the use of horse-drawn plows, cultivators, and harrows, however, it was a struggle to stay ahead of the weeds and to work the ground fast enough to keep it from baking hard and dry under the Kansas summer sun.

With a gasoline or steam tractor, a farmer could plow or cultivate thirty-five or forty acres a day. Steam traction engines, as they were first called, made their appearance in the 1870s—the term *tractor* came into use after the turn of the century. Steam power, including stationary engines that powered threshing machines, feed grinders, and corn shellers, was prevalent until about 1900, but after the turn of the century gasoline engines replaced steam. The gasoline engine was much smaller and more flexible than steam, had a far better weight-to-power ratio, could be operated and fueled much more efficiently, and was an infinitely lesser fire hazard. Grandfather Phipps's first tractor was a steam-powered Bull, which had two big drive wheels in the rear and one small wheel in front.

Tractor technology progressed through the 1920s with the addition of headlights, hydraulic lifts, and the power-takeoff drive, which ran a wide variety of implements from feed grinders to hay balers to small combines. Smaller "tricycle"-configured tractors became increasingly popular during and after World War I and replaced horses on lighter jobs such as working corn and other row crops. A major technological breakthrough was the introduction of rubber tires in 1932, which caught on quickly—95 percent of the tractors in Kansas were on rubber by 1940—because they increased ground speed, fuel efficiency, drawbar power by 25 percent, and operator comfort, and made it possible to move from field to field rapidly on paved roads.*

---

*As obvious as this development seems today, it was the source of some debate; I remember farmers arguing right after World War II about whether six miles per hour was too fast for good field work. My father-in-law, an Iowa veterinarian and farmer, was initially convinced that tractors on rubber were a bad idea and in 1934 distributed handbills to the farms around Sioux City arguing against them. An otherwise liberal and progressive man, he loved to tell this story on himself and ruefully contended that that was the last time he ever tried to stand in the path of progress.

As powerful as the new post–World War II tractors such as the International Harvester W9, the upgraded Model D John Deere, the Model LA Case, and others were, it still seemed as though it took forever to chisel or one-way a quarter section—it took three or four days, in fact. We had to run the tractors almost continually, six days a week, fourteen to sixteen hours a day, sometimes around the clock late in August, to stay ahead of the weeds on the summer fallow and get it ready for planting in September. Today, huge tractors that are nearly as high as a house and have four enormous drive wheels can easily work a half section in a day with implements that cover thirty-five to fifty feet at a swath. At a cost of $100,000 or more, they also come with air-conditioned cabs, two-way radios, and stereos. Even the "smaller" tractors have four-wheel or "enhanced" drive. Implements have increased commensurately in size, which makes sophisticated hydraulic systems necessary just to lift them out of the ground at the end of the day or at the completion of the job.

⚞⚟

The scythe and sickle and cradle as harvesting instruments were replaced by horse-drawn mechanical reapers, which went into production in the 1840s. They operated much like the old-fashioned manual lawn mower. Like the lawn mower, they had a rotary reel that pushed the stalks back into the cutter bar, which had serrated sickle blades that moved rapidly back and forth about an inch in either direction like those on mowing machines. There were two basic types of reapers. One was the "binder," which appeared in the 1870s and tied the stalks into compact sheaves or bundles; the first models used wire but soon were replaced by twine-tie mechanisms. The other was the "header," which was pushed from behind by horses. A broad canvas conveyor belt driven by the machine's main wheels lifted the heads and stalks into a large wagon known as a "header barge," which was towed alongside the header by horses. When the barge was full, the heads were either unloaded onto stacks to await the threshing machine or taken directly to it.

Threshing machines powered by horses and mules were introduced in the 1860s and 1870s and were replaced in the late 1870s by steam-powered machines. This was another major technological development, but it still involved a great deal of muscle power. A threshing machine crew consisted of the operator, known as the machine man; the measure man, who kept track of the amount threshed and the yield per acre on a pegboard; his assistant, who held the sacks into which the grain was loaded; the band cutter, who cut the ties of the shocks; and generally two or three "pitchers," who fed the stalks into the machine with pitchforks. The stalks were pitched by hand into the thresher and the bagged grain was loaded by hand into wagons or trucks, all of which was hard physical work.* Nor was cooking for a threshing crew a minor matter because there could easily be fifteen to twenty hands or more, depending on the number of machines in operation. The farmer's wife either had to have a good-sized kitchen crew of her own or, as happened frequently, joined in a cooperative effort with her neighbors.

The combine, so called because it's a combined reaper and thresher, was first used in California in the 1880s and came into use in the Midwest in the 1920s. It required only a fraction of the manpower needed for the reapers and threshers.

The first combines were pulled by horses or tractors. A pull-type combine crew consisted of the combine man, the horse or tractor drive, the wagon or truck driver, and, before World War II, a couple of hired hands to help scoop the wheat out of the wagon or truck up into the farmer's granaries if he wasn't hauling the grain to an elevator in town for sale or storage. During World War II, gasoline-engine augers that elevated the grain into the bins came into use, replacing the human scoopers. All these implements, plus the self-propelled combine, which eventually replaced the pull-type machines after the war and eliminated the tractor and its driver, greatly reduced the manpower required for harvest.

The self-propelled combine also speeded the harvest process enormously. Whereas a reaper or header could cut 20 acres or so of wheat in a day, a modern self-propelled combine with a thirty-foot swath can cut 80 to 100 acres of wheat and 50 to 60 acres of corn in a normal day, more if they operate at night. Bob Johnson, who raises wheat, corn, alfalfa, and cattle south of McDonald, gets corn yields of up to 200 bushels per acre. With his combine able to run through this at five miles per hour, five or six trucks each with a 400-bushel capacity or two large semis each with 1,000-bushel capacity are hard pressed to keep the combine clear. Ron Bell and his sons also can combine corn with one machine as fast as they can haul it. It takes four trucks each with a 350- to 400-bushel capacity and shuttling constantly between the field and the granaries to keep their seven-year-old John Deere combine clear.

The current combines cost $150,000, and with an eight-row corn

---

*Man wasn't always a slave to the machine, however. Leonard Vyzourek, who is retired and lives in McDonald while his son runs his farm east of town, recalls his days on a threshing crew. When the pitchers wanted a break, they would deliberately speed up their pace in order to overload, or "slug," the machine, which would force a halt while the operator and his assistant dug the excess straw out.

header costing another $28,000, they are a capital investment that many farmers either can't afford or don't consider efficient. Many of the biggest operators, whose wheat acreage is in the thousands, don't feel that they can afford the number of machines their land would require, although some own one or two to help reduce their custom-cutting costs, to clean up loose ends if rain delays keep their custom cutters from completing the job, and to cut corn and milo. Instead, they rely on the custom cutters, entrepreneurs who each own several combines and contract with farmers to cut and haul their wheat and often are farmers themselves. When the wheat harvest begins in May in the Texas panhandle, they move north with the ripening wheat, many ending up in Canada cutting the spring wheat.* They also harvest corn and feed grains in the fall.

As efficient as these machines are, it is certain that they will get better. In 1994, two cousins in central Kansas, in the never-ending search for greater speed and efficiency, were developing a machine in which the concaves rotate in the same direction as the cylinder, although at a lower speed, 50 rpm compared to the cylinder's 800 rpm. They contend that the system cleans the grain better and is smaller than the current ones. The result is a smaller combine with half as many moving parts that still threshes faster; another improvement is that they mount it on caterpillar tracks, which enables it to work when the plants are dry but the ground is too wet for conventional traction, an important factor particularly when corn is ready for harvest in the fall.

In addition to wheat, the combines thresh corn and feed grains such as sorghum and milo, soybeans, and sunflowers. Mechanical corn pickers ended the slow, laborious process of picking and shucking corn by hand and throwing the ears into a wagon to be hauled to the crib or sheller, and the combines have replaced the pickers and shellers. A strong, experienced man could pick 100 bushels by hand in a long, hard day; the new combines can thresh that much in ten or fifteen minutes and are the cause of the disappearance of the traditional slat-sided corncribs in which unshelled ears were stored to dry.

Shelled corn is first stored in granaries, where it is dried by hot air forced through a network of pipes. Arlie Archer, who with his brother and son are the third and fourth generations on the family farm southwest of

---

*The rates, which vary slightly by location, are $12 or $13 per acre for wheat plus about $0.12 per bushel for yields above 21 bushels per acre (bpa); about $18 an acre plus $0.10 or $0.11 per bushel for yields over 67 bpa for corn; and $14 per acre plus about $0.12 a bushel for yields above 36 bpa for sorghum feed grains such as milo. Hauling charges for all grains are about $0.12 per bushel plus $0.11 per mile over thirteen miles.

McDonald (his father enlisted in the Army with my uncle Asa in World War I), has a corn-drying bin with a 5 million Btu burner that can dry up to 10,000 bushels overnight. It is powered by a Chrysler V-8 engine and controlled by a computer on the side of the bin. At intervals, the computer orders the conveyor system to move a small amount of corn past an electronic sensor to test it for moisture content. If the corn is at or below the percentage of moisture Arlie has entered into the computer, the computer orders the conveyor system to move it to a storage granary and monitors it during the process for dampness. If it's too wet, the computer stops the conveyor and turns on the burner, which blows hot air into the drying bin until the corn is dry enough. A tape, which looks much like the one on a cash register, gives Arlie a continuous readout on the operation.

Computers play an increasingly important role on today's farm and many farmers have as many as a dozen performing such functions as analyzing the efficiency of their various operations (cattle, hogs, wheat, corn), regulating customized mixtures and amounts of various nutrients in their feeding and fertilizing operations, and monitoring their machines' performances. Many farmers have computer systems and software that help them to manage their operations and inventory, and to track markets, commodity prices, futures, and weather patterns. Most successful farmers have software that enables them to track the commodities markets in Kansas City, Minneapolis, and Chicago minute-by-minute. At any given moment, the computer can tell a farmer what the result will be if he sells a certain number of bushels of corn on any given day and what the current market price is for sales contracts made for any particular day or days in the future. And there are programs that help them keep track of costs and can tell them at any given moment what a one cent change in fuel costs or beef prices, say, will mean to them. Ron Bell has a degree in electrical engineering from Kansas State and one of his sons, Charlie, is just a semester away from his EE at K-State.* This use of telecommunications is nothing new; in December 1925, the *McDonald Standard* carried a farm column that reported that "radios are becoming as common as telephones and are working a great change in the grain trade. If the morning report is of a poor market, little grain will come in that day, but if the market is good the grain comes flooding in."

---

*Ron and Charlie design and sell computer systems as a sideline. A. B. Fisher's son, Abe, is a Kansas State graduate who was working on a master's degree in computer science and working for a computer company in Kansas City when he decided to return to the farm. Abe has brought the operation's computer system up to speed. His wife, Janet, a former accounting teacher, and A.B.'s wife, Judy, operate the computerized bookkeeping system.

The latest combines have computers that give them "cruise control" similar to those used on autos to maintain a constant speed on interstate highways. On the combine, the computer keeps the internal mechanism running at optimum speed, adjusted to the condition of the grain being threshed, and alters the combine's ground speed to the heaviness of the crop. The modern tractors and combines also have computers that tell the farmer how much land has been covered in a given time, how much grain has been threshed on a given piece of ground, and what the per-acre yield is, both on individual fields and in toto. These systems have sensors that monitor the performance of critical elements and warn of malfunctions and misadjustments that can cause such problems as blowing a portion of the grain out the back along with the straw and chaff or inadequate cleaning of the grain of straw and chaff. Today's grain carts, or wagons, into which the combines unload have scales in the bottom that weigh each load, and computers that also keep count of the amount harvested off each field.

The old horse-drawn farm wagons could haul only 55 to 60 bushels, which made a substantial winter's work for a farmer who harvested several thousand bushels, stored it in granaries on his farm, then hauled it to the elevators in town for sale in the off-season. A long, cold winter's work as well, since each wagon could make only one or two trips a day, depending on the distance to town.* The standard-sized trucks of the 1930s and 1940s, which were rated at a one-and-a-half- or two-and-a-half-ton capacity, could haul about 120 bushels, or two of the old combine bin loads, and make several trips a day. After World War II, the size of trucks grew. Trucks that can haul 500 or 600 bushels now are common and many farmers have semis that can carry nearly 1,000 bushels. Many farmers in northwest Kansas routinely haul their grain as much as fifty miles to terminals such as Colby, which has a complex of enormous elevators and a railroad siding for about 100 cars that carry cargo directly to the ports on the Gulf of Mexico.

One thing is certain. Technology will continue to grow in sophistication. The latest experiments in field analysis use satellites to track equipment moving through the fields, down to the centimeter. Variations in soil composition and fertility can be mapped to a fraction of an acre, which

---

*My stepfather, C. L. Raichart, did a lot of this work as a young man and never forgot how cold and miserable it was. One theory about warding off colds was to eat raw onions, which, he laughingly recalled, "kept our sinuses open—and our dance cards too." Onions were a popular medicine in those days. Roasted onion poultices, applied to the hands and feet for chills and fever, and to the chest for colds and pneumonia, were a common treatment.

will enable the farmer to plant seeds in varying densities depending on fertility and to avoid expensive fertilizing in patches that don't need it. The farmer will be able to add trace chemicals in amounts as small as a pound per acre or a pound per million pounds of topsoil.

✒

Technology is ubiquitous. Many large operators have machine shops that are on a par with many commercial operations. They can do all the repair work on their complex machines except such highly technical processes as turning engine crankshafts, which they take to machine shops in larger towns such as Burlington, Colorado.

Since 1975, several of the big farms around McDonald, the Bells, the Fishers, the Frisbies, Bob Johnson and his sons, Herman Antholz, and Dan and Dave Hubbard,* have been on a UHF line-of-sight radio network. The system was devised and installed by Ron Bell, who is also helping Rawlins County set up communications systems for its emergency services. The radio transmitter, which is on top of the Bells' ninety-foot silo nine miles south of town, can reach as far as Colby and Goodland, fifty miles away, and McCook, Nebraska, eighty miles northeast. Each member of each family on the net has a radio and a call sign (Bob Johnson and his sons and their wives are RJ 1, RJ 2, RJ 3, and so forth).

At first they mounted the radios in their truck and tractor cabs but now carry them on their belts. If someone in the field needs a repair part or supplies of any kind, he can radio home for it. Or he can find out if any of the others is in Goodland or Colby, which have regional implement dealers. Because the system can patch into the phone system, they can also call in orders for parts and material directly from the field to the dealers in Colby or Goodland.

Probably the most dramatic use of the network was when Jim Bell, Ron's son, was combining wheat about a mile and a half west of town and straw in the combine was ignited by an overheated bearing on the return auger. He radioed an alert, which his grandfather picked up. "I told him, Jim, for Heaven's sake, drive the combine over on that worked ground of Fisher's so you don't set the field on fire," Claude Bell, Jim's grandfather, recalled. Jim did. Dave Hubbard, who was at his home in town, just two blocks from the fire station, heard the alarm, raced to the station, and started up the fire truck. Ron Bell also heard the call and reached the

*They inherited the holdings of their father, DeRoy Hubbard, a high school classmate of mine, and are renting Ed Cahoj's land, another classmate, as well.

combine a few minutes later, arriving at about the same time Dave did. Ron put the exterior fire out with his fire extinguisher while Dave flooded the combine's interior with water from the fire engine. Because of their quick reaction, the fire didn't even scorch the combine's exterior paint; the only damage was the loss of some internal vinyl and rubber beaters that help move the straw through the machine.

The newer combines have sensors that detect such mechanical failures. It's an imperfect world, however. At one point, the warning lights on the dashboard of the Bells' new combine malfunctioned because of dirt and had to be removed and cleaned.

In 1994 northwest Kansas began another step in technological upgrading with the construction of transmission towers near Atwood, Oberlin, and St. Francis that will provide access to cellular telephones. It was only in late 1993 that the area got touch-tone telephone service, which is crucial in the age of telecommunications.

⚡

A major downside to technology, beginning with the discovery of fire and the invention of the wheel, is that it's dangerous. Serious accidents are always lurking just around the corner from people working with machinery. Impatience—the temptation to take a shortcut that will save a few seconds—is the killer and maimer of thousands on farms and ranches. An instant's inattention or carelessness can be fatal. Farming and mining are the most dangerous occupations in this country.

Tractors overturn on slopes; arms and fingers get caught in high-speed chains and belts. Horses and other large animals are a peril if a farmer allows himself to unwarily step behind one or be trapped between one and a fence or barn wall. Ed Cahoj, my old friend and classmate, and his family have known their share of tragedy. His older brother, Leonard, was killed by the gas from fermentation of silage stored in one of his silos, and his oldest son, Phil, almost lost a hand when the sleeve of his jacket got caught by a high-speed power-takeoff driveshaft that didn't have the safety guard on it; the injury cost Phil partial use of the hand, years of treatment, and a dozen operations, and it helped drive him out of farming in Kansas. Ed's father, who celebrated his ninety-sixth birthday in 1994, was minus a finger for most of his adult life.

The power takeoffs on tractors and the corn shellers, feed grinders, and other machines they power are all potentially lethal. Harry Archer, Arlie's father, who lived into his nineties, lost an arm at the age of seventy-seven when it was caught in a grain auger and he had to be cut loose with a chain saw. Over the years, such tragedies have been played out thousands of times on the nation's farms. There's no end to the variety of potential disasters.

Fortunately, I never had a mishap, but that was due in large measure to good luck. My only close brush with a potentially serious accident was the summer I was fifteen when I was on the harvest crew for Dal Hughes, a wonderful man whose family were longtime friends of my grandparents.* Dal had a big Minneapolis-Moline tractor which had a hand clutch the operator pushed forward to go and pulled back to stop. The concept couldn't be more simple and logical and it was the arrangement of most tractors that had hand clutches (International Harvester tractors, such as the W9, had foot clutches, like an automobile's). The problem was that the hand clutch on my family's Model L Case tractor, which was the first one I ever ran, operated just the opposite: You pulled it back to engage and pushed it forward to stop.

We had a day off from cutting wheat because of rain and Dal and I were moving some machinery from one field to another. I was trying to hook up to a disk plow known as a "one-way" and taking one of those dangerous shortcuts that lead to trouble. I backed the big tractor so that its drawbar was almost aligned with the one-way's hitch, then stepped down between the tractor and the implement. Reaching up to the hand clutch, I eased the tractor back in reverse gear for the hookup. I momentarily forgot the MM's clutch arrangement, however, and wanting to stop it, I pushed the clutch forward, as I would have with our Case. The MM kept right on coming back at me, of course, and was about to pin me against the one-way and its sharp steel disks. Fortunately, I didn't panic, remembered where I was, and pulled the clutch back before any damage was done.

God knows what could have happened, however, and I'm afraid the episode took several years off poor Dal's life. He was several yards away and saw the whole thing, but I had the tractor stopped before he could take more than a few steps. When he arrived, however, he advised me in unmistakable terms never to back a tractor up to an implement that way ever again. That close call, to borrow from Samuel Johnson's dictum about the imminence of hanging, certainly focused both our minds on the matter and I took Dal's admonition to heart. A gentle and generous man if there ever was one, that was the only time he ever spoke sharply to me, but I didn't take it amiss. I was almost as shaken as he was.

The only close call I had in harming machinery through negligence was on the W9. It had the temperature and oil gauges on top of the engine

---

*His father was a Baptist minister and baptized Grandfather and Grandmother Phipps in 1896.

hood at eye level, which made them pretty hard to miss, but I occasionally managed to do it. Early one afternoon when I fortuitously happened to focus on them, I saw that the temperature gauge was in the red. I shut the engine off and saw that the radiator fan belt had broken. Since I didn't have the pickup and was three miles west of town, I had to walk across the road to the nearest farm (which was the place my grandparents had settled in 1905 and sold in 1920) to phone for help. I had managed to boil the radiator almost dry but fortunately shut down before doing any damage to the engine—not soon enough, however, to avoid getting some hard-eyed looks from my uncle and Claude Pickett and reminders that those gauges were there for a purpose. It also took longer than I care to remember before Claude felt that he didn't always have to be on me to make sure that I was dependable in emptying the air filter, which collected dust, chaff, and other sediment in a glass bowl before it could get into the carburetor, and the sediment bowl, another glass bowl on the fuel line into which dust that had gotten into the gas tank settled before it could get into the carburetor.

⚓

Technology took the really back-breaking work, like pitching hay and scooping wheat, out of farming, but the boredom of long hours on the tractor or combine, twelve to fourteen hours, day after baking, sun-struck summer day, was a major downside of working with machinery. Looking at the air-conditioned cabs with their stereos on today's machines reminds me that I would have killed just for a radio on the tractor—forget the air-conditioned cab (which is a necessity, not a luxury; tractor and combine cabs are mostly glass for visibility, which lets in sunlight and makes air-conditioning a necessity. If the air conditioner breaks down, the combine is shut down). About the only thing we could do to pass all that time on our cabless, radioless tractors was to take our shirts off and work on our suntans.

Having radios to help pass the time on tractors or combines is not the reason for them, however; they have a serious function in helping to increase the farmer's efficiency. From the development of the flint arrowhead to the silicon computer chip, technology has aided and abetted man in his never-ending quest to bend nature to his will. The pace of technological change—and its impact on society—steadily becomes more rapid and more profound.

CHAPTER FOURTEEN

"LAND OF THE UNDERGROUND RAIN"

THE ABILITY TO PUMP IRRIGATION WATER OUT OF THE OGALLALA Aquifer enabled High Plains farmers to raise corn, feed grains, soybeans, sunflowers, edible beans, and other crops in addition to wheat. It allowed them to diversify their crops, which cushioned the blow of a poor wheat crop, and to some extent afforded some protection against the vagaries of the weather, particularly the sparse and unpredictable rainfall on the High Plains. Irrigation wells make water available on demand, although at a cost, and a history of early irrigation by Donald E. Green is aptly entitled *Land of the Underground Rain: Irrigation on the Texas High Plains, 1910–1970.*

Like other technology, irrigation has made a profound impact on farming around McDonald. It greatly increases the farmer's capital investment, as much as doubling it by some estimates, and thus adds to the pressure to enlarge operations. This in turn makes it more difficult for young, independent new farmers to start up. It has also altered the nature of farming in the area.

The ability to raise corn and feed grains gave an enormous boost to the cattle industry on the High Plains. In Rawlins County alone, corn production increased nearly tenfold in the 1980s, from 2,500 acres harvested in 1980 to 22,400 in 1991. By the 1980s and 1990s, the center of the cattle-feeding, slaughter, and packing industries in the United States had shifted from Illinois and Iowa to western Kansas, Oklahoma, and Texas and the new feedlots and packing plants in Dodge City, Garden City, Liberal, and Scott City in Kansas and Guyman, Oklahoma, and Perryton, Texas. The largest meat-packing plant in the world is near Garden City, just outside the little town of Holcomb, which is eight miles west of Garden City; the plant kills and processes 5,000 head a day.* The second largest is in Dodge City. Another reason for the shift is that winter feeding of cattle is more efficient here where the winters are milder than in Iowa and the other corn states farther north.†

About 150,000 wells have been drilled into the Ogallala Aquifer since World War II, about 17,500 in Kansas, due to such technological developments as the turbine pump, lightweight aluminum piping, the center pivot mechanism, and the discovery of cheap natural gas, which fuels the pumps, in the Hugoton field in southwest Kansas. More than 3 million acres are irrigated in Kansas and they produce about one-fourth of the state's crops.

In 1955, a McDonald farmer, Arlie Archer, drilled the first pump-installed irrigation well in northwest Kansas. This was appropriate in a historical sense because in 1885 the state drilled the first irrigation well ever in Kansas on his farm, which was then owned and operated by his grandfather. The well was never used for irrigation, however, but pumped water into a reservoir that for many years supplied water, and ice in the winter, for the town of McDonald.

There are about 200 wells irrigating about 20,000 acres in Rawlins County. So many wells have been drilled in northwest Kansas that it is now almost impossible to get permits for new ones. Only two were issued in 1993 and Jack Poore, the McDonald area's premier driller, has been out of business since the mid-eighties because of this and the recession. "New rights fell off the edge after 1979," said Wayne Bossert, manager of Northwest Kansas Groundwater Management District Four, which includes the McDonald area. "The district all but shut down" in granting new permits. There are 3,526 wells in the management district, which includes all or part of the ten northwest counties, 3.1 million acres.

It is increasingly difficult to make irrigation cost-efficient for a number of reasons. One is that natural gas, the most efficient fuel for pump engines, cost $0.22 per thousand cubic feet (mcf) back in the 1950s but was nearly $4 per mcf in 1994. The Bells, who have holdings east, south, and west of McDonald, estimate that it costs them about $10,000 a month for

---

*Holcomb is the site of the Clutter family murders, which Truman Capote made famous with his book, *In Cold Blood.*

†Garden City, population about 24,000, has had to manage the influx of large numbers of ethnic minority workers in the feedlots and slaughterhouses, particularly Vietnamese and Mexicans. This and the large turnover of these groups—no one wants to work in the abattoirs very long—have caused some stress on the town, particularly the school system, but on the whole it has coped pretty well.

five months to run six pumps, which irrigate 950 acres, 700 of corn and edible beans and 250 of wheat. And as the water level in the Ogallala drops because of the continuing drawdown, the water becomes more expensive to pump.

The hardware also has become more costly. Center pivot units, which most farmers are installing because of their efficiency—they lose less water to evaporation—cost from $35,000 to as much as $60,000 or more each, including the cost of drilling the well and installing the underground pipe. A center pivot is a long pipe on wheels that rotates around a pivot point and waters a circular area of 120 to 130 acres. A ten-inch pipe with a pump powered by an eight-cylinder engine adapted from the oil fields can deliver as much as 1,200 gallons of water per minute.

The initial irrigation technique on the High Plains was to flood the fields, first with ditches, then from gated pipes laid at the high end of the field, which was graded so the water would flow by gravity down the furrows. This method has two major drawbacks: It is labor-intensive because of the need to check the pipes and ditches, and compared to the sprinkler systems, it loses a relatively large percentage of water to evaporation and deep percolation.

Because of the rapid drawdown of the Ogallala Aquifer, in the past several years Groundwater Management District Four has been trying several means of bringing it into equilibrium. One is to require irrigators to bring their systems up to maximum efficiency. The goal, as proposed, is to get farmers with center pivot systems to adopt techniques that are 85 to 90 percent efficient, i.e., that get 85 to 90 percent of the water to the plant roots area rather than having it soak deeper into the ground or losing it to evaporation. The new center pivot systems can do this because they substantially reduce evaporation by sprinkling the water out of drop hoses that hang down from the pipe rather than spraying it up and out under pressure into the air as the earlier ones did. Farmers still using the flood system will be pushed to improve their systems to reach their 75 percent maximum efficiency.

"Our policy will be one of attempting to protect senior water rights, but we have a sort of paradoxical reverse order of priorities because the junior rights have the most efficient technology," said Bossert. The district won't shut down farmers who have older rights and techniques and can't afford the new technology, but it will drive all systems to operate at the top of their efficiency. However, it is currently working on a policy that entails a sophisticated monitoring system which will check all the irrigation operations in the district to determine if any are using more water than they need each year. This will be done by measuring the amount of rainfall and the crops raised on each field, which determines the amount of irrigation water needed, and then checking that against the actual amount pumped. Those who irrigate in excess will be required to upgrade their systems for maximum efficiency or make whatever management adjustments might be needed to ensure efficient use of the water.

District water officials also advocate a weather modification program, primarily cloud seeding, to increase rainfall and reduce hail, which would conserve water and would also have a substantial economic benefit. "The technology is there," Bossert contended. "Some are resisting it, but it can be done." Another means of conserving water is simply to transfer water rights to land that can be more efficiently irrigated, primarily land that is flat and not cut by draws, gullies, and creeks. "We have to be flexible in changing rights so that we can get the right kind of system on the better irrigable land," said Bossert.

Finally, water can be saved by switching federal farm subsidies from water-thirsty crops such as corn to those that require less moisture, such as milo and other feed grains. "One way to slow the drawdown of the aquifer is for the federal government to switch the price subsidies to less water-intensive irrigated crops than corn," Bossert said. A major reason for the quadrupling of corn acreage in Rawlins County is that the price supports for corn make it so profitable even though the country has a surplus of it.

The drawdown of the Ogallala Aquifer has been less in the northwestern counties, Rawlins, Cheyenne, Sherman, and Thomas, than further south in Kansas, Oklahoma, and Texas, where the resulting increase in pumping costs has curtailed or halted irrigation in some areas. This is primarily because irrigation started earlier in the southern areas, and partly because the northwestern counties are cut through by several large creeks and draws, which reduce the amount of flat, desirable cropland that is good for irrigation. It also appears that the aquifer may be recharged somewhat faster by surface streams in some areas north of Interstate 70, which runs east and west about thirty miles south of McDonald.

The Bells reported that the water level under their land has dropped only a foot since they drilled their first well in 1962 and believe that the aquifer in their area is being recharged by the man-made Bonny Reservoir on the Republican River in eastern Colorado, about fifty miles west. In Rawlins County overall, however, the aquifer has been drawn down 10 to 15 percent, according to Bossert. Arlie Archer's operation is typical of the area; in his forty-nine years of irrigation, his water level has dropped 13 percent, from 177 feet to 200 feet, with no reduction in 1993.

In addition to decisions on irrigation, a major management decision area for farmers is in the adoption of tillage techniques that reduce moisture evaporation, prevent wind and water erosion, cut down irrigation and tilling costs—and maximize profits.

Probably the most significant tillage technique development on the High Plains prior to modern technology was "summer fallowing" wheat land. In this process, the ground lies fallow for a year and is planted every other year. This increases moisture conservation by about 15 percent and gives subsoil moisture a year—fourteen months, actually, between harvest in July and drilling in September of the following year—to restore. This is of great importance in an area of meager rainfall such as western Kansas. Wheat yields on "summer till" are about twice those of continuous cropping, so overall production is about the same while labor, fuel, and other costs of continuous cropping are reduced.

Summer tilling was pioneered in northwest Kansas by Asa Payne, or "Ace" as he was known, a highly respected McDonald farmer and business and civic leader who chanced onto it at the turn of the century. A neighboring farmer had planted ten acres to potatoes in the corner of one of his wheat fields northwest of town, but potato bugs killed the plants before they produced anything. Asa Payne noticed the bare patch and at drilling time asked the neighbor if he could rent the ten acres and plant it to wheat. The plot yielded nearly forty bushels per acre, more than twice the norm for continuous cropping, and Asa Payne assumed that there was a connection between the fact that the patch had stood idle for a year and its improved yield. Subsequent experimentation proved him correct.

In 1927, Asa Payne wrote in *Kansas Farmer* magazine:

> During these 25 years of summer fallowing we have never failed to raise a good crop of wheat, having from 100 to 420 acres planted every year and yielding from 27 to 45 bushels an acre. In 1926 we had 240 acres of summer fallowed wheat that averaged 41 bushels an acre. . . . This wheat was grown with [only] 5.06 inches of rainfall from the time it was seeded until harvested.

He went on to note that wind erosion, or "blowing," had been eliminated by using the lister, a double-moldboard plow that dug a furrow, instead of the traditional moldboard plow, which turned the stubble and other vegetation under, and the spring-tooth harrow, which broke the ground into clods rather than pulverizing it. "The disk should not be used at any time and has no place in summer fallow farming where the soil is silty as in Northwest Kansas," he continued.* This historic breakthrough has been widely practiced on the High Plains for nearly a century now and has been of enormous value both to the farmer and the environment. It wasn't the complete answer, however; summer fallow ground blew almost as badly during the Dust Bowl as the rest.

※↓※

Another moisture-saving technique developed in the twentieth century is the construction of terraces, which prevents water runoff and erosion. This involves plowing berms—terraces—along the contour lines of rolling land, which makes it somewhat harder to farm but prevents runoff and stores the water. There are 8,144 linear miles of terraces on Rawlins County's 650,000 farm acres.

An increasingly popular dryland farming technique is "no-till," the practice of leaving wheat stubble intact over the winter and planting it to corn the following spring. Not cultivating the stubble has a big advantage in moisture retention because every time tilled land is worked to kill the weeds, which summer fallow requires, the ground is opened up and moisture is lost to evaporation. No-till has another positive side because rotating crops helps prevent plant diseases, which are more likely when the same crop is planted year after year on the same ground. No-till is another means of soil conservation and a response to the concern over the dwindling Ogallala Aquifer and the increasing cost of irrigation. Properly done, it enables farmers to raise milo and even corn, one of the thirstiest of crops, without irrigation even in western Kansas, where the twenty-inch annual rainfall is only about half the amount needed for corn.

Dryland corn has to be planted in wheat stubble and new drills have been designed to do this. Herbicides are applied immediately after the wheat is harvested in July, which keeps the untilled ground weed-free over the winter until the corn is planted the following spring. With the wheat stubble holding the snow and reducing evaporation by shading the ground and no weeds to draw off the precious water, 60 to 80 percent of the moisture is retained, which is enough to support corn, albeit at a lesser yield than on irrigated land. Another negative of no-till is that while the stubble retains water, it can harbor insects and plant diseases. The trade-off is in the reduction of irrigation and tilling costs.

---

*The lister created small ridges on either side of the furrow, which helped break the wind and the movement of the silty soil.

The drawdown of the Ogallala Aquifer and the resulting increased pumping costs will probably cause dryland farming and no-till corn acreage in the area to continue to increase, but some farmers, like Arlie Archer, are skeptical about the long-term prospects. "It's worked in the past few years when we've had above-average rainfall," he observed. "We'll see how it does in average or below-average moisture."

In addition to corn and milo, irrigation has enabled farmers in western Kansas to raise sunflowers, both the confectionery variety eaten as snacks and those whose seeds are crushed for cooking oil, with the residue processed into livestock feed. This is appropriate since the indigenous sunflower is the Kansas state flower, but there also is a bit of irony; the sunflower only grows wild in ditches, creek banks, and other areas where moisture accumulates and it has to be irrigated to make a crop. There has been a growing market for sunflowers in the 1990s, both domestic and export, and prices have been high enough that they haven't needed the government-support programs such as those for wheat and corn.* Farmers can contract the sale of the seeds in advance of the harvest whenever they think they're at the top of the market, or store the crop and wait for prices to rise; the general contract is for the seeds to produce oil 40 percent by weight, with a discount for those producing less and a bonus for those that exceed the minimum.

Sunflowers exacerbate a serious problem for the High Plains, however. Plants add to and take out elements in the soil, a process that alters the soil's chemistry. Each plant has a different effect and the changes sunflowers work alter the soil's texture in a way that causes it to granulate, making it susceptible to wind erosion. Blowing is a serious matter for farmers in western Kansas, for both ecological and economic reasons. When a field starts blowing, the owner has to get into it quickly to plow it into strips with a chisel, which breaks the crust into clods and helps stop the blowing. If a field frequently blows, it is liable to being classified as erodible or highly erodible by the Agriculture Stabilization and Conservation Service (ASCS), which means serious trouble. Wind erosion obviously can't be kept secret; farmers downwind from a blowing field are anxious to get it stopped before the blowing dirt damages their crops and to that end often help with the chiseling. They will also report it if it becomes a chronic problem.

---

*At the time of passage of the 1993 North American Free Trade Agreement (NAFTA), my first cousin once removed, Greg Doll, was the purchasing agent for the Sun Products company in Goodland. Its crushing plant is a former sugar beet facility capable of processing about 500 tons of sunflower seeds per day. Greg strongly favored NAFTA because of the demand for sunflower oil for food processing and cooking in Mexico.

The market value of land classified as highly erodible is reduced by 50 percent or more because it places severe restrictions on the land's use—and the classification is very difficult to reverse. Erodible land that can be put into crops must conform to a planting plan that has very restrictive rules such as requiring that the crops leave a minimum poundage of residue per acre to inhibit blowing. Some can be put into grass, in which case the farmer bears the expense of seeding and keeping the weeds down and is paid a 5 or 6 percent return by the federal government. He can graze on it—but must get a permit from the ASCS.

Because of wind erosion, the traditional moldboard plow hasn't been used on the High Plains in decades. Turning the ground over and leaving it bare, then disking it, as is done in states like Iowa that get ample rainfall, powders the soil and makes it susceptible to blowing. As a result, implements have been developed for the High Plains. One is the disk plow, or "one-way," which chops the stubble up but doesn't turn it under. Another is the "chisel," which has large harrowlike teeth that break the ground into lumps, or clods, which, like stubble, stalks, and other vegetation—known as "trash"—help keep it from blowing. This tillage reduces evaporation loss by an estimated 15 percent; no-till reduces it by about 25 percent.

Another post–World War II technological development is the enormous increase in the application of chemicals to the soil. The extensive use of chemicals—fertilizers and herbicides—began on the High Plains about 1960. It boosts yields but is expensive. Big operators like the Bells and others buy anhydrous ammonia and other fertilizers by the tank-car load, about twenty tons each, and can apply two tons an hour spraying a fifty-foot swath at six miles per hour. Claude Bell estimated that it cost $50,000 to fertilize and seed 700 acres of corn; other estimates put the figure at twice that.

Another technological development of the early 1990s promises to improve the efficiency of fertilizer and increase corn yields substantially. Corn is fertilized with nitrogen, phosphate, potash, zinc, and sulfur, whose mix and amounts are monitored and adjusted by computers on the implements during operation. One problem has been the inability to inject the mixture deep enough to get it below the root system. Until recently, the farmer could only get it down about two inches below the surface, which meant that he was getting only a fraction of its nutritive value because it needed to be eight to ten inches deep to be fully absorbed by the roots. Arlie Archer bought an implement in 1993 that has chisel blades which penetrate nine inches and have an attached tube through which the fertilizer is inserted below the root level.

"We get about one hundred and sixty bushels to the acre now and I expect this will add ten or fifteen bushels an acre a year for a while at least," Arlie said. "At two dollars a bushel and one hundred and sixty bushels, we can't pay the bills. We have to increase production." Another farmer smiled his rueful agreement. "And we add to the [corn] surplus." he said.*

The use of chemicals, not surprisingly, has led to environmental concerns. Traces of herbicides and fertilizers are appearing in the groundwater, but some agronomists think it's slight. "I don't think it involves much risk because we're using short-lived contact herbicides that don't accumulate in the soil as the earlier ones such as atrazine did," said Richard Wahl, a former farmer and now a Kansas State University extension agricultural economist in Colby. "We're looking at a trade-off. No-till farming [which requires herbicides for weed control] reduces wind and water erosion."

Atrazine, which is a suspected carcinogen, will probably be banned nationwide by 1995 or 1996. "We have to keep it back from the wells and water sources like creeks, but it'll probably be gone in two or three years," said Arlie Archer. Atrazine was a favorite with many farmers because it is enormously effective and very cheap—in some corn states such as Wisconsin it is credited with helping to more than double corn yields since 1960. It costs only about four dollars per acre to apply, which is a fraction of the cost of its suggested replacements, and one application is all that's needed.

🖎

Another post–World War II technological factor is the breakthrough in corn and wheat hybrids, which provide greater yields and are more resistant to disease, insects, and extremes in the weather. The hard red winter wheat strains now planted on the High Plains are descendants of the hardy Turkey Red, which, as previously noted, the so-called "Volga Germans" fleeing czarist Russia in the late nineteenth century brought with them. Because the climate of the Ukraine and southern Russian steppes is similar to that of the High Plains, Turkey Red could withstand the temperature extremes of Kansas summers and winters and the sparse rainfall, and adapted well to the New World. It was also rich in gluten, the

---

*Another technological development of the 1990s, which could reduce the use of pesticides, is cloning a gene from a disease-resistant plant onto others. An early success with the technique was with tomatoes.

sticky, nutritious protein substance that gives dough the tough, elastic quality necessary for making good bread. At first, however, it posed a problem for millers, whose stone grinders and water-driven mills were adequate for the soft native wheats but not the hard Turkey Red. The millers had to develop cold-iron rollers and more advanced sources of power such as steam engines for Turkey Red and its descendants.

The new strains of wheat, known as semidwarfs, have a much shorter stalk than the old ones, about half as much as the old Turkey Red. This makes them less likely to go down in a tangle when hit by wind and rain when they're ripe and ready for the combine, which slows the harvest and often results in crop loss. It also makes them less susceptible to fungus and other diseases, enables them to dry faster, and leaves less straw to be processed. The new strains are also high in gluten. Most of the new wheat strains over the years have been developed by plant geneticists at Kansas State University, so it was something of a blow to state pride that the most popular strain in Kansas—accounting for 70 percent of the state wheat crop in the early 1990s—was a popular new strain called TAM 107, which was named for Texas A&M University, where it was developed.

The search for improved varieties of corn, a pioneer in which was Iowa's Henry Wallace, Franklin Roosevelt's second vice president, continues unabated. Many farmers have as many as fifteen test blocks each, with a different strain of corn in a field, planted by seed companies to see which give the best yield and resist disease and the elements the best.

<hr />

Technology has made the farmer more productive and his work easier, physically if not mentally and emotionally, and it has enabled him to reconcile his economic goals with the need to preserve the environment in ways undreamed of 50 and 100 years ago. At the same time, it has made his operation much larger and more complex and the management of it commensurately more complicated.

Successful operators like the Bells—the late Claude Bell, his son, Ron, and Ron's sons, Charlie and Bob—Arlie Archer, his brother, Ross, and Arlie's son, Alan; C. K. Fisher, his son, A.B., and A.B.'s son, Abe; Bob Johnson and his sons, Rod and Ron; and Don Antholz and his son, Robbin utilize a wide variety of technologies in their operations: machinery, irrigation, new tillage techniques and plant strains, fertilizers, herbicides, and pesticides. They use computers to monitor everything from the commodity markets and weather to the proper mixture of fertilizers and cattle feed to the functioning of their machines. The essence of farm management, as always, is utilizing technology and other resources not necessarily to maximize production but to maximize the bottom line.

The Bells, for instance, have 1,900 acres of cropland and 500 acres of grass. In a typical year, they put in 600 acres of corn, 650 acres of wheat, and 80 acres of edible beans such as pinto and black beans. They irrigate the corn and beans and 250 acres of wheat from six wells drilled down into the Ogallala Aquifer. They irrigate the wheat twice during the spring and summer and in 1993 their irrigated wheat made fifty-nine bushels per acre (irrigated wheat generally yields about ten bushels per acre more than dryland wheat and often has a higher test weight because it's less likely to shrivel in dry, hot weather); wheat requires much less water than corn, which has to be irrigated almost constantly during the growing season.

The Bells plant, fertilize, and irrigate their corn to get a 150-bushel-per-acre yield. They could get 200 bushels but don't feel that the likelihood of losing some of it to the weather makes the additional costs a good business risk. To raise "150-bushel corn," as it's known, they sow each plant seven inches apart and fertilize and irrigate accordingly. Unlike many farmers in the area, they don't raise milo or sunflowers. "The cattlemen prefer to feed corn over milo and pay twenty to thirty cents a bushel more for it," Claude observed shortly before his death. "At one hundred and twenty to one hundred and fifty bushels per acre, it adds up. The difference pays the water [irrigation] bill."

The Fishers, who are incorporated as the Fisher Cattle Company, are one of the biggest family operations in western Kansas; for tax and estate purposes, they actually constitute two corporations, a partnership, and a number of trusts. They own about 24,000 acres and buy, feed, and sell cattle by the thousands. "Do you know what a township is?" C.K. asked as he showed me around his holdings in the summer of 1993. "Yes," I answered. "I own a township," he said with a touch of justifiable pride. A township has two definitions: It is a unit of territory in the U.S. land survey thirty-six miles square, or 23,080 acres; it is also a political subdivision smaller than a county but larger than a town or city. Sometimes the political jurisdiction is the same size as the survey unit but not always and C.K. was referring to the survey unit.

Although eighty-seven years old and suffering from Parkinson's disease in the summer of 1993, he was eager to take me on a tour of his holdings. He derives a historical satisfaction from the fact that he now owns the field in which Asa Payne discovered the summer fallow process. The Fishers own land north, west, and south of town. "You try to spread it around,

238 238 HOME ON THE RANGE

not have it all in one place," he said. "That way hail and other bad weather doesn't get everything." Their holdings span as much as twenty miles north and south. C.K. came to McDonald as a schoolteacher in 1928 with nothing but his brains and ambition and married another schoolteacher. They bought a quarter section and then another and by the time A.B. was married in 1962 they owned 4,000 acres. The 20,000 acres they've added since then have been in large lots of several thousand acres each from the Williams and Dewey ranches and other holdings.

For all their acreage, 75 percent of the Fishers' operation is in cattle. They have three large feedlots, one about five miles south of town in which they can feed about 5,000 head. C.K. and his son, A.B., and their five full-time farmhands designed it. It is divided into sections into which animals in different stages of feeding can be segregated, and the feeding troughs run the length of the lot. They are concrete and run as straight as a die for half a mile. "We had to be very careful to meet the EPA's runoff regulations," A.B. said. "We had a laser [beam] control on the bulldozer to make sure we got exactly the two-and-a-half-degree slope required."

Studies by agricultural economists at Iowa State University during the hard times of the 1980s indicated that the peak efficiency of scale in the corn, cattle, soybean, and hog operations of that state was about 600 acres, with the management and capital-investment capabilities of the farm family becoming overtaxed on operations larger than that. There is no similar figure on the maximum size that can be efficiently managed by a farm family in western Kansas, however. Except for family operations that incorporate for tax and estate-planning purposes, corporate farms haven't made much of an inroad in the Midwest. They have a history of management problems and difficulties in motivating salaried employees, who quickly adopt an eight-to-five attitude. "You can't get them to do the extra things that a family operation will," said A. B. Fisher. "They adopt a city labor union attitude. Abe and I worked almost all day last Sunday, but if something goes wrong on Sunday, they won't do anything, and probably not on Saturday, either."

Another problem is that the average age of farmers in western Kansas keeps rising—in the early 1990s, the average age in Rawlins County was fifty-seven. Studies of Iowa farmers by Professor Neil Harl of Iowa State University show that peak efficiency is reached by farmers between the ages of forty-five and fifty-five who are expanding their operations. It falls off as they begin to pull back, phase out, and either turn it over to their sons or begin selling out in preparation for retirement. The exodus of the young from the High Plains and the increasing difficulty of starting up for young farmers is one of the area's major problems, as it is in other agricultural regions. Farmers like Ron Bell, A. B. Fisher, and Bob Johnson, who went into farming with their fathers, feel twice blessed that their sons are carrying on the family operations.

The pressure on farmers to grow in order to realize the economy of scale necessary for survival continues apace, however. There is general agreement that it takes a minimum of 2,000 acres in western Kansas to support a family operation, but agricultural economists wonder if some of the area's biggest farmers, those whose holdings are 10,000 to 20,000 acres or more, aren't well past their managerial capabilities.

"Some of the big family operations may be at the edge of efficiency," observed Richard H. Wahl, an agricultural extension economist with KSU's Kansas Farm Management Association NW in Colby. "There is a question of how much more growth they can absorb and manage. They just can't supervise it all."

The trend to larger and fewer farms on the High Plains will inexorably continue, however; to survive, a farmer has to achieve a minimum economy of size and those who can expand will. "It's just going to get worse," said Bob Johnson, who took over his father's operation south of McDonald and pools equipment and labor with his two sons, who are independent operators in their own right. "For one thing, people who want to sell are looking for an established operator, not some young guy who's just starting up."

A prime example of this was when 6,000 acres of the old Dewey ranch, which at the turn of the century controlled about 700,000 acres, were put on the market in 1987. The First National Bank of Goodland, which was the receiver, asked C. K. and A. B. Fisher, already the biggest operators in the McDonald area, to buy it. The Fishers had also acquired the 6,000 acres of the George Williams ranch five years before.

As always, financial arrangements are influenced by technology and capital investment. Investment tax credits and accelerated depreciation encourage investment in technology and larger farms; agricultural economists note that farmers with higher incomes receive greater tax incentives for capital investment and are able to bid higher for land, equipment, and buildings than their smaller competitors. Large-scale operators can also negotiate for volume discounts on supplies. In addition, nonfarm capital is attracted to large-scale agriculture, often seeking tax shelters through the depreciation laws. Large farmers also get larger price support payments from the federal government, for the obvious reason that they plant more acres. The payments are based on the average yields of previous years and the target price the government sets for each crop. However, there is a ceiling on dollar payments, with the result that the large operators often get smaller per-acre payments than their smaller colleagues.

Despite the reservations about farmers' ability to manage very large operations, the trend to growth and economy of size is inexorable. Every factor, from technology to the banks to government policy, pushes farmers in that direction.

CHAPTER FIFTEEN

GRASS TO GRASS—THE BUFFALO COMMONS

From the 98th meridian west to the Rocky Mountains there is a stretch of country whose history is filled with more tragedy and whose future is pregnant with greater promise than perhaps any other equal expanse of territory within the confines of the Western Hemisphere.
—Algie Martin Simons, *The American Farmer*

IN THE LATE 1980S A MOST UNLIKELY COUPLE FROM A MOST UNLIKELY place, Frank and Deborah Popper of Rutgers University in New Jersey, burst spectacularly onto the High Plains picture, armed with a bright idea. He is a professor in Rutgers' urban studies department and an internationally recognized expert on land-use planning. She was a geographer at Rutgers who is now teaching in the political science department at the City University of New York on Staten Island.

The circumstances of their inspiration were as unlikely as they are themselves—she is by way of Manhattan (New York, not Kansas), Bryn Mawr, and Rutgers, he is from Chicago, Haverford College, and Harvard. One day in 1987 the Poppers were caught in traffic gridlock on the New Jersey Turnpike heading into New York City. To pass the time they began mulling over various land-use theories, which led them to ponder the use of land that is the diametric opposite of the densely industrialized and urbanized area in which they were temporarily immobilized. They had been traveling on the northern Plains for about a year and a half researching an article on the area and came up with a proposal to convert the most economically declining and depopulating areas of the High Plains into huge open-land national park and wildlife refuges that would total about 140,000 square miles by the year 2020.

Since the High Plains had served as an enormous commons for Indians, wildlife, and then cattlemen before the homesteaders fenced and closed the range, and since part of the Poppers' idea was that the indigenous bison and other wildlife would be reintroduced to roam free in the proposed park and refuge area, the logical name the Poppers came up with for it was "Buffalo Commons." The Commons is more of a metaphor than a concrete land-use proposal, and as such has helped crystalize and focus the debate over the future of the High Plains as no other idea has.

While the Poppers saw the Commons as reverting in some extent to the original state of grass, native game, and predators that Lewis and Clark saw, with the native Plains Indians possibly being allowed to hunt the buffalo again as their ancestors had, they also envisioned the Commons as a workable mixed-use project. They argued that the encouragement of tourism, recreational areas, retirement communities, oil drilling, and other economic activities would be necessary for the idea to work.

Their formula for selecting the areas that would be included in the Commons was: a 50 percent or more population loss since 1930, as opposed to a 100 percent increase in the U.S. population since that time; a population loss of 10 percent or more in the 1980s; a population density of four people or less per square mile, at which point delivery of social services such as schools and medical care becomes difficult; 20 percent or more of the population living under the poverty level; a population with a median age of thirty-five or higher, compared to the national median of thirty; and new and add-on construction investment of only $50 per capita, as opposed to the national average of $850 per capita. Counties that met at least three of these criteria would go on the Buffalo Commons list.

Working primarily from census data, the Poppers forecast a gloomy future for the areas that fit this formula. These areas, which would form the core of the Buffalo Commons, included 110 of the 400 counties in the High Plains and about 413,000 of its 6.5 million residents. The areas are not contiguous—they are scattered throughout all ten High Plains states, with the largest in sparsely populated areas in eastern Montana, the Dakotas, northeast New Mexico, and western and central Nebraska.

After their proposal appeared in *Planning*, a professional land-use journal, it was transformed, to their surprise, from an intellectual academic exercise into a full-scale and often emotional public debate, as local and regional newspapers and radio and television stations picked it up. As one writer noted, the Poppers became "the most controversial pair to wander the west since Bonnie and Clyde.* In fact, many High Plains residents and politicians *did* treat the Poppers like a pair of low-life horse thieves and reacted with fury, scorn, and disbelief.

Rawlins County and its adjoining counties, for instance, are on the Poppers' hit list because of their demographics, but since they are part of one of the most richly productive farm areas in the world, the idea that they will be turned back to buffalo grass is preposterous; the Poppers understand this and note that such areas of stable, profitable farming will continue to be so. There may be fewer and fewer farmers on that land, but those who survive raise more and more wheat and cattle and are prospering. With their tall grain elevators, granaries, and big machine sheds, many of these farms look like small towns themselves.

"The Poppers have tapped into a wellspring of anger and resentment, but they don't flinch," Professor Mark Lapping, also of Rutgers, said admiringly. "The people of the area should be grateful to them for calling attention to the problems. They are carrying out the highest responsibility of teachers."

Many students of the plains, academic and otherwise, scoff at the Poppers, however. "We think things are bad out here, but we are not impressed by the Poppers' research and conclusions," says John Wunder, director of the Center for Great Plains Studies at the University of Nebraska.

Others find the idea intriguing. A major reason is that more and more people on the High Plains are coming to realize that there are marginal areas that never should have been put into agricultural production and should have been returned to grassland long ago. This could be accomplished partly through natural attrition as the land goes into foreclosure, which has already been done in some areas. There are already large national grasslands scattered throughout the ten states—an area about equal to that of New Jersey, in fact—that are part of 11 million acres of foreclosed land that the federal government took over during the Dust Bowl of the 1930s. This is in a way being continued. The Department of Agriculture's Conservation Reserve Program has paid farmers according to a formula based on the pro rata value of their average crops to take erodible land out of cultivation and put it back to pasture, which eventually could affect up to 25 percent of some High Plains counties; about 34.6 million acres have been returned to grassland or forest nationwide under the program. In addition, a number of national and state parks and

*Anne Matthews, *The New York Times Magazine*, June 24, 1990. The article subsequently was expanded into a book, *Where the Buffalo Roam*, published by Grove Weidenfeld.

forests already dot the High Plains. The conservationists, however, have to run just to stay even. About 750,000 acres of marginally arable grassland were broken in Colorado alone during the 1980s, and there have been drought years in some parts of the High Plains in every decade since World War II.

The Poppers suggested that the Commons could be run by a consortium of federal and state agencies and private concerns that already own an interest in the area, such as the Bureau of Land Management, the Agriculture Department, the U.S. Forest Service, the Nature Conservancy, the Farmers Home Administration, private banks that foreclosed thousands of farms and ranches during the 1980s, and others. Making a pudding that has a theme out of such a wildly disparate and in many cases mutually antagonistic conglomeration obviously presents a daunting task. An equally formidable array of experts—agronomists, biologists, botanists, zoologists, economists, sociologists, et al.—also would have to be included in the equation.

In addition, many state and local politicians and their constituents view the Poppers' plan as just another case of patronization and persecution by Eastern urbanites.

The Poppers are not intellectual dogmatists, however. Their plan is intended as a guideline and stimulus to thinking on the issue. Not surprisingly, many residents of these areas take a much darker view and see the Poppers and their ilk as Eastern dilettantes who are trying to destroy their way of life. The historical isolation and loneliness of life on the High Plains, combined with the often justified suspicion that powerful economic, political, and social forces both scorn them and are trying to do them harm, breeds a habit of skepticism of outsiders. It makes some susceptible to conspiracy theories and even crackpot insurrections such as Posse Comitatus, a radical, often armed survivalist movement of the 1980s. Many resent the federal government's interference in their lives and livelihoods, even though this attitude conveniently ignores the federal farm subsidy programs that are a staple of the economy; their dependence on these programs is a subliminal reason for this resentment. Bernard DeVoto, the former editor of *Harpers Magazine* and a historian of the West, described this attitude as, "Get out and give us more money."*

---

*Resentment over the 55 mile-per-hour speed limit that is intended to save lives and conserve fuel is one manifestation of this. In some High Plains states exceeding the limit up to 75 or 80 mph is not cited as a speeding violation, but is ticketed for being an "inefficient use of fuel." The offense doesn't put penalty points on the culprit's drivers license and the fine in South Dakota, where I was caught doing 78 mph in 1986, was $12. In Montana it was $5.

Many High Plains residents, therefore, view the Poppers almost as alien archaeologists of the sort that snoop through the Pharaohs' tombs in Egypt. "People in pith hats are discovering the Plains the way they used to discover New Guinea," complained Republican Representative Pat Roberts, whose Congressional district includes the western two-thirds of Kansas.

Nevertheless, four years after the Poppers came up with their brainstorm, discussion of and growing familiarity with their idea reduced the initial fear and resentment of many. Increasingly, High Plains residents came to understand that Buffalo Commons was a beginning point for discussion, not an imminent prairie *coup d'état*. In addition, there had been substantial initial support for the concept. Many academics in the High Plains predict that economic and environmental factors will result in huge areas of marginal, fragile High Plains farmland being retired and reclaimed, and a number of think tanks and environmental groups are studying it.

In 1993, 300 buffalo were turned loose on the 35,000-acre Tallgrass Prairie Preserve in northeast Oklahoma, the headquarters of the Osage tribe and the last large piece of the 200,000 square mile ocean of grass that once covered the High Plains. The herd, which is expected to grow to 1,800 by the turn of the century, is the result of five years of negotiations between environmentalists, Indians, ranchers, and farmers. There now are about 135,000 buffalo in the United States, in small, scattered herds in the West and Midwest.

The High Plains lies just west of the geographical center of the United States and includes parts of ten states—the Texas panhandle, the western halves of Oklahoma, Kansas, Nebraska, South Dakota, and North Dakota, and the eastern parts of New Mexico, Colorado, Wyoming, and Montana. It is bounded on the east by the 98th meridian*, which is about 380 miles east of Denver and is almost the exact north-south dividing line of the United States, and on the west by the foothills of the Rocky Mountains. It runs from the Texas panhandle north to Saskatchewan and Alberta. It covers about one-fifth of the contiguous forty-eight states, but has less than 3 percent of the population, with the number dropping steadily during the 1980s.

In the nineteenth century, the High Plains was known as the Great

---

*The 98th meridian, which bisects Kansas, is the isohyetal line where the climate changes from humid to subhumid. Subhumid is the geographers' term for areas of twenty to thirty inches of rainfall annually; 170 miles west of the 98th meridian, in Rawlins County, average annual rainfall is about twenty inches. Ten to twenty inches, in turn, is classified geographically as semiarid.

American Desert, a barren stretch to be endured by the pilgrims making the trek to California, Oregon, and Washington. The High Plains was the last area of America to be settled, but the insatiable appetite of the European immigrants for land and the resulting pressure for westward expansion led to the discovery that much of it was arable. In fact, portions of the High Plains are among the richest farmland in the world in good years, which is to say, years of normal rainfall.

The key is "good years." The geographical definition of the High Plains is that it is flat, treeless, and subhumid, or semiarid, which means that its average annual rainfall is about twenty inches—the minimum for dependable farming—or less. By comparison, the average annual rainfall in the eastern Kansas counties along the Missouri River is about forty inches, and in Iowa, a humid state, it's forty to fifty inches and sometimes more. This is sufficient for corn and soybeans, which have to be irrigated on the High Plains.

Some geographers today use the terms High Plains and Great Plains interchangeably. However, it is useful to define the High Plains, as Walter Prescott Webb did, as a part of the Great Plains region of the United States. The Great Plains is the area west of the great forested region that once covered the eastern one-third of the nation. It includes most of the United States west of the Mississippi River—and some areas of Illinois and Indiana east of the Mississippi—with the exception of such obvious areas as the western mountain ranges and the timbered regions of the Rocky Mountain and Pacific Coast areas. The geographer's difference between the High Plains and the Great Plains is that the Great Plains includes any two of the three characteristics of the High Plains—flatness, treelessness, and subhumidity—but not all three.

In the mid-nineteenth century, the High Plains was advertised by hyperfervid boosters and shysters as a new Garden of Eden, a pastoral paradise with a balmy year-round climate, an inexhaustible underground water supply, and fertile soil from which bumper yields of any crop that prospective settlers were pleased to put in would spring eagerly to fruition with no toil or effort other than the casual scattering of seed. Some of those hucksters may even have believed their nonsense.

By definition, however, the High Plains is ecologically fragile and as we have seen subject to cycles of drought and other weather extremes. It is an area of austere beauty whose vulnerability is underscored at the beginning of each spring when the first tender green shoots of grass and winter wheat peep up into their harsh environment. It suffers the nation's greatest extremes of heat and cold. It is windswept and frequently scourged by violent thunder- and hailstorms and blizzards that are all the more awe-some in their absolute visibility when they blow up across the immense, vast emptiness of the prairie.

In stark relief, these oncoming storms reveal the puniness of man's pres-ence, the precariousness of even his most imposing structures. Outlined against the vast, gathering forces of nature that loom and boil across the horizon, man's grain elevators, silos, water towers, church steeples, farm-steads, and stark, tiny towns look as though they could be swallowed up without a trace. However, there is a poignant irony in the fact that these farms and towns are dwindling and disappearing in number not due to Mother Nature's powerful dispensation but due to man's own advance-ments in technology and changes in lifestyles.

Only on the seacoasts does the wind blow as hard and as constantly as on the High Plains. The dry furnace blasts of the summer exacerbate the aridity by accelerating the evaporation of what moisture there is. In the winter, the arctic gales that howl down out of Canada on the jet stream, the "Alberta clippers" et al., can make zero and subzero tem-peratures seem forty to fifty degrees colder. The area is pocked with de-pressions in the ground, some as large as several acres, commonly known as "buffalo wallows" from the mistaken notion that they were formed by the enormous herds of bison that used to inhabit the country; they actually are areas where the grass cover was thin and in dry times the ever-probing wind scooped them out, so that today they form sloughs and lagoons. "Ain't nothin' between us and the North Pole but a bob wahr [barbed wire] fence" was a common saying in the area. Another popular joke went: "When the wind stopped blowing, the chickens all fell over."

What spared the High Plains from disastrous wind and water erosion over the aeons was the sod cover—the native short grasses, including the buffalo grass of my area—until the white settlers began plowing it under in the late nineteenth and early twentieth centuries. These grasses also formed the area's fertile soil. The constant dying, decomposition, and re-newal of the grass roots over the centuries formed a soil rich in organic matter, much more fertile than that of forestland, where the tree roots were permanent and the soil's fertility went into the trees.

Prior to the white man's arrival, the Plains Indians and the buffalo co-existed quite well on this land. The buffalo by some estimates numbered as much as 60 million on the Great Plains in the 1860s, possibly as many as 30 million alone on the great grass commons between the Arkansas River in Kansas and the Platte River in Nebraska, both of which run west to east from the Rockies to the Missouri River. Because both the Indians and the animals were nomadic, the ecology was able to renew itself between their presences. The European settlers disrupted this process, however, and with harsh justice, Mother Nature in due course presented them and their descendants with an appalling bill for their sins, the Dust Bowl of the 1930s, the "Dirty Thirties." About 85 percent of the High Plains' native grasslands has been plowed under and the area has lost much of its wildlife and biodiversity. The High Plains has suffered from what Elwyn Robinson, a historian at the University of North Dakota, has described as the "Too Much Mistake"—too many people, farms, ranches, towns, roads, and railroads for the land to support.

Conservation farm techniques have helped prevent a recurrence of the Dust Bowl, although there have been lesser versions of it in nearly every decade, but there may be another bill down the road. While the area's farmers have succeeded in slowing soil erosion, they have rapidly depleted the underground water of the High Plains since World War II. Because of agricultural irrigation in eastern Colorado and Nebraska, the Platte River, the historic route of the Oregon Trail and a major flyway for migrating birds, runs at just 25 to 30 percent of its original flow in many stretches, with trees and brush now choking much of its dry streambed. An estimated 4,000 miles of creeks and rivers in Kansas are drained or dammed off for irrigation and near Hays, Kansas, brush in the dried-up Smoky Hill riverbed recently caught fire.

As noted earlier, after World War II, technology made it possible to pump water out of the Ogallala Aquifer, the enormous underground lake that underlies much of the High Plains and that by some estimates is equal to the volume of Lake Huron. There were about 250 wells in Kansas in 1950; now there are about 17,500, 200 in Rawlins County alone. The good news is that this has enabled farmers to irrigate and thereby stabilize crop yields as well as diversify their crops. The bad news is that although the pumping slowed substantially with the increase in fuel prices stemming from the oil shocks of the 1970s, the aquifer is still being tapped at an estimated twenty times its recharge rate. High Plains farmers face serious problems with irrigation and water rights.

Some farmers in the Texas panhandle, on the southern edge of the aquifer where the water-bearing formation is thinnest, have had to revert to dryland farming and it is likely that eventually everyone will. How soon this comes to be depends on the adoption of efficient irrigation techniques, new farming methods, and drought-resistant crops that slow the depletion rate. In 1989, Kansas state officials estimated that there was another fifty years of water in the aquifer, but scientists' calculations put it at closer to thirty-five years. It wasn't until 1989 that Kansas finally came up with a water use plan, which some students of the problem considered too little too late, but hopefully better than nothing.

᨞᨞

Walter Prescott Webb identified five weather phenomena of the High Plains, four of which are bad: the hot winds of summer; winter blizzards; hailstorms; "northers" (the cold waves from the north that blow suddenly into warm areas and cause precipitous temperature drops, sometimes as much as fifty degrees in a few hours); and the warm, dry winter winds, known as "chinooks," which blow down the eastern slope of the Rockies onto the cold regions below. Only the chinooks are benevolent; the other four bring economic ruin and physical suffering in their wakes. The poet Kathleen Norris, a South Dakotan, noted that one thing that can be said about the High Plains weather is that it keeps the riffraff out.

The ever-present winds still blow enough dirt in dry years to serve as a reminder of the Dust Bowl even for those too young to have lived through it. One National Park Service scientist described the High Plains as an area where people take an emotional and economic risk just by getting out of bed every morning. My uncle Wayne used to joke that a Kansas farmer always seemed to be either just two miles from a million dollars or a million miles from two dollars.

As harsh as this environment is, the area is ever more productive due to constantly advancing technology. In the 1980s, Kansas produced record wheat crops, with many fields frequently yielding fifty and sixty bushels to the acre, and occasionally as high as seventy and eighty, something unheard of fifty years ago, when yields of twenty-five or thirty bushels per acre were considered outstanding. The High Plains region is the world's fourth-largest wheat producer, the sixth-largest oil producer, and as of 1990, with a herd of about 40 million cattle, the seventh-largest beef producer.*

At the same time, however, much of the area's social fabric and culture is dying off. In addition to the smaller number of farmers and workers needed in agricultural production because of technological advances, changes in transportation have hurt the small towns. The interstate highways have bypassed many small towns and the increased use of trucks to move freight, greatly encouraged by the interstates, has caused

---

*After India (195 million), Brazil (136 million), Russia and the Russian Federation (118 million), China (77 million), Argentina (50 million), and the rest of the United States (58 million).

the railroads to discontinue much of their service. The smaller towns are caught in another vicious cycle as the bus lines, which in many cases are their last source of public transportation, also have cut back because of dwindling populations. Deregulation of trucking and buses, the airlines, and telephone companies have contributed to the growing isolation of the area.

And, every time a national discount store such as Wal-Mart sets up in a county seat or regional town or urban center, it draws retail trade from the surrounding towns.* The automobile and its concomitant, the suburbs and their shopping malls, have revolutionized the social organization of the United States, and the big discount chains are bringing this process to the rural areas. Ironically, the automobile has helped give people the opportunity and independence to leave the High Plains—and opportunity and independence were what our forebears were seeking when they settled the area a century ago.

Many small towns have withered away to little more than a grain elevator and a grocery store surrounded by boarded-up storefronts with broken windows and peeling paint and homes occupied by steadily aging—and dwindling—populations. Some High Plains towns and counties have lost 50 percent or more of their populations since 1930; many lost 10 to 15 percent during the drought of 1956–57; and some, like Rawlins County (17 percent), lost more than 10 percent in the drought and farm depression of the 1980s. The savings and loan crisis contributed to this depression, and the end of the Cold War and its hundreds of missile silos was an economic blow to Montana and the Dakotas. Many of these areas, including my home county, have populations of only four people per square mile—or less. The result is that people in many communities have to drive fifty miles or more to shop for groceries or to see a doctor. Many have lost their schools, which are the core of their social organizations and functions and the loss of which is a death knell to a small town. There are hundreds of ghost towns on the High Plains and an estimated 5,000 to 10,000 abandoned farmhouses in Nebraska alone.

---

*Wal-Mart, particularly, is admired for bringing a wide range of discount-priced goods and the most sophisticated marketing organization and techniques in the country to rural areas. It has also been somewhat romanticized because of the common touch of its founder, Sam Walton, a Bentonville, Arkansas, boy. Ironically, however, the chain is one of the great ravagers of small-town Main Street business districts. Some small towns have organized to try to keep Wal-Mart out of their areas, and advising small Main Street merchants on how to survive alongside the big discounters has become a growth industry. When he died in the spring of 1992, Sam Walton's family fortune was estimated at $23 *billion.*

The sense of isolation, of being exploited, neglected, and part of a dying culture, along with the economic shocks that periodically rock the area, are sources of enormous stress for many on the High Plains. These are culturally conservative people in whom the belief in self-reliance and wariness of change are almost as ingrained as breathing. Many have the same mind-set as their forebears who settled the High Plains more than a century ago. And for many, the slings and arrows of outrageous misfortune have become almost more than they can bear.

"What's scary about Kansas is that they have played by the rules and still they're getting screwed," observed Professor Lapping, now dean of the School of Planning and Public Policy at Rutgers University, who held a similar post at Kansas State University in the 1980s. "They have a strong work ethic and general sense of ethics. I've done consulting work all over the United States and in other parts of the world, such as India, and the sense of betrayal by the people of Kansas is the strongest I've ever encountered. That and the sense of defeatism, that they've been passed by and ignored. And they've been let down to a great extent by their leaders. Even Kansas State has some culpability. We have not always given them the best advice and often they've literally bet the ranch on it. And yet, Kansas is one of the safest environments I've known. It is a much warmer environment, on a personal level, than most."

⚎

In his book, *In the Center of the Nation*, Dan O'Brien wrote: "When you get the feeling that the whole world can see you but no one is watching, you have come to the grasslands of North America."

In McDonald, population now about 200, the Reverend Gregory H. Moyer, pastor of the Federated Church, estimated in 1989 that about 10 percent of his congregation had sought counseling due to economic stress. Bird City, nine miles west and population 670, had two teenage suicides that year. In Goodland, population 5,700, fifty miles southwest of McDonald, Greg Hubbard, the Baptist minister (and son of one of my high school classmates), then about thirty years old, worked to prevent four threatened suicides in one year in the late 1980s. In some cases, the strain becomes so acute that the clergy themselves seek counseling.

Great stress caused by loneliness, economic and psychological insecurity, hard work, and hard times is a historical fact of the High Plains—its past is rife with accounts of settlers, particularly women, driven to madness and suicide by these strains, particularly isolation and loneliness. This is of no comfort to these people today.

⚔

Many institutions and organizations in the country, including the major universities in the High Plains states, are beginning to address the problem of the area's decline and are endeavoring to help small towns expand and diversify their economies.

State governments don't have the resources to help every small town, however, and some have adopted a de facto policy of economic "triage," similar to the system of identifying and treating battlefield casualties who have the best chance of surviving. This is a proposal of Professor Lapping and a Kansas State University research team, the idea being to concentrate governmental and other resources on towns with populations of 2,500 or more and let the rest go their own ways. One result could be what the president of a Denver think tank, the Center for the New West, foresees as an "archipelago society" of a few urban islands in an ocean of wheat and grasslands, linked by the interstate highways.

There is some historical irony in this. In November 1933, the *McDonald Standard* carried a story about what was perceived as an unfairness in the Roosevelt administration's easing of the National Recovery Administration (NRA) regulations on merchants in small towns, those with populations of 2,500 or less. The purpose of the NRA rules was to benefit workers by raising wages, improving working conditions, and shortening work hours, thereby spreading work and employment around. The *Standard* story went on to argue that maintaining the NRA regulations in such relatively large nearby county-seat towns as Goodland and McCook, Nebraska, would put them at a competitive disadvantage with their smaller neighbors because they (Goodland and McCook) were just "overgrown farm towns surrounded by live [small] towns."*

Despite this dire prediction, those "overgrown farm towns," Goodland (population 5,700) and McCook (population 8,400), are doing very well sixty years later, while those "live" small towns such as McDonald are dying. Goodland and McCook both are on major highways and railroads, and in addition to being their county seats, both have airports served by major feeder airlines, both have hospitals (McCook has a CAT Scan), and both have diversified economies with businesses that are not related to agriculture; McCook has a community college and Goodland has a major

---

*The NRA was known as the "Blue Eagle," which was the symbol merchants put on their products and in their windows to advertise that they were in compliance with its policies.

U.S. Weather Service station and a food-processing plant. They are the sorts of towns that will survive at the expense of the small-town merchants, partly by drawing small-town shoppers into their larger stores, both the traditional ones on Main Street and those in the malls that are increasingly being built near them.

Totally unsuspecting of this future development, however, in January 1934, the McDonald city fathers drew up plans for a new high school building to be built with federal funds. The original plan called for a building that was designed for 150 students and teachers, but that could accommodate 170 if necessary "without crowding." This was rejected on the grounds that "a 150-student building does not sufficiently anticipate the future and the building should at least be large enough for 200." The new building, completed and dedicated just twenty-two months later, in November 1935, was designed for 200 and would hold up to 240 without crowding.

High school enrollment never got near these optimistic projections; it inched up into the seventies for the four grades during World War II as a result of the baby boom of the 1920s (the largest graduating high school class was twenty-four in 1945) and got into the eighties in the 1960s with the World War II baby boomers. In 1976, however, with enrollments falling, McDonald's schools were merged with those of nearby Bird City. In 1994, the combined high school enrollment for the two towns was eighty-one, about what each of the two high schools had at the time of the merger. The McDonald high school building, an attractive, well-lit blond-brick edifice with clean lines and beautiful hardwood floors, is now used for storage, administration, and club activities. In 1995 it is scheduled to be torn down because modifying it for the handicapped is too expensive.

⚖

Population in nearly every western county in Kansas has steadily declined since World War II, some precipitously during the hard times of the 1980s. Of the 105 counties, 37 had a population loss of 10 percent or more, primarily in the western half of the state. Even Ellis County, whose county seat, Hays, has a state university branch and a regional medical center, lost population, although Hays itself gained slightly. Of the 4 counties in the northwest corner of the state, Rawlins County's population declined from 4,123 to 3,404, or 17 percent; Cheyenne County dropped 11 percent; Sherman County went down by 10 percent; Thomas County dropped by only 2.3 percent primarily because its county seat,

Colby, held steady. Only 7 Kansas counties experienced population growth of 10 percent or more and they were in the northeast corner of the state, the Wichita metropolitan area, and the southwest Kansas counties, where the large beef-feeding, slaughtering, and processing plants have located around Garden City, Dodge City, and Liberal.

"If these trends continue, we will have major, major problems in northwest Kansas," said the Reverend Delbert Stanton, pastor of the United Methodist Church in Atwood and president of the Rawlins County Economic Development Commission. "It may be that the farm population will become the base for these counties [instead of the towns]. We have to think about county-wide development, maybe even development of the entire northwest Kansas area, because it's all interconnected and regional growth will raise everyone."

The census reports chart the steady attrition of population on the High Plains in the twentieth century. In 1930, Rawlins County had grown to its peak population, 7,362; in 1940, it was 6,618, and in 1950 it was 5,728; by 1990, it was down to 3,371. This decline was due to a number of reasons, two of which were the end of the modest oil boom of the early 1960s and the drought of 1956–57, which was short-lived but as severe as the Dust Bowl of the 1930s while it lasted. It is worth noting that the population loss in the Great Depression and the Dust Bowl of the 1930s was 10 percent.

The 1970s, however, were very prosperous due to good crops and the huge Soviet wheat sale. Wheat reached a record high of $5 a bushel and the price of Kansas wheat land soared to $1,100 per acre, about twice its normal value. Land values precipitously returned to reality in the 1980s in Kansas as well as other agricultural areas, however, and in the resulting recession many overextended farmers who had borrowed heavily against their inflated land prices went the way of thousands of their predecessors since the first white settler broke the first strip of sod in the 1870s.

In the early 1990s, however, the perpetual economic roller coaster that the people on the High Plains have ridden over the past century was on the upswing again. Farmers were buying new machinery, and civic leaders noticed more new automobiles and newly painted homes in town. The farmers who had survived the wring-out of the 1980s recession were doing pretty well. Average annual net income of medium-sized farms enrolled in the Kansas State University farm management program was up more than 20 percent, from $39,249 in 1985 to $47,872 in 1990, the value of their farmland was up by about 30 percent, and the ratio of loans to net worth was 45 percent in 1990 compared to 80 percent in 1985. Median annual income in Rawlins County, which was about $17,000, also was on the upswing. However, the long-term prognosis for the area is that the population will continue to decline as farms become ever larger. This is true of most areas such as the High Plains that depend on extractive and manufacturing industries rather than the much faster growing high-tech, communications, and service industries.

"If the cycle continues—and we believe that it has so much momentum and such profound roots that it will—then in approximately a generation large parts of the rural plains will extensively empty," the Poppers predicted. "They will not totally empty, but they will be far emptier, more frontierlike, than they are today."

The entire country has a stake in the future of rural areas like the High Plains, for a number of reasons. Primary, of course, is the need to guarantee an efficient—and cheap—food production system, which underlies the nation's agriculture policy. Another is America's global competitive position, including its trade balance. Much of the increasing economic competition by other countries is in the extractive and low-tech, low-wage manufacturing areas that are the basic economic activities of rural areas in the United States. Diversification of rural economies into service, information, and high-tech manufacturing, which are in growing demand, would improve the nation's global economic position.

One Kansas State University study draws similarities between Kansas and Appalachia based on their almost exclusive reliance on extractive industries. The study predicts that with the steadily declining groundwater level in the Ogallala Aquifer, which is being heavily tapped for agricultural irrigation, there will be future legal battles over water usage similar to those over coal rights in Appalachia. Although Kansas has a much higher education and socioeconomic level than Appalachia, there are several similarities between the two regions, primarily the lack of economic development, diversification, and opportunity. The result is out-migration of the young, which continues apace in Kansas, and the concomitant aging of the remaining population, which has lower income levels. This, in turn, results in a lower tax base and declining levels of services, the loss of a "critical mass" of population, which jeopardizes towns, churches, schools, and businesses and contributes to the downward spiral.

"Farming needs a certain amount of agribusiness support and when fewer producers remain there will, in time, likely be fewer suppliers, thus threatening the viability of those who remain on the land," said Professor Lapping. "This could jeopardize profitability and even survival."

"Kansas does a tremendous job of educating its young people and exporting them somewhere else," writes Steve White of KSU, a student both of Appalachia and of water usage and irrigation on the High Plains. The average age of Rawlins County farmers in 1994 was fifty-seven and with the constant development of technology the capital investment required for modern-technology-intensive farming makes it almost impossible for young farmers to start up as they did in the past. Some business and civic leaders talk of a program similar to those in a number of communities in Iowa in which the banks and business community establish a sort of clearinghouse to help young farmers buy out the retirees.

For all of this, many small towns on the High Plains are doggedly working to diversify their economies, bolster individual incomes, and halt their population slide. The bases of these efforts are tireless determination and a plan to create and attract new businesses, particularly enterprises that are not related to agriculture and its periodic economic crises—with the emphasis on tireless determination. It is a never-ending struggle and, to paraphrase Thomas Jefferson, the tree of economic diversification, like that of liberty, must be fertilized by the sweat of a town's citizens.

A 1989 study of North Dakota by the Council of State Policy and Planning Agencies found that almost one-fourth of the people in the state were employed by businesses that had come into existence since 1980 and that less than 5 percent of the new enterprises were agricultural or agriculture-related. Another study, of rural Midwest towns that have enjoyed economic growth and prosperity in the 1980s and 1990s, identified a number of factors such as organization and infrastructure. It discusses what sort of businesses such towns should seek out, but there is one constant factor—long-term, sustained local economic development activities, unrelenting effort, and the willingness to take economic risks. The study, done for the National Governors' Association, was funded by the Ford Foundation and the Aspen Institute.

"Not every town will survive—or should survive," Professor Lapping said. "One approach is to get towns to work together in a regional fabric. What happens in southwest Kansas, for instance, will be determined by what happens in regional centers such as Garden City, Liberal, and Dodge City. But some towns defy the formula.

"Sharon Springs [the Wallace County seat, which is seventeen miles east of the Colorado line and has a population of about 1,000], for instance, is the most fascinating town I know. Everything I know as an academic social scientist tells me that it should have died years ago. But the human spirit rises above such formulations. They have faith in each other, they invest in each other. They really have taught me something."

There are other towns in western Kansas like Sharon Springs that can teach the social scientists something.

CHAPTER SIXTEEN

THE NEIGHBORS—ATWOOD AND COLBY

SHARON SPRINGS ISN'T THE ONLY WESTERN KANSAS TOWN THAT'S working to beat the academicians' odds and could teach them something. Not many towns in western Kansas are passively going gentle into that good night, although towns like McDonald, which are not county seats, face the hardest struggle.

One of McDonald's neighbors, Colby, fifty miles to the southeast, fits the academicians' formulas for population and resources and has a relatively promising future. Atwood, the Rawlins County seat, is much like Sharon Springs—outside the formula's parameters but doing well, regardless. One characteristic all these towns share is simply the determination to make it.

ATWOOD

The population decline in western Kansas has taken its toll on all the towns in Rawlins County, not only on McDonald, Herndon, and Ludell, but on Atwood, as well, despite the inherent advantage of being the county seat and its longtime, diligent efforts to attract new business and light industry in order to diversify its economy. Atwood's population was nearly 2,000 in 1960 and held at about 1,650 for the next two decades, but the 1990 census showed that it slipped to 1,388 in the 1980s. More and more, the future appears to rest with towns like Colby and Goodland, which are thirty miles south on Interstate 70. This happy accident of location on a major transportation artery gives them a greater potential for prosperity and growth than towns that are off the interstate.

One of Atwood's great civic prides is one of its sons, Mike Hayden, a Republican who was governor of Kansas from 1987 to 1991 and was speaker of the state House of Representatives for four years before that. The town has a great deal more than this distinguished native son going for it, however, starting with the civic-mindedness and hard work of its citizens, who have developed a number of impressive assets over the years.

Atwood has a twenty-four-bed general hospital, although keeping doctors in small towns is a never-ending struggle. It has a senior center and a fifty-bed Good Samaritan nursing and residential care center. It has an airport with a lighted, hard-surface, 5,000-foot runway that was upgraded to accommodate jets, particularly for the medical emergency "Flight for Life" aircraft. The upgrading was a $1 million project, of which the Federal Aviation Administration contributed 90 percent. "It's the same size as Lawrence's [the site of the University of Kansas]," Bob Creighton, a lawyer who served as mayor for eight years, noted with pride. Creighton, a KU undergraduate and law school alumnus and former chairman of the Kansas Board of Regents, is a member of the Board of Trustees of the Atwood Second Century Development Fund, a civic organization; he is a second-generation graduate of KU, his wife, Barbara, is a fourth-generation alumna, and their two sons are fifth-generation graduates.

Atwood sits in the Beaver Creek valley, a tributary of the Republican River. In 1987, the citizens restored Lake Atwood, a forty-three-acre man-made lake that is fed by Beaver Creek. The lake went dry in the drought of 1955 and never fully recovered; a study in 1972 showed that its average depth was only fourteen inches, and the lake bed was planted to crops in the early 1980s. When a grant to restore it was denied, the residents financed it themselves in a typical community-minded effort with a bond issue and volunteer involvement. Engineering estimates of the cost were $1.5 million, but with residents volunteering their labor and tractors the project cost only $150,000 and was done in a year and a half. Now the lake is available for fishing and canoeing and has a playground and camping area with recreational vehicle hookups. When Don Beamgard, a member of a longtime civic-minded family, learned that the Burlington Northern Railroad was going to tear down the old depot, he arranged for the town to acquire the building. They moved it half a mile to the lake, and began a two-year renovation program. Now it is a gallery for about thirty local artists and handicrafters who display and sell their creations and take turns running its daily operations.

The town did the same with the old Jayhawk movie theater, which closed in 1979 because small-town populations can't support movie theaters on a free-market basis in the age of television. Former councilwoman Marion Frye bought the property for $800 at a sheriff's sale in 1987 and donated it to the town, which made it part of the municipal park system. A "big band" dance organized by Rod and Teresa Beamgard raised about $9,000 at $100 per ticket, $5,000 of which funded a new roof; the Beamgards picked up the tab for the band and the other expenses for the dance, which was attended by then-governor Mike Hayden and his wife.* After the new roof was on, architects estimated the cost of restoring the rest of the building at $150,000, but it was done for $68,000, partly because the city maintenance crew worked on it over the winter. The work was financed by private investors and a $30,000 loan from the Rawlins County Development Company, Inc. The theater, which is subsidized by the community, is used for movies, live stage productions by the schools and the Rawlins County Community Players, presentations of the Western Plains Art Assocation, and other civic activities and projects. This sort of civic participation is commonplace in Atwood.

The Atwood Second Century Development Fund was created in the late 1970s when the town's two banks each contributed $50,000 to start a civic projects fund. It now has assets of about $800,000, having been increased by several substantial donations, including one from a former State Bank teller, Mary David, who bequeathed $500,000 to it. The fund has an annual budget of $35,000 to $40,000 for various civic projects that otherwise would go unfunded. In 1994, these included $10,000 to the Rawlins County Hospital, $6,000 for a new Jayhawk Theater movie projector, $5,000 for new carpet for the library, $6,000 for equipment for the new fire truck, plus a variety of scholarship, recreational, youth leadership, and other programs. Prior to 1994, Second Century disbursed more than $228,000 to various community projects and programs. It is administered by a seven-member board, which includes Barney Horton, president of the Farmers Bank; Chris Hovey, vice president of the State Bank; and the senior partners of the town's two law firms, Bob Creighton and Robert Lewis, Sr. Ruth Kelley Hayden, a historian of Rawlins County and Mike Hayden's mother, is executive director.

Atwood also has one of the best county historical museums in the state, which features a historical mural on one wall that is thirty feet by nine feet; it is the creation of Rudolph Wendelin, a native of Rawlins County

---

*Both Rod and Don Beamgard are former mayors as is one of their cousins, Doyle, and a third brother, Bill, currently is mayor. Bob Creighton is the only former mayor who is not a Beamgard who is still living in Atwood.

and an artist for the Department of the Interior who popularized Smokey Bear, the national forest fire prevention symbol. Atwood is the site of the Beamgard Learning Center, a regional school for handicapped children, and the Prairie Development Center, a training center for handicapped adults. It has a 25,000-volume public library and a nine-hole golf course; a trust set up by the estate of a brother and sister, Francis and Lucille Obert, gives about $20,000 annually to the library plus donations to churches, the Masonic temple, the historical museum, the Girl Scouts and Boy Scouts, and other civic projects.

Atwood boosters also cite their school system and the fact that their students' academic test scores are higher than both the national and state averages for every grade, kindergarten through high school. They are also proud of the neighboring town of Herndon (population 170), which has the second-smallest high school in the state, with an average of just five graduates a year in the early 1990s. They consistently post high scores in scholastic competitions such as the Academic Bowl and Odyssey of the Mind; in 1983, Herndon's Future Problem Solving team, another intellectual competition, beat out Lawrence, the largest high school in the state, to place first in the state competition and compete in the national contest.

"A study by a member of the Kansas Board of Regents showed that classes of twenty-five students or less get higher average ACT scores than larger ones," Bob Creighton said. "Another study of one-room schools in Nebraska concluded that they provide an excellent learning environment."

Atwood High School's athletic programs also are highly successful— the football team won three straight state championships in its division (2A) in 1989, 1990, and 1991, and is a consistent contender; it was reclassified 3A in 1994. The basketball teams are often championship contenders and the wrestling teams are consistently good. The football coach is Dan Lankas, another Atwood native son, who was a star linebacker at Kansas State, where he holds the single-season record for tackles (Kansas State, alas, was long storied for its bad football teams, and its defensive players had ample opportunity to make lots of tackles); two nephews were stars on his state championship teams in 1990 and 1991. His son, Mike, also a linebacker and holder of Atwood's record for tackles made, was all-state and named Defensive Player of the Year after his 1993 senior season and received a football scholarship from Fort Hays State University.

Under Lankas, Atwood dominates conference rivals from larger neighboring towns such as Colby, Goodland, and Scott City despite their larger enrollments and higher division (4A). His program is remarkably sophisticated for a town of Atwood's size, or any high school program, for that matter; he has a half-dozen assistant coaches, and a weight room and lifting program that would do justice to a college. There are junior varsity, junior high school, and grade school football programs and a variety of other sports, including track—both boys' and girls'—golf, and girls' basketball and volleyball.

Partly because of the teams' successes, the townspeople are ardent boosters. Sizable numbers of Atwood fans wearing red are in evidence at all the Buffalos' out-of-town games, a fact that is noted with pride in the local newspaper, the Rawlins County *Square Deal*. Atwood businesses and citizens, including Pat Carroll, the sports editor and his wife, Madge, take out ads in the paper praising the various teams for their efforts and successes and rooting them on.

This emphasis on athletics, however, is a cause for concern by some residents, such as Wayne Harper, a retired farmer, two of whose grandsons were Atwood High School football stars and went on to play in college but who worries about overemphasis. Bob Creighton, a good friend of Wayne's, defends it, however. "The athletic program sets a standard of excellence that carries over into academics," he contended. "You can see it in such activities as the Academic Bowl competition and the band."

⚜

For fourteen months, from October 1992 to December 1993, Atwood was one of the relatively few two-newspaper towns in the country, and almost surely the smallest. Almost since the town's founding in 1885, it was served by the weekly *Citizen-Patriot*, but in 1988 the local *Citizen-Patriot* owners were bought out by a small newspaper chain, Gozia-Driver Media, of Crystal City, Missouri. Gozia-Driver owns small daily papers in Missouri, Iowa, Kansas, and Nebraska, including those in the neighboring towns of Colby, Goodland, and McCook, Nebraska. In the inimitable style of outside ownership, Gozia-Driver immediately drove the *Citizen-Patriot* into the ground, trying to maximize the bottom line by cutting costs, including the size of the staff. The news stories dwindled to nothing as the paper was filled with boilerplate and press releases.

In October of 1992, a number of the *Citizen-Patriot*'s former staff members started up a new paper, the *Square Deal*. The charge was led by sports editor Pat Carroll, who moonlights (or "daylights," rather) as the head meat cutter at Williams Brothers supermarket. Pat, who refers to himself in his weekly sports column as "the Dago," takes enormous pride in the fact that his three oldest sons have played for Atwood, one of whom won a football scholarship to Fort Hays State. The lead paragraph in his column, "Dago's Sports Corner," is a progress report on his youngest son, Roman, who suffers from leukemia but, like his father, is an ardent sports fan; the paragraph always concludes, "As always, we leave things in the Lord's hands." The other staffers were Rosalie Ross, now the *Square Deal* publisher; Kathy Davis-Vrbas, the editor; associate editors Mary Holle and Joe Snydstrup (who are co-owners with Ross); assistant editor Joe Matisek; Mary Chessmore, the composition and production editor; and darkroom technician Keith Reunitz. All had been with the *Citizen-Patriot* but left one by one out of disgust with the new owners' operations. After its first year and a half, this staff was still intact.

Rosalie Ross was one of the last to leave, hoping somehow to maintain the traditional standards of the *Citizen-Patriot*, but it was not to be and she was instrumental in the formation of the *Square Deal*. Pat Carroll stayed with the *Citizen-Patriot* the longest out of his intense loyalty to the high school sports program, which he thought deserved coverage. An ardent rooter whose ambition is to write a book about the Buffalos' championship seasons, Pat frequently refers to the young athletes as "our heros." When the new management wouldn't run his sports stories, however, Pat drafted a letter to a number of citizens asking them in effect if they wanted their local newspaper back.

The enterprise was a classic Atwood civic project. In the summer of 1992, about 100 people met in the conference room of the State Bank of Atwood. Among them were Lonnie Wells, then the bank president and a former newspaper publisher in South Dakota; state representative Fred Gatlin, an Atwood boy; Arden Hale, a former editor of the *Citizen-Patriot*; and Bob Creighton, who were named to a committee to explore the options of either buying the *Citizen-Patriot* or starting a new paper. Gozia-Driver put the selling price of the *Citizen-Patriot* at $300,000; Randall Braden, publisher of the neighboring *Oberlin Herald*, was interested but couldn't arrive at an acceptable price with Gozia-Driver. A new paper it was.

A mailing financed by the Farmers Bank and Trust, which was repaid in advertising, brought in 550 advance yearly subscriptions at twenty dollars each and twenty-four of the *Citizen-Patriot*'s advertisers bought space in advance. "Whenever we encountered an obstacle, we had help," Mary Holle recalled, and laughed at the memory. Women in the community volunteered to help with the mailing. "My mother-in-law sold subscriptions door-to-door and by telephone," she said. Everyone was promised their money back if the first edition didn't come out as promised on October 1, which turned out to be a touch-and-go matter. The enlarger for the photo printing process was late in arriving and when it did it had a broken bulb, for which someone managed to find a replacement at the last moment. "We worked all night to get everything over to the paper in Norton, which did the printing, by eight-thirty A.M. and then I had to go cover the county commissioners' meeting at nine," Mary Holle remembered.

There was another problem—100 years of tradition of the *Citizen-Patriot*. A lot of people feared that the new paper would "tear the town apart," as one staff member put it. But the *Citizen-Patriot* no longer was covering the county commission, the schools, or the hospital board meetings and other public and governmental functions. Gozia-Driver hired out-of-town reporters from Wichita, Great Bend, and Colby, and people could read the difference in its coverage and that of the *Square Deal*. Gozia-Driver made an effort, hiring the daughter of an Atwood couple as publisher, but it was a case of too little too late. The *Square Deal* drove the hapless outlanders out of business in just fourteen months, although the staffers suggest with considerable justification that Gozia-Driver put itself out of business.

There was no feeling of triumph in this, however. "There was that feeling of tradition and the people they hired were nice people," Kathy Davis-Vrbas said. "We hated to see the *Citizen-Patriot* go and we were sorry to see people lose their jobs." To close the breach in tradition, they resurrected the name of a former weekly. "I was determined that 'Rawlins County' would be in the title and we put the picture of the walking plow in the nameplate as a reminder of our pioneer past," said Rosalie Ross.

The Rawlins County *Square Deal* is now a newsy publication, sometimes as large as sixteen pages and often with a six-page supplement on topics such as conservation. Just eighteen months after its inception, it won three Kansas Press Association prizes—one to Mary Holle for a feature story, one to Keith Reunitz for photography, and one for editorial page excellence. It's made an impact in other ways as well. Shortly after the *Square Deal* began publishing, Rosalie Ross testified on behalf of a bill sponsored by Fred Gatlin to eliminate the requirement that a newspaper must have been publishing for at least five years before it could print the county public notices, a major source of small town newspapers' income. Gatlin's bill passed; the law it replaced obviously was designed to protect established papers from upstart competitors and would have made it impossible for a paper like the *Square Deal* to get started. If the bill had failed the Rawlins County notices would have been published by the papers in neighboring counties. Ms. Ross and the paper got the attention of the Kansas press, not all of it favorable.

Certain problems are peculiar to publishing a small-town newspaper. A typical example arose when three young men, former high school athletic stars and members of prominent families, broke into the high school building on New Year's Eve 1993, and stole some articles, including athletic gear. The county prosecuting attorney reduced the felony charges to misdemeanor possession of alcohol, which undoubtedly was a major factor in the matter in the first place. Running such stories presents a problem for small-town newspapers because of the intimacy of their communities, but the *Square Deal* staff knew they couldn't ignore this one. They ran the story but made no editorial comment on the reduction of charges. In any event, the *Square Deal,* like nearly every other small-town paper, carries the sheriff's log each week so anyone who's interested can keep posted on every barking dog, stray calf, and arrest for public drunkenness that takes place in the county.

Perhaps the biggest challenge small papers like the *Square Deal* face, however, is how to realize enough income from a small advertising base to cover the news the way the staff wants to. One knotty problem is news of the activities of local organizations, who would like regular free news columns, which forces a choice on which is more important, space for receptions and chicken dinners or for the fire department or the hospital.

My uncle Wayne encountered similar problems in his years as owner and editor of the *McDonald Standard* (another is dunning subscribers for late payments). They're not issues for journalists in impersonal big cities, but they loom large in a small town.

⚞⚟

For all its efforts and accomplishments, Atwood, like every other small town on the High Plains, is still faced with the inexorable decline of the rural population. In 1960, it had four implement dealers, Case, International, John Deere, and Allis Chalmers, but it now has just the Allis Chalmers and a Hesston dealership. It lost its Sears store when Sears cut back its small-town operations. Atwood didn't take these setbacks lying down, however. Mike Schnee, the Sears franchiser, stayed in business as an independent appliance dealer; a local merchant, Dan Timm, expanded his variety store, moving into two adjacent buildings, one of which had been the old Sears store; and a national auto parts chain, NAPA, located a franchise in Atwood.

Because of the energy and determination of its townspeople, Atwood has a variety of small businesses—a recent National Governors' Association study noted that this is more desirable than having just one large business or branch operation. It is also desirable to have businesses that aren't tied to the vagaries of agriculture and other extractive industries.

However, Atwood was dealt a stunning blow by its leading employer, Bell and Carlson, which manufactures rifle and shotgun stocks out of fiberglass, Kevlar, and graphite. The episode is a classic example of the up-hill problem such towns face. B&C was started in 1984 by two local men who financed it with $210,000 in stock bought by local investors. In 1992 the company was sold to a Dodge City owner, which inspired occasional rumors that it might move because of difficulty in finding workers; in August, 1994, these rumors came to pass when B&C announced that in fact it was moving to Dodge City no later than the end of 1994. The company, which had a payroll of about fifty and manufactured about 145 stocks a day, cited its inability to attract enough workers to Atwood and the local housing shortage. B&C's owners contended that they would need at least 150 workers through 1995, probably 300 to 500 in the next five years, and that it already had a market for twice the production of which it was capable in Atwood; its owners said it could realize profits of $10 million to $15 million annually in Dodge City compared to possibly $1 million in Atwood. The town offered to build a climate-controlled building for B&C and contends that its low wage and lack of benefits was a factor in hiring. B&C's base wage is five dollars per hour plus production incentives, with no benefits, and its annual payroll was nearly $1 million. The company offered a raise of one dollar per hour plus health coverage and a profit sharing plan for workers who moved to Dodge City with them. If a majority make the move it also would have an adverse effect on the schools, which could lose as many as twenty students.

One hope, encouraged by passage of the North American Free Trade Agreement, is for a proposed superhighway from Canada to Mexico, which is a major market for High Plains farm products ranging from beef to sunflower oil for food processing. This highway would go through or near the big meat-packing-plant towns of Garden City, Dodge City, and Liberal, in western Kansas, and those on the Oklahoma and Texas panhandles. Rawlins County boosters hope it will be routed through Atwood, although Oberlin, which is thirty miles east, would appear to have an advantage because it's on U.S. Highway 83, as is Garden City. The plan is being pushed by the Huck Boyd Foundation in Phillipsburg, named for a prominent regional political and civic leader and newspaper publisher, which is working on it with Kansas State University.

Like other small rural towns, Atwood sees a retirement community as a major opportunity for a region that is free of crime, crowding, and pollution. "There's some talk that Good Samaritan might build some retirement apartments," said the Reverend Delbert Stanton. "One possibility is to build garden apartments so the elderly here in town could put their houses on the market and move to places that are easier to maintain."

"Our situation really shows in the problems of the hospital," said Bob Creighton. "We have to downscale." This means the Atwood hospital provides emergency and outpatient treatment and sends acute care patients to neighboring towns like Hays and Colby or to Denver, Kansas City, or Wichita. The Atwood hospital has survived more perils than Pauline in recent years, but by 1993 it appeared to be solving its financial troubles and was showing a profit. One reason for its fiscal health is an annual $500,000 county tax subsidy, a remarkable contribution of nearly $150 per capita each year from the county's 3,400 residents. This, however, will expire in 1995.

Recruiting doctors is an agonizing, never-ending problem for small towns and many are forced to rely instead on highly trained physician assistants and nurse practitioners. Atwood pools doctors and dentists through a local three-county organization (Rawlins, Cheyenne, and Dundy, Nebraska, just across the state line) known as the State Line Health Network.

The problem is exacerbated by the fact that few medical schools have programs for primary care doctors. This includes the University of Kansas and in the early 1970s, when Mike Hayden was in the state legislature, he pushed through a loan program for medical students at KU under which the loans were forgiven for those who practiced for five years in underserved rural communities. The program was undercut, however, when medical centers in cities like Phoenix and Dallas started buying out the loans, which generally came to about $100,000 each, to lure the doctors away. The availability of doctors and adequate health care facilities is crucial in attracting new businesses and retirees to small towns. "Doctors want three things in a hospital: equipment similar to what they've been trained on, access to specialists, and a situation in which they don't have eighty-hour work weeks," Bob Creighton pointed out.

Creighton and other community leaders such as Marcille Currier, executive codirector of the Atwood Chamber of Commerce, see telecommunications in medicine, education, banking, telemarketing, and other businesses as a major hope for towns in western Kansas counties like Rawlins. Some states, including Kansas, Oklahoma, and North Dakota, have programs using interactive television to unite small schools in a "learning region" to teach important elements of a modern curriculum in areas of large distances and small populations. "Smaller schools seem to hold up rather well, but I think there is a problem in terms of programs like art and music, language instruction, and in keeping science laboratories up to date," said Professor Lapping of Rutgers. The Bob Dole Center at Kansas State University is the center of that program in Kansas.

Rawlins County is a leader in a medical telecommunications project that involves fifty counties, most of which are in the sparsely populated western half of the state. The participants have raised $200,000 from the counties and area banks and utilities to finance drawing up and raising the money for a $3.5 million plan to plug into a medical, educational, and commercial fiber-optic telecommunications network. The $3.5 million will be used to design the network, educate the people in the area on it, and assess its use. "We also have to educate them on how to use the technology we already have," said Bob Creighton.

The plan, to be completed in 1996, is to be funded by a $1 million grant from federal and state sources such as foundations, $2 million from businesses and industries, including utilities and the telephone companies, and $500,000 from state agencies such as the Department of Commerce. The seven-member executive committee includes Creighton, Dr. Robert Cox of Hays—a consultant for the KU and Hays medical centers*—and hospital administrators and health care officials from Colby, Garden City, Phillipsburg, Salina, and Cedar Vale. Rawlins County has taken the lead in this project, including engaging a telecommunications consultant, from Lenexa in eastern Kansas. Atwood already has a telemarketing business, which is run by the wife of the high school music teacher and markets products for children in wheelchairs.

In medicine, high-tech telecommunications can have many applications. One is two-way interactive video, with voice, graphics, and data transmitted over digital telephone lines, which enables the primary care physician in a rural hospital to consult with specialists in larger hospitals on diagnosis and treatment. Others include computers to transfer X rays and pathology slides and for bookkeeping and administration; satellite-delivered educational programs tailored to preventive medicine and other

---

*Dr. Cox was orphaned at the age of three when his parents died in a hotel fire in Atlanta in 1946. He survived when he was thrown from the hotel window and landed on an awning below. His father was the brother of Nell Fisher, the wife of C. K. Fisher of McDonald, one of the most successful farmers in the state. Nell and C.K. raised the boy and Dr. Cox subsequently graduated from McDonald High School in 1961 and medical school at the University of Kansas.

rural priorities; telefacsimile networks between hospitals and libraries; and bedside terminals to allow computer monitoring of both hospital and home health care regimes. One of the greatest benefits would be in reducing the professional isolation felt by doctors in rural areas, a major problem in recruitment.

"It's probably five or ten years away, but if it succeeds, it will be historic in the developmoent of rural counties," Creighton said. He has no difficulty operating in such a time frame because he is thinking in a much longer term. His view on technology's role in the area is clear and unambiguous: "Telecommunications is the last hope for communities this far out."

COLBY

Colby is an attractive, progressive town that, with its broad, tree-lined streets and large, attractive houses, could be a movie set for life in an idyllic small town. Through hard work, foresight, and good luck, it has another tangible, more practical asset: a bright future as a regional hub in northwest Kansas. I have a soft spot for Colby because my mother taught English in the high school there in the 1942–43 school year, commuting the fifty miles home to McDonald on weekends. I attended the spring semester of sixth grade in Colby, which turned out to be a thoroughly pleasant as well as broadening experience.

Colby has a lot going for it. It is on Interstate 70, and U.S. Highway 24 runs through it. It has a 5,100-foot jet-capable airport. It is a regional railroad and grain shipping center and has the only railroad container cargo dock between Kansas City and Denver. It has a forty-bed hospital in which it has generally managed to keep six doctors. It has a seventy-two-bed privately operated nursing home. The county is building a new sixty-bed nursing home for long-term care plus a twenty-unit assisted-living project, which will be completed in 1995 and will replace the current county facility. There is a community college, which is filled to capacity with an enrollment of about 1,200 and offers nurse's training and night and extension classes. In addition to providing jobs and a large group of shoppers during the academic year, the college draws people to cultural, educational, athletic, and other events.

Colby has an art gallery, the Northwest Kansas Cultural Arts Center, and an excellent county historical program. This includes the Museum of Prairie Living, which in addition to its exhibits has regional books and artifacts for sale. It also offers a couple of locally published paperback books that are a mark of the town's civic pride and are something every small town would do well to produce. One features group pictures of every

Colby High School graduating class, the other has team pictures and the scores and records of every one of the high school's football teams since its inception; the football book tells which boys on each team went on to play in college and where. From these books, I learned that one of my sixth-grade friends, Claude Herron, had stayed on to farm in the area and has been very active in Boy Scout activities; that, tragically, Dean Young, a good-looking, modest kid who was the best athlete in the class at the time, had died in 1984; and that Dick Pratt, whose family owned the hardware store, had played freshman football at the University of Kansas. The book is a few years out of date, but there is a move to update it.

Colby's major asset is probably its location on the interstate highway. The major element of luck that Colby has enjoyed in its growth and development efforts is the fact that I-70, which was opened in the mid-1960s, was originally routed along U.S. Highway 40, which runs twenty miles south of Colby and on west to Kit Carson, Colorado, where it makes a forty-five-degree angle northwest to Denver. That 20 miles is a long and crucial distance for the town, however. I-70 follows the U.S. 40 route west from Kansas City for about 300 miles to Oakley, where it leaves the highway route and angles sharply northwest 22 miles up to Colby. I-70 then proceeds west along the U.S. 24 route through Goodland to Limon, Colorado, where it intersects again with U.S. Highway 40 and angles northwest into Denver.

This bending of the route up from Oakley was the result of effective lobbying by Colby, led by its then–state senator, August Lauterbaugh, who also was president of the Farmers Merchant State Bank in Colby and one of the most powerful men in the state legislature. The original I-70 route was through Goodland but at a more oblique angle from Oakley, which bypassed Colby. Good luck is often the fruit of hard work and planning and this is true of Colby. Whatever the cost and effort, getting the highway rerouted has paid off enormously for Colby and will continue to do so. Colby's success certainly brought no pleasure to Goodland, which is thirty-seven miles west, because it makes Colby a strong commercial rival.

"The big difference simply is I-70," said Larry Barrett, chairman of the Colby Economic Development Commission and owner of a company that designs and sells computer programs for businesses such as accounting firms as far away as Virginia. "That was very good luck for us. This region will continue to struggle, but there will be pockets of prosperity like Colby and Goodland." The critical importance of location on or near the interstate becomes increasingly apparent with each example. "Suffice it to say that planners of the interstate system didn't realize the significance of interchange location when they laid out the system, although some townspeople did," said Professor Lapping.

The major negative Colby faces is the same one nearly every other town and county on the High Plains is struggling with—the area's steadily declining population. Despite its prosperity and promise, Colby's population dropped by 148, from 5,544 to 5,396, between the 1980 and 1990 censuses. However, this was one of the smallest declines both in number and percentage suffered by any of the towns in the twenty-one northwesternmost counties of Kansas. Colby boosters contend that its population has grown since the census, one sign of which was its housing shortage, due in part to the cessation of building during the economic recession of the 1980s. Only Hays, which is 110 miles east of Colby and is the largest town in the region (population 17,767), grew during the 1980s, by 1,466, or 9 percent. Hays is the site of a major medical center and a branch of the state university system.

Colby has a reputation for progressive and aggressive development programs. A quarter of a century ago, the Colby Development Corporation, a private organization run by business and civic leaders, was formed for the purpose of buying up land that could be made available cheaply for development sites; this encouraged Pepsi, Coors, and United Parcel Service (UPS) to make Colby a warehouse-and-distribution center and helped lure Wal-Mart into Colby.

The town's Main Street and business district runs six blocks north and south, but the town is laid out east and west along U.S. Highway 24, which runs through the center of it, and there are businesses along the highway the length of the town. However, since the advent of I-70, which is about a mile south of downtown, the town has developed southward toward the interstate; that's where the hospital, the historical museum, and the community college are located, and a new high school is scheduled for completion there in 1995. There are national franchise restaurants and hotels and a factory outlet complex of national retailers at the interstate intersection; Ramada Inn and McDonald's came in, which also helped prompt Wal-Mart's move in 1987. Wal-Mart was followed by other national franchises, including Long John Silver, The Sirloin Stockade, Burger King, Days Inn, and Econo Lodge.

The factory outlet center, a U-shaped complex next to the interstate, was built by a local boy named Larry White, who is an architect and a graduate of KU, where he was a scholarship football player. It is home to twenty quality national brand names, including London Fog, Corning, Ralph Lauren, Bass, Van Heusen, Florsheim, Revere, Swank, and B.U.M. During the tourist season, the parking lot is filled with automobiles from states as far away as Pennsylvania and Virginia to California and Oregon, and from neighboring counties year round.

London Fog was the first big name brand to locate at the outlet center. In the fall of 1990, White heard that Harry Lazarus of London Fog was looking for an outlet in the area and invited him to Colby. "Harry wanted to be on the interstate and he needed five thousand square feet, which I had," White recalled. "We put on a good show for him and he opened sixty days later." Lazarus also met with business and civic leaders in Goodland, but they didn't have the space immediately available. In 1994 White and London Fog were negotiating a second, larger building to meet the company's expanded needs and he and Lazarus have become something of a team on the High Plains. After Lazarus retired from London Fog he became White's leasing agent.

"He wanted to go into North Platte [Nebraska, 150 miles north of Colby] but couldn't find property to develop, so I helped him with that," White said. With London Fog as a tenant, White has developed franchise outlets similar to the one in Colby in North Platte (population 22,600 and twelve stores) and Blackwell, Oklahoma (population 7,538 and sixteen stores), and is negotiating the leases for one in Webbers Falls, Oklahoma (population 722), which he projects will open with ten stores. He also was planning to begin construction of another in 1995 in Rosenberg, Texas, about thirty miles southwest of Houston on U.S. 59. All have master plans under which they can expand to thirty or forty outlets and most are on interstates: North Platte is on I-80, Blackwell is 100 miles north of Oklahoma City on I-35, and Webbers Falls is 140 miles east of Oklahoma City on I-40. "This is a good example of how a local leader was able to use a connection with an external actor, London Fog, to make things happen," noted Professor Lapping. "People in rural development are just beginning to pick up on ... the importance of leadership which networks both within and without the area and region."

At first, the national franchises on the interstate, which regularly attract shoppers from about 150 miles around, had a negative impact on Colby's downtown business district. "There were seven or eight vacant buildings on Main Street, but now there's only one," noted Carolyn Armstrong, the city manager. "The businesses in town are ones that aren't on the interstate, specialty stores that Wal-Mart and the others don't have.

Lots of out-of-town people come on into town after they've shopped at the outlets. We have two quality jewelry stores, men's and women's clothing shops, a new Dollar Days store, and an expanded wood furniture and crafts store."

The art of competing with the big discount stores like Wal-Mart has become an industry in itself. The secret is to carry goods and services the discounters don't and to try to be competitive in prices and service. Smith's Pharmacy in Colby is an example of how it's done. Randy Smith, the owner, computerized his operation and was able to offer service, including home delivery, that Wal-Mart couldn't match. He set up a patient board for the residents of the nursing and assisted-living homes showing each day's medication for each patient. He has a computer printout for each drug he dispenses, including side effects and cross-referencing of possible interactions with other drugs a patient might be taking.

The interstate is also the focus of future development. "We have a fourteen-year-old plan that we're in the process of reviewing, but the next growth area will be the second exit," Carolyn Armstrong noted. The second exit is about a mile east of the first one and initially will probably be the site of a truck stop with a restaurant and a service station and related services. Other businesses are also considering the location.

For towns on the High Plains, the struggle just to stay even is neverending, however. There is the constant effort to diversify the economic base. "We need manufacturing, prime wage, technical jobs," Carolyn Armstrong said. "The key is medical services. We have six doctors; Goodland has one." And, there is always the hope of food-processing plants, "vertical integration" of the area's agricultural produce. Colby has a confectionery sunflower packing plant, and development leaders are talking about other possibilities, such as a paper plant using milo residue as its raw material. As the Reverend Delbert Stanton in Atwood noted, every community wants diversified manufacturing and doctors but they are hard to come by.

In the nineteenth century, the key to a farm town's survival was being located on the railroad and telegraph line, on the main lines of communication. That principle holds just as true 100 years later, with the addition of the internal-combustion engine, the interstates, and the developing telecommunications "information superhighway." Colby has as much access to these means of communication as any community in the area. It also has a citizenry that appears capable of making the most of its assets.

CHAPTER SEVENTEEN

ON THE WALL OF THE FROSTY MUG, MCDONALD'S LONE CAFÉ (AND tavern and pool hall), is a sign that reads:

> Sadly, our small village can no longer afford the luxury of a full-time town drunk, so we have agreed to take turns. When it's your turn, BE HERE!

Sadly, there is as much truth as barroom humor there, even though the Frosty Mug is one of the town's few thriving enterprises. It isn't open for breakfast, but it does a brisk noontime dinner trade, both with townspeople and farm crews whose wives can't or don't feel like cooking for them on a particular workday. It also enjoys a brisk evening supper and postprandial business with farm crews as well as with people who simply feel the urge to get out of the house or off the farm and come to town on a week night. It has a booming supper trade on Friday and Saturday nights, attracting customers from neighboring towns as well as the locals.

There are a number of reasons for this. One is that Dee Dewey, the co-owner of the Frosty Mug with her husband, Chauncey Dewey, Jr. (known universally as "Junior"), is a superb cook. Another reason for its success is simply that places in northwest Kansas where people can gather for food and drink are few and far between. There are precious few locations, unfortunately, where people can congregate for any purpose and such places are crucial to a community.

I was having coffee there one morning with Leonard Vyzourek and my cousin Wally Ritter, when three men from Bird City walked in. Leonard

introduced us and I recognized the name of Lee Amsberry. He was the
Bird City High School quarterback when we played them my freshman
year in 1945, forty-eight years before, and he had stayed on to farm and
run the Bird City Co-Op filling station after graduation. We started remi-
niscing about our teammates and I asked about Neil Hamm, who was an
all-state guard and Bird City's star lineman that year. Lee said he thought
Neil was in Nebraska somewhere but would check it out. A couple of days
later, I was having dinner in the Frosty Mug with Vernon and Bertie Davis,
two friends from school days, when Lee and his wife and two other couples came in. He came over to our table to report on Neil when Bertie
broke in. "I could have told you about Neil," she said. "He and I dated for
two or three years after we got out of high school." I'd known that and for-
gotten. The lives of people crisscross constantly in places like the Frosty
Mug and it's hard for someone to get lost out there.

In the view of the Reverend Clarence Swihart, who is retired as pastor
of the Federated Church but still functions as an active and compassionate shepherd to his former flock, there are only three places in McDonald
where an individual can "engage in a retail transaction"—the grocery
store, Perry Larson's Conoco station on U.S. Highway 36, and the farm
implement parts store. The Reverend Mr. Swihart's inventory, under-
standably, doesn't include the Frosty Mug or the liquor store up on the
north end of Main Street in his inventory.

There is also the post office, a communal gathering place first thing in
the morning after the mail is delivered and put up in the people's boxes;
this is a major social medium in all small rural towns. In addition, there
are the Peoples State Bank, the Cheylin Unified School District middle
school (the district was formed by the merger of the McDonald and Bird
City school districts and is a meld of their respective county names, Rawlins and Cheyenne), the American Legion Hall, the senior citizens center
in the old Masonic and Eastern Star temple, three beauty parlors, Pete
Holub's auto-and-tractor-repair garage, two service stations on the highway, Les Loker's insurance office, the grain elevators, and, of course, the
Federated Church. And that's about it.

Without question, the people of towns like McDonald are fighting an
uphill battle because the tides of history are running against small rural
towns on the High Plains. Since 1953, the year the Reverend Clarence
Swihart moved to McDonald, the town has lost two of its three grocery
stores, the drugstore, the weekly newspaper, the high school, the movie
theater, the clothing store, the hardware store, three cafés, the appliance
store, the Chevy and Chrysler-Plymouth dealerships, the International

Harvester, Case, and Oliver implement dealerships, the barbershop, the pool hall, two blacksmith/machine shops, two filling stations, the Church of God, and the Masonic/Eastern Star Lodge. Several of those, including the drugstore, the hardware store, the clothing store, and Hattie West's grocery and notions store, disappeared during the 1980s. The death in 1984 of Alfred Buck, the drugstore proprietor, was a grievous loss to the community. He was a tireless civic activist, was organizer of the annual alumni reunion weekends, which draw remarkably large turnouts from all over the country (he was class of '21), and was legendary for his "green rivers," the green syrup and soda water concoctions that he dispensed across the soda fountain bar, which are still remembered by many with something akin to reverence.

McDonald's population is now about 200, down from a high of about 480 in 1935, and it seems to be slowly sliding into oblivion. One can only imagine what life would be like without the grocery store, the church, the post office, the school events, and the Frosty Mug, particularly for the elderly should the time come when they have to drive to the next town for things as basic as a bottle of milk or loaf of bread. This unpleasant prospect, unfortunately, is not someone's hyperfervid bad dream; unfortunately, there already are all too many such towns in Kansas and the rest of the Midwest.

The key to survival of any small town, however, is its school system, and McDonald took a major hit when its schools were merged with Bird City's in 1975 to form the Cheylin Unified School District. Bird City got the advantage because it got the high school, which is a major source of social activity in small towns. McDonald's junior and senior high students are bused nine miles west to Bird City, while Bird City's grades 1 through 6 pupils are transported to McDonald. The high school football games are played in Bird City; the basketball games are played in the McDonald field house. Some McDonald residents such as Don Antholz, a farmer northwest of town whose son, Robbin, was a member of McDonald Rural High School's last graduating class, still refer to the merger as the time "when we gave the school away."

The merger was forced by the area's dwindling population and enrollments. McDonald had the option of merging with Atwood, the Rawlins County seat, and Bird City could have combined with St. Francis, the Cheyenne County seat, but neither town cared much for that idea. A Cheylin Unified School District seemed the lesser of two evils and the class of 1975 was the final one for the McDonald and Bird City high schools. The Reverend Swihart's son, Steve, was last alphabetically in the class of 1975 and his diploma was the last ever awarded by the McDonald Rural High School. After fifty-nine years, MRHS had come full circle, from the one-member class of 1917, Roy (Link) Lyman to Steve Swihart of the seventeen-member class of 1975; in 1994 Steve was working and taking seminary courses in Denver, possibly to follow in his father's footsteps.*

There was some irony in the merger because of the intense rivalry between the two towns, which goes all the way back to their foundings. High school athletic contests with other neighboring towns such as Brewster and Sharon Springs paled by comparison to those between Bird City and McDonald. It was Bird City's goalposts that we dragged back to McDonald to burn in the homecoming pep rallies, and vice versa. However, citizens of both towns take equal pride in the high school teams; in the fall of 1994 there were slogans soaped on their store and car windows in both towns cheering on both the once-beaten football squad and the girls' volleyball team ("Chew The [Brewster] Bulldogs Up Cougars!" "Go Big Blue!"). Despite this, the old feelings hang on.

"At the home games, the Bird City people are on one side and those from McDonald are on the other," says Richard Cain, the school superintendent and high school principal. "It doesn't make any difference to the kids because it's always been this way for them, but the adults reflect the old rivalry." This also manifests itself in jealousy over school funds. If money is spent on the football field in Bird City, there had better be an equal amount for the baseball diamond or basketball court in McDonald. A referendum on building an entirely new school complex out in the country midway between the two towns failed, partly because the school board changed building types shortly before the election. The result is redundancy and cost inefficiency. "We pay two heating, insurance, bus, maintenance, and insurance bills," Cain notes.

Enrollment in kindergarten through the 12th grade was 235 in the 1993–94 school year, eighty-one of whom were in the four-year high school, up from just fifty four years before due to a baby boom. The fact that this is about the enrollment McDonald and Bird City *each* had at the time of consolidation less than twenty years before is a measure of the

---

*Other distinguished graduates of McDonald's schools include Leland Caswell, who was president of the Columbia University Teachers College in New York; Claude Bell, a successful farmer, high school teacher, and long-time state senator; Ray Frisbie, a president of the Kansas Farm Bureau Association, candidate for governor of Kansas, and football star at Colorado State who also taught high school and coached football; and many others, including several graduates of the Air Force Academy.

ongoing population decline. Based on the numbers in kindergarten and the lower grades, however, Cain sees enrollment holding stable for the next few years.

"The state is not forcing further consolidations by setting minimum enrollment figures," he says. "The fact is that education is better in small schools, although it costs more." This is a widely held belief in the area. The state funds the schools in Kansas on a per capita basis, $3,600 per student per year. Many schools get considerably more than this, however, when weighted for factors such as busing and "at risk" students, those who come from troubled and/or emotionally deprived families, although this formula has recently been challenged in court. Primarily because of busing, the Cheylin school district is weighted at double its actual enrollment, which qualifies it for about $1.6 million annually in state funds rather than the $800,000 under the basic formula. It also could tax itself up to an additional 25 percent of this for the schools if it chose.

Some disagree with Cain's predictions and see darker times ahead. "School enrollments will probably fall off in the next five to ten years because there are no child-bearing families on line," predicts the Reverend Gregory Moyer of the McDonald Federated Church. The late Claude Bell, a former state senator and member of the McDonald school board, foresaw eventual county consolidation in sparsely populated western Kansas.

"The school aid formula is written to consolidate counties with populations of less than 5,000," Claude pointed out in the summer of 1993. "The teachers, the National Education Association, want county consolidation and so does Joe Harder, from Mound Ridge, the chairman of the Senate Education Committee. The NEA does all this electioneering for him. I know him and where he stands on this." City council member Brenda Johnson foresees the same problem "We're determined to keep our schools," she says. "But the governor and the legislature want to consolidate at the county level, maybe even regional. It could be that the kids will wind up going to regional schools in Colby and Goodland and commuting home on weekends." This would be a catastrophe for small towns.

⚌

Schools aren't the only institutions on the High Plains that face consolidation. The electronic age is helping turn many small town banks into branches of larger banks. "You have one person out in the small town branch with the central staff and accounting functions at the main bank," says Elroy Osborne. "As the banks get better computers they need fewer people." The bank in Herndon is now a branch of the State Bank of Atwood, Ludell's bank was bought by one in Phillipsburg, which is about 80 miles east, the Cheyenne County State Bank in St. Francis is now a branch of the First National Bank of Goodland. Two banks in Colby are branches of larger institutions, one in Wichita, the other in Salina.

Be this as it may, the people of McDonald are not waiting for the end with passive resignation. In the spirit of their forebears who broke the sod and founded the town, many are working to upgrade the community and keep its people together. "The spirit of the people in McDonald is marvelous," said Kathy Davis-Vrbas, editor of the *Rawlins County Square Deal,* the weekly newspaper in Atwood. "They're educated, activist, and, unlike some other towns, are completely open to people from out of town."

At the time of this writing, six years after its centennial celebration in 1988 and the sprucing up it got for that occasion, McDonald appears to have had held up very well and it still looks far better than it did before the celebration. Most of the houses are occupied and well kept up, but it is a struggle to keep the yards of the abandoned ones mowed and maintained. And, many of the buildings on the three-block Main Street are now vacant, with some empty lots where buildings once stood.

Still, like the workings of nature on the apparently still expanses of the prairie, which are often not visible to the casual viewer, there is a remarkable amount of activity in this quiet town, both civic and social and often a combination of the two. In the spring of 1994, the civic activists began work on a new city park on a vacant lot on main street. They were working to get a state grant to pave the streets, beginning with the one the school and the Federated Church are on, which is the most heavily traveled except for main street. They have refurbished the "Tongish Building," a one-time auto-and-tractor-repair shop on main street named after its former owner, into a city headquarters and shop building. They have held sausage and pancake suppers to raise money to upgrade the fire truck and ambulance equipment and buy uniforms for the sixteen volunteer firemen. They had raised the money to buy the ambulance in the first place with dinners at the Legion hall, pancake suppers, and quilt raffles (I wonder how many hundreds of quilts Grandmother Phipps and her friends worked on every Thursday afternoon in the church basement for similar projects during her lifetime).

The plan for the city park included building a gazebo for picnics and band concerts, planting trees and flower beds, and installing picnic tables, playground equipment, a small log cabin for children to play in, and split-rail fences and lilac hedges around the park. The McDonald Area Development Committee (MAD), a combination chamber of commerce and community service organization, Xeroxed copies of its proposed layout for people to pick up at the grocery store, the bank, and other business establishments and sketch in their suggestions for the park's design and equipment. City officials were gratified by the large number of responses, from teenagers to the elderly; one was to plant a variety of trees for schoolchildren to identify in nature and science classes. Following its tradition, MAD held hamburger and pancake suppers at the Legion hall to solicit ideas and raise money for the park, which was to be built by city employees and volunteers.

The town, which has held an ambitious tree-planting program in recent years, was also pushing to get the U.S. Forest Service and the national Arbor Day Association to designate it as a "Tree City, U.S.A.," which requires, among other things, spending at least two dollars per person annually on planting and maintaining the town's trees; the district forester from the state forestry extension service in Manhattan advised the community on what trees would do best in the new park. "We may make it a memorial park where people can plant trees and flowers in memory of loved ones," said Vera Kacirek, the McDonald correspondent for the *Square Deal* and a garden club officer. "We'll have a registry book and possibly put up honorary plaques." Not many towns on the High Plains have a "Tree City" designation; the closest is Hays, 160 miles east. The garden club is also encouraging residents to replace trees killed by the big hailstorm of June 1989 and the unseasonal freeze of May 26, 1992.

"We're pushing for projects like the city park as a means of getting people together and keeping the town alive," said Brenda Johnson, the president of MAD and a member of the city council. In addition to her civic duties, Brenda helps run the McDonald grocery store, which is owned by her husband's aunt, Lois Johnson. Brenda moved to McDonald fifteen years ago when she married Ron Johnson, who farms in partnership with his father and brother.

Some community leaders like Les Loker, who was chairman of the centennial committee and is an independent insurance district broker, are pushing to pave all the streets—main street is the only paved street in town—and replace the curbs and sidewalks on main street. Until the town gets new sidewalks, it adheres to a principle it learned during the centennial celebration: Eradicate the grass that grows in the cracks in the sidewalks on Main Street, a sign of a dying community. Les also advocates property tax breaks to encourage new businesses to either put up new buildings or take over vacant ones. In the spring of 1994, he bought the old movie theater building and an empty building that once housed an insurance office with the idea of restoring the theater for movies and live productions much as Atwood did with the old Jayhawk Theater. He also made arrangements to lease space for an auto body shop (the nearest are fifty miles away) and a custom T-shirt and sign-painting shop.

MAD was formed by Elroy Osborne, executive vice president of the Peoples State Bank and currently the mayor, shortly after he moved to McDonald in 1974. "The town didn't have a chamber of commerce and I thought it needed one to promote business, because we could see the decline and consolidation of small towns, the trends working against them," Elroy recalled. People like Elroy and Brenda are crucial to change and progress. It is often difficult for people who have spent their entire lives in a community to see its needs and opportunities, particularly the latter. Possibly the most important principle in small towns' efforts to grow and prosper is not to lose sight of their assets. While their small size is a liability in one sense, it can be an asset in another, in that just a few people demonstrating leadership and initiative can have a major impact.

Since its inception, MAD has promoted a host of civic projects: the senior citizens center; the erection of street signs and assignment of house numbers; a "Yard of the Month" competition during the good weather months; the "Helping Hand" award to citizens who perform outstanding civic service;* an annual Pheasant Hunters' Breakfast at the Legion hall at the beginning of the season in November, for out-of-town hunters who rent rooms with the locals or stay with relatives, an effort to encourage tourism (more than 50 attended in 1993 and more than 300 turned out a few hours later for the Lions Club ham and bean lunch, both in the American Legion Hall); the home and yard Christmas light contest; the Girl Scout troop; the Easter egg hunt; the annual MAD Day for Kids, a sort of fair and track meet that features bicycle races, balloon throws, sack races, and other contests; planting trees around the athletic field on the east end of town; and other activities, including two unsuccessful efforts to establish a medical clinic attended part-time by a doctor from a neighboring town.

The Lions Club promotes a number of similar projects, including Santa's Day the Saturday before Christmas, when the jolly old elf descends on the

---

*A typical award was the one to Bob Banister, eighty-six, for mowing and cleaning up the untended yards of empty houses in his neighborhood.

town to distribute candy to the children and fruit baskets to the adults. It erected and maintains a picnic area and tennis court in a school-owned park near the school buildings. It also raises money for worthy causes, such as the $2,000 for Phil Cahoj's family after Phil nearly lost a hand when his jacket sleeve got tangled in a tractor's high-speed power-takeoff shaft.

"Success is in expanding and reaching more people," Elroy said of these efforts. There have been modest gains—Blaine Hubbard opened a farm supply store that is still thriving under new ownership—but such advances come hard. Even the news of a new family moving to town and buying or building a house—although moving an existing house from a farm or another town is much cheaper and therefore more common—is counted as a gain.

Nevertheless, the people of McDonald soldier on and stay busy. In the course of one week in the fall of 1993, they turned out on a Thursday night to cheer on the final regular season victory of their undefeated high school football team, the Cheylin Cougars. On the following Sunday evening, more than 100 gathered at the Legion hall for the annual Halloween Soup Supper and children's Spook Parade led by the fire truck prior to their trick-or-treating (a number of parents also were in costume). The next day, Monday noon, the Senior Citizens Club's annual pre-Thanksgiving dinner drew a record turnout of more than 100, also in the Legion hall. Monday night was the Lions Club meeting. Tuesday night, the Cougars played highly favored Quinter in the first round of the substate high school football play-offs, and lost a thriller on a last-minute touchdown, 38–34. On Wednesday, MAD held its monthly luncheon meeting and reviewed plans for such programs as the annual home and yard Christmas lighting contest and the proposed city park.

These activities were great opportunities for a native son who long ago had moved away to renew old friendships and acquaintances. I was introduced at the senior citizens' Thanksgiving luncheon by Owen Wingfield, the president of the Peoples State Bank and a longtime friend. Owen had been one of my mother's favorite students when she taught English at McDonald Rural High School and had worked for my uncle Wayne on the weekly newspaper while he was in high school and then during harvest several summers after he got out of the Army.

The *really* senior citizens were a generation older than I and still called me "Dickie," which had the somewhat surprising and rather pleasant effect of making me feel young again, or younger anyway, and able to ignore the awkward fact that I am just an all-too-few years south of Social Security eligibility myself. Others there were my contemporaries, some of whom, not to put too fine a point on it, are already eligible for Social Security. The fact that I was there to write a book about the town, although I stressed the fact that it was also about my family, was received with the politeness with which people of that area habitually receive outsiders. They extend it even to those from cities back east who come into town to ridicule or to patronize them and their way of life, which many outsiders seem to find as exotic as anything they'd find on the far side of New Guinea. These visitors, in turn, might be surprised if they could hear the comments *they* inspire.

Actually, I didn't feel like an outsider for very long as, one after another, people whom I hadn't seen in years came up to renew our acquaintanceships. One, who was helping serve, was Vivian Curry, a lovely and graceful woman who has long been one of my aunt Margaret's best friends; her late husband, Dal, had managed one of the grain elevators, and a son, a few years younger than I, has a Ph.D. in psychology from the University of Kansas and is on the faculty of the University of Wyoming. At the Halloween supper, I sat with Amelia and Bob Banister, whose Uncle Jim had been a good friend of Grandfather Phipps's and in the hard early pre–New Deal days of the depression made a loan to Grandpa that helped save his farm.

I was also at the table with Vernon and Roberta "Bertie" Davis, both of whom I went to school with, and Laverne and Ruth Klepper. Laverne, a retired rural mail carrier, was a man I admired a lot when I was growing up. In those days, he and I spent a lot of time in the local cafés rolling dice for coffee. A short, still powerfully built man in his early eighties, Laverne's sense of humor is as quick and puckish as ever, and he fell immediately into the affectionate teasing that marked our friendship.

"Well, Dickie, how long have you been back there in Washington now?" he started out, his blue eyes lighting up with their old mischief as he tried to distract me long enough to steal my mincemeat pie. "Thirty years? Seems to me we sent you back there to fix things up and it doesn't seem that you've made much progress. Things seem to be getting worse, in fact. What have you been up to all these years?" He professed to have missed me, primarily because he remembered winning regularly when we rolled dice for coffee at Chet's Café. "Your moving away cost me a lot of money," he joked. I had the same teasing friendship with his father, Orval, and his younger brother, Audrey, who had worked on the farm for Grandfather and Grandmother Phipps back before World War II.

Vernon is a husky, handsome, retired Kansas Highway Patrol officer who hasn't changed much physically in the past forty years except for a touch of gray and a few added pounds. He and Bertie moved back to McDonald to be near her mother, Dorothy Walter, who is elderly and frail but still alert and spirited. We got caught up on our contemporaries, including a pretty girl a couple of classes behind us whom I dated a few times when I was eighteen. Vernon was the one who brought the matter up. "I seem to remember that you were kind of sweet on her," he teased. I laughed. I had no idea that he even knew that I had taken her out, let alone remembered it, but memories are long in small towns. It reminded me that the romance, if it could be called that, had made me the object of some envy by my contemporaries.

Bertie and Vernon's commitment to her mother is a common phenomenon in a community where family ties are strong and tenacious. I had lunch one day at the home of Vance and Betty Lewis, who also had moved back to McDonald, from Grand Junction, Colorado, after Vance had retired from his position as a plant manager for Texaco, to be near her father, Claude Pickett, who subsequently died at the age of eighty-five in June 1993. This left Vance and Betty with the decision whether to move back to Grand Junction, where they still own a home, or to stay in McDonald, where they have strong ties. Vance is on the city countil and Betty has a number of school friends and former classmates in town, including Bertie and Joan Tongish; Betty and Joan were also best friends of my cousin, Jo Ann Ritter Wilford, when they were in high school. Betty, Joan, and Bertie see a lot of each other in various civic activities, such as making regular trips to Atwood to do the hair of the elderly women who live at the Good Samaritan retirement home, a service they share with the women of Atwood's churches.

Les Loker has a somewhat different take on the parental situation. A 1969 graduate of McDonald High School, he was recently offered a promotion, which would have required him to move to San Antonio, but he turned it down. Instead, he began expanding his operations by organizing a regional consortium of several major insurance companies, each of which would write a different line of insurance, with the regional headquarters to be in McDonald and branches in Colby and Goodland. "My dad's near seventy and I want to be near him," Les said. "Besides, I like it here. This is a nice place to live."

⁂

This is an oft-sounded theme. When the Reverend Clarence Swihart retired from the Federated Church in 1979, he and his wife, Eleanor, lived in

Illinois for four years, then in Bailey, Colorado, for four more, before moving back to McDonald in 1987. He serves as the Federated Church's associate pastor for senior citizens, stands in when needed for the regular pastor, the Reverend Gregory H. Moyer, and frequently fills in for ministers in neighboring towns. "We moved back to McDonald because of the people," he said. "It's a stable, fear-free community. My son, Steve, once said that Heaven must be like one big Kansas."

It is a community unaccustomed to locking its doors. If Grandmother Phipps had a key to her front door, which had a skeleton key lock, I never saw it; when she was out of town, one of her children or grandchildren dropped by every day to leave the mail and check on things. It's a community where juvenile delinquency is still more along the old storybook lines of stealing watermelons and playing hooky than the troubles common to urban areas, although it's not completely immune to the larger social trends and problems. There was a drug scandal several years ago involving a handful of young men who were a few years out of high school, and some of the elders worry about reports of teenage drinking (a problem with which I was familiar at that age) and occasional rumors of high school pregnancies and abortions.

Generally, however, a small town's social cohesion still exerts a powerful cultural control over youthful behavior. The price for this stability and continuity is that the residents enjoy considerably less privacy than people in urban areas, but they don't consider that a very difficult burden. One of the most striking aspects of high school football and basketball games in the area—in addition to the fact that the young people are generally much better athletes than in my day—is the complete absence of hotdogging and demonstrations of the sort that are commonplace on television today after a score or outstanding play. The only venting of emotions is self-scolding for a botched play or being called for a foul, not an argument with the referee. At a 1994 high school basketball game between Cheylin and Brewster, a town thirty miles south of McDonald, one Cheylin player hit a shot at a critical moment when his team desperately needed a score to keep the game from getting away from it. Cheylin's best players were the stars of its undefeated football team, but Brewster's starters, all sophomores, including their spectacular six-foot five-inch center, were primarily basketball players and had been playing together since grade school. The Cheylin player pumped his right fist in a short, belt-level gesture of satisfaction as he retreated on defense. A couple of McDonald farmers sitting behind me, one of whom had a son on the squad, didn't like even this minimal gesture: "He better watch that hotdoggin'," one said to the other.

As powerful a communications medium as television is, it still doesn't override these tight-knit communities and their mores.

⚞

Some in the community feel that McDonald's problems have been exacerbated by the conservatism of its civic leaders since World War II and point to a number of opportunities the town missed in the past when its future and that of towns like it seemed much brighter.

One was the refusal to allow the Northwest Kansas Rural Electrification Administration (NWKREA) to put up a maintenance shop and vehicle storage building on main street because of the fear of noise and vehicle movement; the NWKREA put its garage—and payroll—in Bird City instead. Another was the decision not to put a swimming pool in the old city park on the east end of town and to let the park itself just disappear for lack of maintenance funds. The town also decided against paving any of the streets except main street.

Even that may have to wait, however, until the remaining balance of about $85,000 on the bonds that financed the new sewer system, which was installed in 1985, is called in 1995. In retrospect, some of the town's leaders think the decision not to install a sewer system back in the 1950s, when Bird City, Brewster, and other neighboring towns did, may have been the biggest error. "I think we may have missed the boat on that one," said Raymond Johnson, who was mayor for eighteen years and served on the city council for another six years and is still a cheerful and energetic community activist. "We may have been too conservative in not wanting to assume the indebtedness."

The result was a depression of property values because the lack of a sewer system made houses hard to sell. Several McDonald area farmers moved to Atwood or Bird City when they retired from farming rather than to McDonald. "Bud Frisbie said he wasn't going to move from the farm into town just to dig another hole in the ground for a cesspool," Ray Johnson recalled.

Also, when Ray and other town fathers were scouting out the possibility of getting federal grants to build low-cost housing in town for retirees, as several neighboring towns did back in the 1970s and early 1980s, they found that the lack of a sewer system disqualified them. By the time the sewer system was installed, the funds were no longer available.

Retirement communities are widely viewed as a promising area of economic activity for small towns on the High Plains because of the wish of urban retirees to escape the crime, crowding, pollution, and high costs of city living. This is an area where the region's demographic situation could be an asset instead of a liability. "We get lots of inquiries from people in Phoenix and Denver, places like that," said Ray Johnson.

The town's position was finally forced in the early 1980s when the federal Environmental Protection Agency cracked down on the grounds that municipal cesspools and septic tanks were potential polluters of the drinking water supply. The city council drew up a $580,800 plan, in which the federal government paid 80 percent under a matching grant, with McDonald raising the rest through a municipal bond issue that is being paid off with a property tax levy. Construction of the sewer system began in August of 1985 and was completed six months later.

The steady and inexorable contraction of the town makes a place like the Frosty Mug loom larger in the community than it would have twenty or thirty years ago. Except for the events at the American Legion Hall and the senior citizens center—of which there are many—it is the only place where people can gather socially, for coffee in mid-morning and afternoon, and, for some retirees, a midday game of snooker. Or to dine, a basic social ritual.

The bill of fare is standard for that part of the country—prime rib, fried chicken, cheeseburgers, pork tenderloin, beef and noodles, and, a Friday night special, "lamb fries"—deep-fried lamb testicles. Nouvelle cuisine has not made profound inroads in western Kansas; I tell my eastern friends that the "diet special" is chicken-fried steak with mashed potatoes and cream gravy. The beer on tap is cold and the mugs are iced, apropos the establishment's name, and the pool and snooker tables are first-rate.

The ambience, a word that isn't bandied about a great deal by the clientele, also is apropos. The Frosty Mug is on the ground floor of the old two-story red-brick McDonald Hotel on Main Street. The wall paneling is well-weathered barn wood, the tables and chairs are sturdy dark hardwood, there is a U-shaped bar with high stools, and no one is a stranger for more than a few minutes.

Junior and his brother, Otis, were the heirs of the once-fabled Dewey ranch. Junior is a former national rodeo circuit bull rider, with photos, trophies, gimpy legs, and a painful walk attesting to it, and an enthusiastic cockfight promoter; there still are cages and pits near the ranch's main buildings. At the turn of the century, the Dewey family owned 300,000 acres and leased 400,000 more from the federal government, an area of about 1,100 square miles. As we've seen, the Deweys aspired to ownership of most of the rest of the northwest corner of Kansas as well, which would have included parts of four counties, Rawlins, Thomas, Sherman, and Cheyenne. Because of the fallout from the Deweys' shoot-out with the Berrys and the press of homesteaders and other settlers, however, this grandiose scheme was not to be. The ranch, whose headquarters is eleven miles south of McDonald, was sold off piece by piece over the years and Otis has the last 6,000 acres. Dee and Junior still own 240 acres, which includes the main house and buildings. Without question, Dee and Junior have made a good thing for themselves with the Frosty Mug. As a social center, it also is a good thing for the town, probably better than many realize.

The programs that MAD, the Lions Club, the garden club, and other civic groups put on are fine as far as they go, but more substantive efforts that will bring systemic change and strengthen the town's economic base are needed, given the area's gloomy long-term prospects. "Every community in America is after some kind of industry," said Reverend Delbert Stanton of Atwood. "Generally, we're not dealing with an established or expanding business. Most are start-ups and they involve erecting a new building or renovating an old one and they often require local investors. That means there's risk involved because the big majority of new enterprises don't make it." Much of the development talk is along the lines of "vertical integration" or "value added" operations, which generally means processing agricultural products, such as making packing material out of residue from corn and other crops.

All the towns in the area are involved with organizations and efforts to attract businesses, professionals, and others to move in; the state requires every county to have a long-term strategic planning council to draft plans both for the short term and for ten years ahead. The strategic planning meetings for Rawlins County development are held in places like the old Buffalo Cafe in Atwood, attended by representatives of the county's four towns, Atwood, McDonald, Ludell, and Herndon, often with outside specialists from the state government or Kansas State University in attendance.

Among the possible business components they discuss at a typical meeting are a retirement center, fiber optics, a medical center, a housing development, a full industrial park, businesses run out of homes, and a brewery. They review the county's strong points: a good school system, a low crime rate, good land, strong family values, a clean environment, and a low cost of living. Among its weaknesses are low per capita income, lack of job opportunities, a small labor force, and negative citizens' attitudes toward change. Typical issues include health care and the hospital, county cooperation and commitment to economic growth and survival, lack of local leadership, youth leaving the county, the shrinking population, and lack of support for businesses in the county. They list these issues by priority and form committees for each to formulate plans on how to address them. It was noted that only three of the citizens in attendance at a recent meeting were born in Rawlins County, which illustrates the point that newcomers are often more alert to the need and opportunity for change than more conservative long-term residents.

A number of factors are involved in these efforts. Leadership and a progrowth attitude are essential. So is the ability to provide the necessary infrastructure—roads, utilities, schools. Most High Plains towns that are prospering, or at least staying even, have a base that includes such elements as a government employer or employers, a college or technical school, medical center, retirement and recreation facilities, and access to transportation, preferably an interstate highway and a jet-capable airport.

Simply upgrading the telephone systems of areas like Rawlins County would make a big difference; these communities need improved access to long-distance, touch-tone, and custom-calling systems, data networks, and even a service that most of the nation takes for granted, 911 dialing for emergencies. Rawlins County didn't get touch-tone, which is needed for many data base programs, and 911 service until late 1993; even so, the new 911 service still isn't the top-of-the-line technology which automatically shows where the caller is, obviously a major factor in emergencies and with the elderly.

The congressional Office of Technology Assessment (OTA) suggests that telecommunications may be the salvation of small-town rural America and has listed possible uses of new technologies to help these areas diversify their economies. Computer, modem, fiber optics, facsimile, video, satellite, digital radio, and other communications technology make it possible for insurance, telemarketing, software systems, financial, information, and other industries to locate and function almost anyplace that has an adequate infrastructure of transportation, schools, and medical services. Telecommunications and modern transportation offer a second chance to communities whose sites were dictated by the location of the railroads and the ability to transport farm produce to them by horse and wagon and which have been left behind by progress.

McDonald's failure to establish a medical clinic was a particular disappointment because it is extremely difficult for any small town on the High Plains to attract and keep a doctor. This is a major obstacle to any effort to attract businesses and professionals, particularly given the aging of the area's population. For this reason, the national debate on health care reform that began in 1993 was mostly irrelevant to the folks on the High Plains. They weren't worried that under a reform plan they might lose their choice of doctors, or about the possible creation of a health care bureaucracy. Their concern is recruiting and holding almost any doctor—or hopefully, doctors—and paramedical physician's assistants and nurses, for that matter. "The question here isn't 'Will I have a choice?' but 'How do I find a doctor?'" one hospital administrator noted.

The OTA envisions communications and information technologies as the means of "reducing the barriers of distance and space that have disadvantaged rural areas" by making it impossible to assemble the skills, information, and capital required for development. These technologies allow isolated rural businesses to link with other businesses and have access to major markets, even in other countries, as easily as urban businesses do. They have the capability of linking rural communities to all the state's educational and informational resources, colleges and universities, libraries, vocational and technical schools, government agencies and programs, private specialists and consultants, and the other rapidly proliferating data bases.

The OTA suggests possible federal-support programs based on the Agriculture Department's Cooperative Extension Service, creating a Rural Development Service to help develop communications technology, and the use of other federal agencies such as the Rural Electrification Administration, with its technological and financial expertise in rural areas.

"We need help," said Ron Bell, a McDonald farmer, chairman of the Rawlins County hospital board, and an electrical engineering graduate who works with the town, the county, and the Cheylin school district on developing electronic technology. "The cost is too high for sparsely populated communities like us right now. We need to share the costs of hooking into the fiber optics line."

Technology, of course, is a double-edged sword and businesses in small communities have experienced the deployment of technology to their areas and the disadvantages they have suffered with the arrival of new and powerful competitors—the discount chains such as Wal-Mart, mail-order firms, and department stores driven by mass media advertising, communications, and other technologies. Skeptics also warn that technology is not a panacea and cannot bring about development by itself.

Still, opportunity is there for communities that focus on their assets—quality of life, sense of community, a population that is generally healthier and better educated than the national average. A small-town rural society that is slowly dying due in great part to modern technology, particularly in agriculture, has little to lose in turning to technology for survival. If you're dying by the sword, you might as well try to live by it.

It may be, however, that the ultimate answer is an element much older than any of the technology that has been brought to bear on the High Plains: the drive that brought the settlers to western Kansas in the first place, or, as one student of the problem put it, "the will of the people." Tireless, long-term efforts pay off. "The key," said Susan Sechler, a former director of the Aspen Institute's Rural Economic Policy Program, "is simply a town's will to do it."

Although of a different nature, the challenges facing the people and towns on the High Plains today are just as difficult and daunting as those of their forebears who settled the area a century ago. The most hardy and resourceful first settled the country and solved the problems of its development. The most hardy and resourceful are turning out to be the last to leave and have bent their energies to solving the problem of their society's survival. Mayor Elroy Osborne put it in plain English: "You have the choice of fighting and continuing to progress or to just fade away."

INDEX